COMMUNITY AND IN-HOME BEHAVIORAL HEALTH TREATMENT

Learn how you can cut down on rapport-building time, make your services accessible to more people, and put your consumers at ease during treatment by offering in-home and natural community-based behavioral health services. This book examines the impact that the environment can have on the comfort level, perception, ability to connect, and general mindset of consumers during treatment. Home and natural community-based services have the potential to help adults, youth, and children live in their own homes and natural communities with specific supports in place that can address their behavioral health needs. Lynne Rice Westbrook examines these treatment settings from the most restrictive to the least restrictive, and demonstrates how such services can be implemented to bring coverage to remote, rural, and underserved areas. Providing services in the consumer's community allows children, youth, adults, and families to receive treatment they may not be able to access otherwise, and to stay together in their own community. This book provides a detailed map of the benefits, challenges, and proposed solutions, and the steps professionals need to take in order to help change the tapestry of behavioral health provision *one home, one healing* at a time.

Lynne Rice Westbrook is a Licensed Professional Counselor (LPC) in Georgia. *Community and In-Home Behavioral Health Treatment* originates from her passion for serving children, youth, families, and adults experiencing behavioral health and substance abuse challenges. She contributes over 15 years of experience as an in-home therapist, a clinic-based therapist, a clinical licensure supervisor, and a quality improvement director.

T0333855

COMMUNITY AND IN-HOME BEHAVIORAL HEALTH TREATMENT

Lynne Rice Westbrook

Routledge
Taylor & Francis Group

NEW YORK AND LONDON

First published 2014
by Routledge
711 Third Avenue, New York, NY 10017

and by Routledge
27 Church Road, Hove, East Sussex BN3 2FA

*Routledge is an imprint of the Taylor & Francis Group,
an informa business*

Library of Congress Cataloging-in-Publication Data

Westbrook, Lynne Rice, author.
    Community and in-home behavioral health treatment / Lynne
Rice Westbrook.
        pages cm
    1. Home-based mental health services.   2. Community mental
health services.   3. Behavior modification.   I. Title.
    RC439.57.W47 2014
    362.2′4—dc23
    2014000937

ISBN: 978-0-415-73559-9 (hbk)
ISBN: 978-0-415-73560-5 (pbk)
ISBN: 978-1-315-81887-0 (ebk)

Typeset in Sabon
by Apex CoVantage, LLC

Printed and bound in the United States of America by Publishers Graphics,
LLC on sustainably sourced paper.

CONTENTS

List of Figures, Tables, and Boxes   viii
Preface: Why I Wrote This Book   ix
Acknowledgments   xi
List of Abbreviations and Acronyms   xii

1 Behavioral Health Needs   1

Behavioral Health: A Changing Landscape 1
Current Behavioral Health Needs 5
Identifying Trends in Treatment 7

2 Traditional Treatment Settings   10

Continuum of Treatment Settings 10
Restrictive Settings Are Not the Best Option for Most
    Behavioral Disorders 17

3 Behavioral Health Treatment in the Home, School,
  and Natural Community   22

Why Treatment Setting Is Important 22
Coverage Considerations 26
Home-, School-, and Natural Community-Based Services 34
Consumer Case Examples (Home-, School-, and
    Natural Community-Based) 35
Providers Working Together 38
Specific Services 39
Applying Skills in the Real World Environment 48

4 Evidence-Based Intervention   51

Evidence-Based Practice 51
Types of Evidence-Based Practice 54
Cultural Considerations 75

5 Assessment and Treatment Planning   78

   *Building Rapport in Home- and
      Natural Community-Based Settings 78*
   Early Identification and Strengths-Based Assessment 84
   Person-Centered Treatment Planning 88
   Treatment Planning Components 92

6 Resource Support Meetings and Identifying Informal
   Support Systems   102

   Resource Support Meeting Process 102
   *Identifying Informal Support Systems the Consumer
      Can Utilize in His or Her Own Community 105*

7 Discharge Planning   112

   Nuts and Bolts of the Discharge Process 112
   Step-Down in Services 118
   Discharge Summary 118
   Areas of Support 126

8 Challenges and How to Overcome Them   129

   Logistics 129
   Expense 132
   Documentation 133
   HIPAA in the Field 134
   Job Stress 138
   Safety in the Field 142

9 Success in My Own Environment   151

   Home and Community Services Work 151
   Service Setting Case Study 153
   *Expanding Home-, School-, and
      Natural Community-Based Services 155*
   International Spotlight 162
   Consumers and Providers Working Together for Change 164
   Putting It All Together 165

   *Appendix A   Evidence-Based Practice Resources That Are
      Accessible on the World Wide Web*   169

CONTENTS

Appendix B   *Evidence-Based Recommendations for*
                Implementation of Behavioral Health
                and Substance Use Interventions by
                Non-Specialist Providers   176
Appendix C   *Evidence-Based Programs and Practices*
                Evaluated in Home-Based Settings for Children
                and Adolescents (Behavioral Health and
                Substance Use Issues)   182
Appendix D   *Evidence-Based Programs and Practices*
                Evaluated in Home-Based Settings for
                Adults (Behavioral Health and Substance
                Use Issues)   188
Appendix E   *Evidence-Based Programs and Practices*
                Evaluated in Other Community-Based Settings
                (e.g., natural community settings, schools, juvenile
                justice, community meeting rooms, multimedia)
                for Children and Adolescents (Behavioral Health
                and Substance Use Issues)   191
Appendix F   *Evidence-Based Programs and Practices*
                Evaluated in Other Community-Based Settings
                (e.g., natural community settings, jail or detention
                settings, community meeting rooms, multimedia)
                for Adults (Behavioral Health and Substance
                Use Issues)   199
Index   211

FIGURES, TABLES, AND BOXES

Figures

2.1 Continuum of Treatment Settings   11
3.1 SAMHSA's Findings Regarding Reasons Adults Needing
      Behavioral Health Services Did Not Seek Treatment   26
4.1 Evidence-Based Practice Integration Model   52
5.1 SNAPS (Strengths, Needs, Abilities, and Preferences)
      Used in Person-Centered Treatment   88
6.1 Equation for Consumer Success: Identification
      of Informal and Formal Supports   106
7.1 Sample Discharge Summary   121

Tables

3.1 Behavioral Health Collaboration With Traditional
      Folk Healers   29
5.1 Treatment Planning Comparison for Home and Natural
      Community Service Provision   90

Boxes

3.1 Behavioral Health Consumer in Southern California:
      Consumer Experience   24
5.1 Assessment Case Study   81
5.2 Strength Identification Dialogue   87
6.1 Resource Support Meetings   103
6.2 Case Example for Resource Support Identification   107
6.3 Resource Planning Guide   109
9.1 Systems of Care Core Values   157

PREFACE: WHY I WROTE THIS BOOK

As a budding counselor, straight out of graduate school, I had aspirations of having a corner office with a view. Having seen many episodes of sit-coms with a psychologist or therapist with the Freudian couch and hour-glass timer, my visions of a therapeutic environment were quite skewed. My first jobs did consist of an office with my degrees on the wall, soft lighting, a waiting room, and the aforementioned couch. Some behavioral health consumers loved this environment and enjoyed the plush setting and professional environment my office provided. I soon began to realize, however, that some consumers spent a large amount of time scanning the room and focusing on degrees hanging on the wall, books on the shelves, and various items on my desk. Consumers would often ask me "Where do I sit? What do I do?" For these individuals, my office was a foreign environment, full of academia, full of professional references, full of many things that served to drive a wedge between them and myself as the professional.

Several years later, I was employed by an organization that had a unique approach to behavioral health services. This organization provided services in the home of the consumer and in the natural community surrounding this consumer. This out-of-the-ordinary concept was not one that I had really explored in any depth in graduate school or in previous practicums, internships, or first career employment sites. I experienced an interesting "table turn" the first time I went into a consumer's home for services. I realized I was on that person's turf, in that person's environment, with that person's personal effects on the walls and tables. No longer was the consumer in my environment with my own personal items, but rather, I was in the consumer's world. I found myself scanning the room, just as my consumers had in my office. I looked at the pictures on their walls and saw the items they chose to display in their homes. I had a glimpse of what it felt like to live in their world. I began to understand what it felt like to go into a foreign environment and be vulnerable.

When we realize what is involved in someone seeking treatment for behavioral health issues, this vulnerability becomes a strong factor in treatment. For some consumers it may have taken them years to find the courage and ability to come in and seek treatment for a disorder or issue that was causing them distress. For those individuals, setting an appointment, ensuring insurance coverage and payment, getting transportation to an office and navigating directions, having the courage to walk into a facility, waiting for treatment, walking into a provider's office, and sitting down to discuss their most intimate thoughts, vulnerabilities, and fears, can be monumental. Now imagine that the professional comes to the consumer and eliminates some of the details of planning and strange environments and meets the consumer on his or her own locale. Imagine the possibilities!

In over 15 years of in-home behavioral health service provision, I saw firsthand the difference treatment location made to my consumers. In my office, many consumers were hesitant to be themselves and were focused on my environment versus the issues at hand. Building rapport in a somewhat sterile environment could take months for some consumers, while others did thrive on the professional setting. My quest was, how do I reach those individuals that don't respond to the professional office setting? How do I build rapport in a manner that is free from artificial hurdles? How do I see my consumers in the environment in which they live?

A funny thing happened when I began to do in-home-, school-, and natural community-based behavioral health; my rapport-building time was cut by weeks and in some cases months. Consumers showed more of their authentic selves. How can you not show more of your true self when daily distractions are happening in front of you: phone ringing, neighbors coming over, dad returning home from work upset, the infant crying, dinner burning, and so on? True life environments produce more accurate reactions and scenarios. In my office, my consumers could say or do anything, why not? We all want to make ourselves appear in our best light, and those seeking services are no different. However, a professional can only treat the issues they understand accurately and with full information.

One small change, such as changing the environment, can make a world of difference to someone seeking treatment for behavioral health issues. This change can bring about expedited rapport-building, trust, insight into the environmental factors contributing to issues, and a "leveling of the playing field." If professionals feel they can't go into the community, then how can they expect consumers to feel comfortable coming into their environment? I am a proponent of bringing services to our consumers and hope this book provides a detailed map as to how other professionals can help change the tapestry of behavioral health provision one home, one healing at a time.

ACKNOWLEDGMENTS

Since the beginning of literary time, authors have taken a moment to put pen to paper (or finger to key) to acknowledge the contribution of others to their process and to recognize those that served as an inspiration to their work. In my case, I want to assign special acknowledgment to the many behavioral health consumers that have helped mold my views on behavioral health treatment far beyond the walls of my own professional education and training. Thank you to each and every consumer who welcomed me into their home, walked me across the threshold of their door and their lives, and gave me the gift of their trust in working with them, often in their most vulnerable moments.

My professional journey would have lacked depth and experience without the guidance and expertise of my co-workers, supervisors, and administrators at Transitional Family Services and Providence Service Corporation. My early professional experiences with in-home counseling gave me a different perspective of the field and I am thankful for those opportunities.

Most importantly, thank you to my family who joined me on this journey and allowed me the space and time to form my thoughts and document them. To my daughters, Sophia and Jordan, who often played at my feet as I typed and were patient with my dedicated time, I will be forever grateful.

ABBREVIATIONS AND ACRONYMS

ACT	Assertive Community Treatment
ADA	Americans with Disabilities Act of 1990
ADHD	Attention Deficit Hyperactivity Disorder
AFSP	American Foundation for Suicide Prevention
AHRQ	Agency for Healthcare Research and Quality
ANSA	Adult Needs and Strengths Assessment
APA	American Psychiatric Association
ASAM	American Society of Addiction Medicine
BERS	Behavioral and Emotional Rating Scale
BPD	Borderline Personality Disorder
BSFT	Brief Strategic Family Therapy
CANS-MH	Child and Adolescent Needs and Strengths–Mental Health
CBR	Community-Based Rehabilitation
CBT	Cognitive Behavioral Therapy
CCMD	*Chinese Classification of Mental Disorders*
CCMHS	Comprehensive Community Mental Health Services
CEBC	California Evidence-Based Clearinghouse
CEU	Continuing Education Units
CHIP	Children's Health Insurance Program
CMCS	Center for Medicaid and CHIP Services
CMHC	Community Mental Health Centers
CMHS	Center for Mental Health Services
CMO	Care Management Organization
CMS	Center for Medicare and Medicaid Services
CSU	Crisis Stabilization Unit
CTI	Critical Time Intervention
DBHDD	Department of Behavioral Health and Developmental Disabilities
DBT	Dialectical Behavior Therapy
DSM	*Diagnostic and Statistical Manual*
EAP	Employee Assistance Program
EBP	Evidence-Based Practice

EBT	Evidence-Based Treatment
EMDR	Eye Movement Desensitization and Reprocessing
ERP	Exposure and Response Prevention
EST	Empirically Supported Treatment
FFT	Functional Family Therapy
FPE	Family Psychoeducation
GAD	Generalized Anxiety Disorder
GAF	Global Assessment of Functioning
GLADP	*Latin American Guide for Psychiatric Diagnosis*
GPS	Global Positioning System
HCBS	Home- and Community-Based Services
HHS	U.S. Department of Health and Human Services
HPSA	Health Professional Shortage Areas
HRSA	Health Resources and Services Administration
HUD	U.S. Department of Housing and Urban Development
ICD	International Classification of Diseases
ICM	Intensive Case Management
IDDT	Integrated Dual Diagnosis Treatment
IFI	Intensive Family Intervention
IOP	Intensive Outpatient Program
IPT	Interpersonal Therapy
LAI	Long-Acting Injectable
LTSS	Long-Term Services and Supports
MET	Motivational Enhancement Therapy
MFP	Money Follows the Person
MFPG	Multifamily Psychoeducation Group
MH	Mental Health
mhGAP	WHO Mental Health Gap Action Programme
MHPA	Mental Health Parity Act
MHPAEA	Mental Health Parity and Addiction Equity Act
MI	Motivational Interviewing
MST	Multi-Systemic Therapy
MTFC	Multidimensional Therapeutic Foster Care
NAMI	National Alliance on Mental Illness
NCTSN	National Child Traumatic Stress Network
NET	Medicaid Non-Emergency Transport
NGC	National Guideline Clearinghouse
NIH	National Institutes of Health
NIMH	National Institute of Mental Health
NIRN	National Implementation Research Network
NOS	Not Otherwise Specified
NPP	Nurturing Parenting Program
NREPP	National Registry of Evidence-Based Programs and Practices
OCD	Obsessive Compulsive Disorder

PCIT	Parent Child Interaction Therapy
PCP	Primary Care Physician
PDD	Pervasive Developmental Disorder
PE	Prolonged Exposure
PMT	Parent Management Training
PRTF	Psychiatric Residential Treatment Facility
PSL-AB	Profiles of Student Life: Attitudes and Behaviors
PTSD	Post-Traumatic Stress Disorder
R/O	Rule Out
SA	Substance Abuse
SAMHSA	Substance Abuse and Mental Health Services Administration
S-CHIP	State Children's Health Insurance Program
SCIE	Social Care Institute for Excellence
SDQ	Strengths and Difficulties Questionnaire
SE	Supported Employment
SMART	Specific, Measurable, Attainable, Realistic, Time-Specific
SNAPS	Strengths, Needs, Abilities, and Preferences
SPA	State Plan Amendment
SPRC	Suicide Prevention Resource Center
SPSI	Scales for Predicting Successful Inclusion
SSI	Supplemental Security Income
SUD	Substance Use Disorder
TFC	Therapeutic Foster Care
TF-CBT	Trauma Focused Cognitive Behavioral Therapy
VA	Veteran's Administration
VRP	Virtual Residential Program
WHO	World Health Organization
WMR	Wellness Management and Recovery
YMCA	Young Men's Christian Associations

1

BEHAVIORAL HEALTH NEEDS

Behavioral Health: A Changing Landscape

The last 60 years have brought about huge strides in the approaches we use in behavioral health[1] diagnostic methodology and treatment. We have gone from an age of using insulin shock therapy to treat schizophrenia, using lobotomies to address mental illness, epilepsy, and even chronic headaches, and the use of very restrictive service environments to a more novel approach as to how we view behavioral health needs and mental illness. This new approach to behavioral health is based on how we view consumers.[2] *How we look at consumers with behavioral health needs dictates the approaches we take in treatment.*

If we were to roll the clock back to the 1950s, we would see that treatment for behavioral health issues was typically provided in large state hospitals and other similar types of institutions. Affordable community-based mental health[3] did not exist at this time and the pharmaceutical treatment of mental illness was in its early stages. While in generations past family members would often care for their own relatives with behavioral health issues in their own homes, this era witnessed an increase in the number of individuals who were sent to institutions for care (often spending many years there). At the time, these state-run institutions were viewed by many as compassionate alternatives to the reality of other options such as imprisonment or homelessness.

The attitude toward behavioral health issues during this era was best encapsulated by the U.S. Surgeon General, in his first Report on Mental Health, when he stated, "In the 1950s, the public viewed mental illness as a stigmatized condition and displayed an unscientific understanding of mental illness." (The public) "typically were not able to identify individuals as mentally ill when presented with vignettes of individuals who would have been said to be mentally ill according to the professional standards of the day. The public was not particularly skilled at distinguishing mental illness from ordinary unhappiness and worry and tended to see only extreme forms of behavior, namely psychosis, as mental

1

illness. Mental illness carried great social stigma, especially linked with fear of unpredictable and violent behavior" (U.S. Department of Health and Human Services, 1999, p. 7). The general lack of understanding and discernment regarding behavioral variances and more severe mental illness, represented in the Surgeon General's quote above, contributed negatively to the way consumers were perceived and treated during this era.

There have been many milestones in our progression in attitudes about behavioral health throughout history. Just 50 years ago, however, we began to see some of the early changes in perception of mental illness and behavioral health issues that have helped pave the road to more dramatic changes in how we now view consumers with behavioral health needs. At this time, U.S. President John F. Kennedy delivered a message to Congress, in which he called for a bold new community-based approach to mental illness that emphasized prevention, treatment, education, and recovery. This was innovative and called the country to task in how people perceived behavioral health, consumers with these issues, and how treatment was provided. The result of these efforts was the signing into law of the Community Mental Health Act of 1963. This act would provide federal funding for community health centers[4] across the United States. These community mental health centers were an integral part of the movement for community-based mental health. Concurrently, with the advent of new pharmaceutical advancements that made it possible to moderate the extreme behavior of many who lived in institutions, it was thought that allowing patients to leave institutions and be treated in the community would be more humane. This movement from institutions to treatment in the community was referred to as deinstitutionalization and occurred gradually in the Western world. However, this increase in the number of deinstitutionalized individuals, along with funding and coverage issues, resulted in some challenges for providing community-based mental health care for all those who had been reintroduced into the community at large. In later years, however, advancements in payer coverage would bring about increased coverage for consumers suffering from behavioral health challenges and serve to increase options for treatment.

Consumer-based movements have also had a strong effect on the landscape of behavioral health, how it is defined, and the recognition of particular behavioral health disorders. After the Vietnam War, for example, military veterans fought for years to gain recognition of the diagnosis of post-traumatic stress disorder (PTSD) as a diagnosable and treatable behavioral health disorder. Later, it was recognized that other sufferers of trauma, sexual assault, or torture; children who witnessed violence; and others throughout the world, could also be affected by PTSD. Consumers themselves have been instrumental in bringing about recognition of the importance of accurate diagnosis and treatment of several disorders

2

throughout the behavioral health care system. Consumers are undoubtedly some of the best sources of input into the system as they are the ones that face the daily challenges of their disorders and can best describe what it means to have mental and substance abuse issues. Perhaps one of the most influential changes we have seen over the years is this recognition of consumer perception and experience in the way behavioral health issues are elicited, diagnosed, experienced, and treated.

Consumer organizations, and organizations of family members of those with behavioral health disorders, have also been instrumental in recent years in raising awareness among policy makers and health care leaders regarding needs in treatment. Beginning in the 1960s, the feminist movement helped redefine women's behavioral health. Similarly, communities representing cultural minorities pressed for respect for cultural differences in behavioral health care and began to insist on cultural competence by behavioral health providers[5] so that providers would have the ability to develop rapport and a healing relationship with their consumers. This advocacy further resulted in legislature like the Americans with Disabilities Act of 1990 (ADA). This act supported parents' and consumers' insistence on an appropriate response to mental illness in the workplace, treatment settings, and public accommodations (United States Department of Justice Civil Rights Division, 1990). All of these advances in recognition, identification, and diagnosis of disorders were reflected in the criteria-based classification systems adopted by the World Health Organization's (WHO) *International Classification of Diseases (ICD)*[6] (WHO, 1992) and the American Psychiatric Association's (APA) *Diagnostic and Statistical Manual of Mental Disorders (DSM)*[7] (American Psychiatric Association, 2013). These diagnostic systems provided a standard for classification of mental disorders and were adopted by many countries as a standard in the diagnostic process. Each of these diagnostic manuals has undergone multiple revisions from the time of their origination to present day. Different regions have also developed standardized diagnostic alternatives, such as the *Chinese Classification of Mental Disorders (CCMD)*[8] (Chinese Society of Psychiatry, 2001) or the *Latin American Guide for Psychiatric Diagnosis (GLADP)*[9] (Berganza, 2001). These alternatives are similar in structure to the *ICD* and *DSM*, but include important variations in the main diagnoses and additional culturally related disorders. There are also other culturally relevant alternatives and diagnostic augmentations available worldwide representing multicultural issues. So, not only have there been advances in the recognition and diagnosis of behavioral health issues and how consumers are perceived, but also in the way specific cultures have impacted this process.

Consumer advocacy, family member efforts, and public initiatives have all been instrumental in changing how the community at large views behavioral health challenges and mental illness. So many groups, individuals, and organizations have contributed to the patchwork quilt that makes up our current understanding of behavioral health. As society changed many preconceived notions of mental illness, the courts also became more understanding of the unique challenges of those with mental disorders. Over the years, civil commitment proceedings were reformed and criminal mental health courts were developed to deal with the needs of the mentally ill offender who had been arrested. Today's mental health courts vary from jurisdiction to jurisdiction, but generally consist of a specialized court docket that uses a problem-solving approach to guide how they process defendants with mental illness. They offer judicially supervised, community-based treatment for each defendant participating in court in lieu of traditional jail sentencing.

Another important change in how the public views behavioral health is reflected in the growing understanding of the relationship between child and adult behavioral health. School districts became aware of the barriers to success in education that mental illnesses created for children and as a result introduced support services into the educational system. Adult and children's services recognized the family unit and how each individual has a role in treatment that affects the overall process. Adult services also looked at how employment and housing are important considerations in overall treatment and the behavioral health of each consumer. Consequently, specialized programs for both children/adolescents and adults were created with a recognition of the difference and similarities of providing services to these consumer groups.

Particularly since 1990, advances in brain science, brain scans, growing understanding in brain biochemistry, advances in psychological therapy, electrical brain stimulation, and the role of the genome in brain development and functioning have brought important new understandings to health care providers, policy makers and the public. The brain and other bodily organs interact in numerous ways. This new understanding was reflected in the Mental Health Parity Act (MHPA) of 1996 and further elaborated upon in the Mental Health Parity and Addiction Equity Act of 2008 (MHPAEA). Ultimately, these acts required group health plans or health insurance issuers that provide mental health and substance use disorder benefits to offer equally favorable benefits for MH/SUD (mental health/substance use disorders) as for medical/surgical coverage. In addition, the Children's Health Act of 2000, which reauthorized the Substance Abuse and Mental Health Services Administration (SAMHSA), was instrumental in reform efforts. The Children's Act called for a greater focus on measurement of behavioral health care outcomes. Together, these far-reaching laws, along with many other efforts and legislature over the years, placed the larger health care reform efforts in sync with behavioral health system transformation.

4

Along with changes in how professionals viewed brain chemistry came another big change in how behavioral health issues were treated and viewed. Prior to the 1990s, there was a split between the treatment of behavioral health and substance use disorders. There was stigma associated with both sets of issues, and the failure to understand their interrelationship often led to a situation where consumers with co-occurring behavioral health and substance use disorders had as their only option parallel treatment in separate programs. Often the consumer with co-occurring behavioral health and substance issues received treatment from two completely different systems because neither system was fully able to treat both disorders. Dual-diagnosis treatments are now available as an option to the consumer with both behavioral health and substance use issues, and have reflected this overarching change in how the two issues are now perceived and treated.

How we view behavioral health and substance use challenges, consumers, and approaches to treatment has changed vastly since the 1950s. Advances in scientific research and policy, in more recent decades, have been a catalyst for the behavioral health community to take a vastly different approach as to how behavioral health issues are viewed. A norm of very restrictive service environments has changed to less radical means of treatment. These treatments include psycho-pharmaceutical interventions, more comprehensive assessments, and consumer-driven treatment. While more restrictive treatments and treatment environments are certainly needed for some cases, many interventions can be performed in community-based settings and with less restrictive treatments and environments, to include more intensive therapeutic intervention by teams of professionals often in home-, school-, or natural community-based settings.

Current Behavioral Health Needs

Numbers of Americans Affected by Mental Illness

So let's look for a moment to see who is in need of services. According to SAMHSA National Survey on Drug Use and Health, it is estimated that in an average one-year period, approximately 17.8 percent of the U.S. adult population (41.4 million adults) will have a diagnosable mental illness. Of those, 3.9 percent (9 million adults) live with a serious mental illness such as schizophrenia, major depression, or bipolar disorder (Substance Abuse and Mental Health Services Administration, 2013). About 45 percent of adults are estimated to have a co-occurring mental health and addiction disorder (SAMHSA, 2012). Then, of adults with mental illness, approximately 60 percent received no mental health services in the previous year (SAMHSA, 2012). The percentage of youth, ages

8 to 15, that experience severe mental disorders in a given year is approximately 13 percent (National Institutes of Health (NIH), 2010), and almost one-half of those youth, ages 8 to 15, received no mental health services in the previous year (NIH, 2013).

If we look further, we can see how these statistics play out in the community at large. The U.S. Department of Housing and Urban Development has estimated that 26 percent of homeless adults staying in shelters live with serious mental illness and an estimated 46 percent live with severe mental illness and/or substance use disorders (U.S. Department of Housing and Urban Development, 2011). If we turn our focus to the prison system, statistics show that approximately 20 percent of state prisoners and 21 percent of local jail prisoners have a recent history of a mental health condition (James & Glaze, 2006). In fact, the U.S. House of Representatives Special Investigations Division reported that two-thirds of juvenile detention centers hold youth who are waiting for community mental health treatment (2004). It reported that in 33 U.S. states, "youth with mental illness are held in detention centers without any charges against them. Youth incarcerated unnecessarily while waiting for treatment are as young as seven years old" (United States House of Representatives, 2004, p. 3). In the education system, similarly, statistics show that over 50 percent of students with a diagnosed mental health condition age 14 and older, who are served by special education, drop out. This is the highest dropout rate of any disability group (U.S. Department of Education, 2006). What all of these statistics have in common is that they show us that there is a large number of individuals with behavioral health and substance use issues that are in the community and either can't easily access traditional services or may benefit from service provision in their current placement setting or in their own homes, schools, and natural communities.

Worldwide Population Affected by Mental Illness

It is estimated that worldwide more than 450 million people suffer from some type of behavioral health or substance abuse disorder. It is important to realize that behavioral health and behavioral health treatment around the world still vary greatly. According to the World Health Mental Health Atlas (2011), published by the World Health Organization, only 62 percent of countries worldwide had a mental health policy in place and just 71 percent had a mental health plan. Still, more countries had no mental health policy that included children and adolescents. The statistics become further varied when a comparison was made between low- and high-income countries. Only 36 percent of people living in low-income countries were covered by mental health legislation, while the rate for high-income countries was 92 percent. Similarly, outpatient mental health facilities were 58 times more prevalent in high-income countries compared to low-income countries. There are many factors that feed into these statistics. For many countries, for example, there is still a perceived stigma around behavioral health issues and consequently human rights violations are still happening across the globe. For still others, financial resources have not been allocated or are not available for behavioral health programs (World Health Organization, 2011).

Identifying Trends in Treatment

Current trends in treatment include the recognition that children, youth, and adults can successfully live in their own homes and natural communities with specific supports in place that can support them with their behavioral health needs. A joint CMCS (Center for Medicaid and CHIP Services) and SAMHSA (Substance Abuse and Mental Health Services Administration) Information Bulletin (2013) states that "these services (community-based services) enable children with complex mental health needs—many of whom have traditionally been served in restrictive settings like residential treatment centers, group homes, and psychiatric hospitals—to live in community settings and participate fully in family and community life" (SAMHSA and CMCS, 2013, p. 1). This recognition and trend in the field potentially changes the process, treatment, and outcomes of those in treatment for behavioral health issues. This trend is based on evidence from major U.S. Department of Health and Human Services (HHS) initiatives that show that services in the community are not only clinically effective, but cost-effective as well (SAMHSA and CMCS, 2013, pp. 1–2). This trend will be explored in further detail in Chapter 3, "Behavioral Health Treatment in the Home, School, and Natural Community."

Notes

1. Behavioral health is a general term now commonly used in place of the term mental health in many geographic areas. In some cases the terminology behavioral health and mental health are used interchangeably.
2. Consumer is the preferred language in many states and countries to represent someone who utilizes behavioral health services. Note that the descriptors *patient* and *client* are also used in some venues and geographic areas to represent the same concept as behavioral health consumer.
3. Community-based mental health as an initial concept referred to services offered in non-hospital and institutional settings.
4. Community mental health centers (CMHC) were structured to provide inpatient, outpatient, partial hospitalization, emergency care, and consultation/education services in community settings versus traditional psychiatric hospitals.
5. Provider is the term used to describe those who work in the behavioral health field. The term providers includes doctors, clinicians, professional counselors,

social workers, psychologists, marriage and family therapists, addictions counselors, nurses, paraprofessional aides, peer supports, and any other similar providers of services.

6. *ICD (International Statistical Classification of Diseases)*, published by the World Health Organization, is a standard diagnostic tool for epidemiology, health management, and clinical categorization. The *ICD-6* edition, published in 1949, included the first section on mental disorders. The eleventh edition of the classification has already begun and will continue until 2015 (WHO, 2013).

7. The *DSM (Diagnostic and Statistical Manual of Mental Disorders)* is a standard classification system of mental disorders used by mental health professionals in the United States. The *DSM-I* was published in 1952 and the most recent update is the *DSM-V* update for 2013.

8. The *Chinese Classification of Mental Disorders (CCMD)* is published by the Chinese Society of Psychiatry and is a clinical diagnostic guide used in China. The first publication, the *CCMD-I,* was made available in 1979. It is currently in its third version, published in both Chinese and English (Jinan: Shandong Science & Technology Press, 2001).

9. The *Latin American Guide for Psychiatric Diagnosis (GLADP)* is a manual developed by the Section of Diagnosis and Classification of the Latin American Psychiatric Association (Berganza, 2001).

References

American Psychiatric Association (APA). (2013). *Diagnostic and Statistical Manual of Mental Disorders* (5th ed.). Washington, DC: Author.

Berganza, C. E. (2001). *Latin American Guide for Psychiatric Diagnosis: A Cultural Overview.* H. F. J. E. Mezzich, Ed. Philadelphia: Psychiatric Clinics of North America.

Chinese Society of Psychiatry. (2001). *Chinese Classification of Mental Disorders* (3rd ed.). Jinan, China: Shandong Science & Technology Press.

James, D. J., & Glaze, L. E. (2006, December 14). *Special Report: Mental Health Problems of Prison and Jail Inmates.* Retrieved October 1, 2013, from Bureau of Justice Statistics: http://bjs.ojp.usdoj.gov/content/pub/pdf/mhppji.pdf

National Institutes of Health (NIH). (2010). *Any Disorder among Children.* Retrieved October 14, 2013, from National Institute of Mental Health: http://nimh.nih.gov/statistics/1ANYDIS_CHILD.shtml

National Institutes of Health (NIH). (2013). *Use of Mental Health Services and Treatment among Children.* Retrieved October 14, 2013, from National Institute of Mental Health: www.nimh.nih.gov/statistics/1NHANES.shtml

Substance Abuse and Mental Health Services Administration (SAMHSA). (2012). *Results from the 2010 National Survey on Drug Use and Health: Mental Health Findings.* NSDUH Series H-42, HHS Publication No. (SMA) 11-4667. Retrieved October 14, 2013, from SAMHSA: www.samhsa.gov/data/nsduh/2k10MH_Findings/2k10MHResults.htm#3.2

Substance Abuse and Mental Health Services Administration (SAMHSA). (2013). *Revised Estimates of Mental Illness from the National Survey on Drug Use and Health.* Retrieved November 19, 2013, from SAMHSA: www.samhsa.gov/data/2k13/NSDUH148/sr148-mental-illness-estimates.htm

Substance Abuse and Mental Health Services Administration (SAMHSA) and Center for Medicaid and CHIP Services (CMCS). (2013). *Coverage of Behavioral Health Services for Children, Youth, and Young Adults with Significant Mental Health Conditions.* Information Bulletin. Retrieved November 15, 2013, from www.medicaid.gov/Federal-Policy-Guidance/Downloads/CIB-05-07-2013.pdf

U.S. Department of Education. (2006). *Twenty-eighth Annual Report to Congress on the Implementation of the Individuals with Disabilities Education Act.* Vol. 2. Washington, DC: Author.

U.S. Department of Health and Human Services. (1999). *Mental Health: A Report of the Surgeon General.* Rockville, MD: U.S. Department of Health and Human Services, Substance Abuse and Mental Health Services Administration, Center for Health Services, National Institutes of Health, National Institute of Mental Health.

U.S. Department of Housing and Urban Development. (2011). *The 2010 Annual Homeless Assessment Report to Congress.* Retrieved October 14, 2013, from Homelessness Resource Exchange: www.hudhre.info/documents/2010 HomelessAssessmentReport.pdf

United States Department of Justice Civil Rights Division. (1990). *ADA Laws and Regulations.* Retrieved October 21, 2013, from Americans with Disabilities Act: www.ada.gov/pubs/adastatute08.pdf

United States House of Representatives. (2004). *Incarceration of Youth Who Are Waiting for Community Mental Health Services in the United States.* United States House of Representatives, Committee on Government Reform—Minority Staff, Special Investigations Division. Retrieved November 1, 2013, from House of Representatives: www.reform.house.gov/min

World Health Organization (WHO). (1992). *International Classification of Diseases (ICD)-10.* Geneva, Switzerland: Author.

World Health Organization (WHO). (2011). *Mental Health Atlas 2011.* Retrieved October 30, 2013, from WHO: http://whqlibdoc.who.int/publications/2011/9799241564359_eng.pdf

World Health Organization (WHO). (2013). *International Classification of Diseases (ICD).* Retrieved October 31, 2013, from WHO: www.who.int/classifications/icd/en/.

2

TRADITIONAL TREATMENT SETTINGS

Continuum of Treatment Settings

Communities usually offer a range of services and programs to consumers with behavioral health needs. This range of programs and services is referred to as a continuum of care. These services and programs are provided in different settings. Traditionally, many behavioral health service settings have been restrictive in nature. In fact, past treatment of mental illnesses often included sanatorium settings, which were used for treatment for individuals with physical and behavioral health illnesses. These very restrictive settings have fallen out of use due to more varied treatment options for individuals struggling with behavioral and physical illness. While not every community has every type of service or program on the continuum, many communities do offer some of the identified treatment settings to be discussed.

It is important to note that each service type and setting has an important place in behavioral health treatment since all individuals do not benefit from the same type, frequency, or intensity of intervention. Each person, disorder, and set of circumstances requires careful consideration as to the best treatment fit for those needs presented. This chapter will explore the continuum of settings as it pertains to behavioral health services beginning with the more restrictive treatment settings. As a caveat, not every geographic area will have a full range of services, and each state and country may have its own preferred program types and terminology. It is also crucial to clarify that detoxification and substance abuse treatment can take place in a full array of treatment settings, but that the choice of treatment setting and intensity of treatment is traditionally influenced by ASAM (American Society of Addiction Medicine) placement criteria. The services listed below, however, are intended to be a generalized representation of the treatment settings offered across geographic regions and are not intended to provide comprehensive coverage of every service and setting represented in every state, country, and community. See Figure 2.1 for a continuum of general treatment settings representing the most restrictive to least restrictive service types.

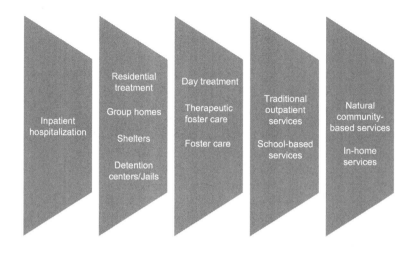

Most restrictive services   Least restrictive services

Out-of-home   ⟶   Community   ⟶   In-home

Figure 2.1 Continuum of Treatment Settings
Adapted from NAMI (2009)

Inpatient Hospitalization

Inpatient stays are used in some situations where 24-hour care is war-ranted. In circumstances where a consumer's symptoms are severe enough to pose an immediate safety need to the consumer or those around him or her, an inpatient stay may be considered. Inpatient hospitalization can be the safest and most secure treatment setting for an individual needing this more intense level of intervention. Admission to an inpatient hospital can be on a voluntary or involuntary basis. If the consumer and the pro-vider agree that inpatient treatment is the best placement, the consumer may be admitted on a voluntary basis. It is important to clarify that some private hospitals will only accept voluntary admits. Involuntary admis-sion to an inpatient hospital, however, is also practiced and is against the will of the consumer and intended to reduce an immediate safety risk. Involuntary admission does involve denial of civil liberty, so there are strict laws in place in many (but definitely not all) states, countries, and other geographic areas to protect the rights of an involuntarily admitted consumer. Each geographic area may differ in regulations that determine

11

how long someone can be civilly committed,[1] but inpatient stays are usually limited to a few days. If the commitment order[2] is to be renewed, there are specific state and country laws that specify terms of renewal. These laws are in place to prevent abuses of this system.

While inpatient, a consumer can expect to receive an evaluation and treatment. Oftentimes, the treatment is guided by a team of professionals. Psychiatrists, physician's assistants, psychologists, professional counselors, social workers, marriage and family therapists, psychiatric nurses, occupational therapists, paraprofessional supports, peer supports, and other behavioral health workers may all work with the consumer while in the hospital setting. This high level of collaborative and integrated care makes possible the monitoring of a consumer's behavior on a 24-hour basis. If the consumer is at risk of harming himself or herself or someone else, hospital staff will be assigned to monitor the consumer around the clock until the crisis passes (often using an observation room). Some hospitals use restraints or isolation rooms to manage physical aggression or self-injury. Many hospitals, however, are moving to alternative methods to manage aggression and self-injury, since seclusion and restraint are considered last-resort strategies to maintain physical safety. If seclusion or restraint is utilized, the hospital is required by law, in many geographic areas, to check on the consumer at regular intervals and to release the consumer as soon as the risk of harm has passed.

Most hospital-based treatment programs will also provide some type of psychotherapy, in the form of individual and/or group therapy, to allow the consumer to process the issues or behaviors that led to the hospital admission. This level of intervention may also include family participation in the assessment, treatment, and planning stages. Family input can allow the behavioral health team to augment gathered information about the consumer's history, ongoing stressors, and what strengths and obstacles are relevant to the individual's care. Pharmacological treatment, as indicated, can also be provided for the consumer during inpatient treatment. Medication management, however, may take different forms while a consumer is inpatient. The psychiatrist may prescribe a new medication (or dosage) or discontinue current medications altogether to allow nursing staff to observe the consumer's symptoms and conduct analysis. Additionally, inpatient hospitalization may offer educational groups, social skills development training, resiliency and recovery skills education, and respite opportunities for the consumer in an environment that is fully supported. As the consumer is leaving inpatient stay, hospital staff should meet with the consumer to plan treatment continuity for services ranging from behavioral health care, support groups, safe housing, to income and health care coverage.

Residential Treatment

Residential treatment as a service varies widely from state to state, as well as country to country, and provider to provider. Residential treatment can be in highly structured institutions that function somewhat like a psychiatric hospital or in less medically oriented facilities that provide a supportive place to live. Some residential treatment centers are lockdown facilities, while others allow the consumer the option of retaining a job or going to school during the day. Usually, residential treatment is considered if the individual's needs are too intense to be managed in outpatient treatment, but do not rise to the level of severity requiring inpatient treatment. Individuals that may be considered for residential treatment include someone who has an unstable living condition; is trying to transition to independent living; was recently discharged from inpatient hospitalization; or is deemed to no longer be a danger to himself or herself or those around the consumer. Additional residential treatment referrals may be made because outpatient treatment has not reduced the impairments that go along with the consumer's behavioral health symptoms, or simply because available emotional resources from existing formal supports (therapists and psychiatrists) and informal supports (friends and family) have been depleted. Finally, residential treatment may be utilized when the consumer's behaviors are severe, but do not justify inpatient hospitalization, or when there are safety issues that may be reduced in a controlled environment that provides around-the-clock behavioral observations (e.g. cutting behavior, purging, substance abuse escalation).

Many residential treatment options are available, and each varies in terms of theoretical orientation and treatment paradigm. Some residential sites have four to six beds within a single family residence, and some are much larger having dozens of beds in a more institutional-type campus setting. Geographic location, cost, and length of stay also vary to a great extent from one residential treatment venue to another. Some residential treatment locations recommend a minimum of one to three months, whereas a few facilities have lengths of stay from six months to two years or more. While some residential treatment settings offer round-the-clock intervention and support, others may have counseling staff that provide more temporary limited daytime support augmented with evening meetings to review the day's events and provide additional support. Other residential treatment programs include psychosocial rehabilitation services and offer skill- and resource-building activities to deal with the practical and realistic needs for transitioning back into the community. However, a full range of mental health professionals may not be on staff in all residential treatment settings, so the consumer most often visits a therapist or psychiatrist elsewhere.

Partial Hospitalization/Day Treatment

In some regional areas there is a "step down" from inpatient hospitals that is termed *partial hospitalization*. This option is also sometimes referred to as a day program. Partial hospitalization can be provided in either a hospital setting or in a free-standing community mental health center. Partial hospitalization is very similar to inpatient hospitalization, except the consumer gets to go home at the end of the day. Most of the programs are based on a Monday-to-Friday schedule and allow the consumer to attend one to five sessions per week. Some programs, however, do run up to seven days a week. These programs still allow strong structure and support to plan and monitor treatment, while helping the consumer make the transition back to life at home and in the community in which the consumer lives. Day treatment for the child/adolescent population often includes intensive psychiatric treatment with special education. The child usually attends five days per week.

Emergency Treatment/Crisis Stabilization

Emergency treatment is utilized to mitigate a crisis. If a consumer is already utilizing non-emergency services, the therapist or psychiatrist can address emergency situations by providing extra appointments for psychiatric support or for medication management in a traditional hospital or clinic-based office setting. Urgent situations, for example, with suicidal or self-destructive thoughts present, may be best served through local hospital psychiatric emergency rooms or local mental health center's emergency services.

Crisis Stabilization Units (CSU) provide another emergency stabilization option. Crisis Stabilization Units are a voluntary service that offers 24-hour, seven days a week, intensive, short-term stabilization (usually up to 72 hours). CSUs also offer behavioral health treatment for the consumer with a condition that does not meet the criteria for involuntary commitment to a psychiatric hospital or other treatment resources. Many communities also have mobile crisis teams. Mobile crisis teams actually fall on the least restrictive end of the treatment setting spectrum as they often provide services in the consumer's natural community setting, but they are considered a type of crisis stabilization. Mobile crisis teams provide community-based crisis supports as an alternative to inpatient hospital stays, emergency room care, or involvement with law enforcement personnel that could result in incarceration for the consumer. Most mobile crisis teams have a licensed clinician (professional counselor, social worker, or marriage and family therapist), a behavior specialist, and direct support staff. Other team members may include nurses, safety officers, and additional clinical and behavioral support staff. Physicians are traditionally available by consult. Each state, region, or country varies in its specifications for mobile crisis teams, but they all will have some set requirement as to maximum elapsed time from time of initial call to when a crisis situation must be assessed. The mobile crisis team travels to the consumer in crisis situations. Following the assessment, the team will coordinate in and out of home supports for a limited time to resolve the crisis (DBHDD, 2013).

Therapeutic Group Home

The therapeutic group home usually includes three to ten consumers per residence-based home, and may be linked with a day treatment program or specialized educational program. These sites are often located in a neighborhood setting with intensive staffing levels and services offered within the context of an around-the-clock, home-like environment. They are traditionally highly structured programs that create a physically, emotionally, and psychologically safe environment for consumers with complex behavioral health needs who need additional support and clinical intervention to succeed in either a family environment or independent living situation. Therapeutic group homes are often designated by gender and age group categories. For many child and adolescents consumers, this treatment level may allow them to attend a local school while a member of the group home. Likewise, adults may be able to retain employment in the community while members of the group home. The programs often offer individual, group, and medication therapies and are designed to help support the consumers' transitions back to their family, the community, or in some cases independent living. This level of care is usually considered to be a step-down in acuity of services from inpatient treatment or residential treatment.

Additionally, there is the option of therapeutic foster care, which is a service designed to provide individualized behavioral health services within a single, residence-based foster family setting. Therapeutic foster care is a long-term, out-of-home placement for children with needs that may not be met in traditional foster care. This model utilizes specially trained and intensively supervised foster parents. The foster parent assumes the duties of caregiver for the time the child is enrolled in the program. Therapeutic services, support, and training are provided to help maintain the consumer's placement. Therapeutic foster care is traditionally one of the least restrictive out-of-home therapeutic placements for children with more severe emotional disorders.

Respite Care

Respite care provides an opportunity for the consumer to stay briefly away from home with specially trained individuals. Respite care is short term and is intended to provide temporary relief for family members and/or caregivers. The term *short break* is used in some countries to describe respite care (Community Care Division, Health Department, Scotland, 2013). Typically a caregiver providing care for his or her own family member may experience the physical and emotional strain of day-in and day-out care for a loved one. Respite care provides a temporary break for those caregivers to help them have an opportunity for self-care and a much needed break that may reduce the possibility of out-of-home placement for the consumer. Respite care also reduces the risk of abuse toward consumers due to caregiver burnout. Respite care can be provided in a variety of settings: in-home respite—where the caregiver comes to the consumer's residence; facility respite—where the consumer stays for a few days or weeks (often used with specialized needs); emergency/crisis respite; sitter-companion services; and therapeutic day care (usually during standard business hours to allow caregivers to work outside the home).

Crisis Residence

The crisis residence is classified as short term (fewer than 15 days) crisis intervention and treatment. Consumers there receive 24-hour per day supervision. Crisis residences provide services to consumers transitioning from acute, inpatient psychiatric units who may need additional, structured recovery time. These sites often also serve consumers experiencing a situational crisis such as family problems, loss of relationships, neglect, or homelessness. Crisis residence services usually include diagnosis, assessment, treatment (including medication stabilization), rehabilitation, and links to community-based services. Crisis residences are generally viewed as a voluntary alternative to hospitalization.

Traditional Outpatient Treatment

Outpatient treatment is defined by the fact that it does not require an overnight stay. Outpatient treatment may involve a combination of psychotherapy and medication management. The typical outpatient practitioner may be a psychiatrist, physician's assistant, psychologist, professional counselor, social worker, marriage and family therapist, or another mental health professional in a private office, clinic, or hospital-based office setting. In this type of treatment the frequency of sessions is quite variable. The consumer and provider decide together what the type and frequency of treatment will be. The type and frequency of treatment is often based on testing, initial evaluation, and treatment planning direction that results from the evaluative process. A clinic or office practice may have a dedicated intake coordinator who is seasoned in the art of building rapport with a new consumer and providing initial assessment of the consumer's presenting issues, diagnosis, and in documenting potential treatment needs. Services are typically scheduled in advance, but may occur during crisis without a scheduled appointment. Outpatient treatment may involve evaluation, diagnosis, and treatment of individuals, families, or groups, as well as medication management.

Intensive Outpatient Programs (IOP) are similar to traditional outpatient therapeutic intervention; however, the frequency and intensity of services is higher due to the specific needs of the consumer. Traditionally, Intensive Outpatient Programs offer three or more hours of treatment in a given day and may run for five days a week. Intensive Outpatient Services also typically occur in a private office, clinic, or hospital-based office setting.

Home-, School-, and Natural Community-Based Treatment Services

Home- and community-based treatment services are designed to meet the needs of the consumer in his or her home, school, and/or natural community setting. These services may be provided in the consumer's natural home (or community placement), school, or in the community where the consumer lives. Home- and natural community-based services typically incorporate strength-based assessments, crisis services, case management, clinical teams, and individualized supports. The set of providers may include the same professionals that provide traditional outpatient services: psychiatrists, physician's assistants, psychologists, professional counselors, social workers, marriage and family therapists, other mental health professionals, peer specialists, and paraprofessional staff who provide skill development and resource coordination. The difference between traditional outpatient services and home-, school-, and community-based services is that the services are not provided in a clinic environment, but rather in the consumer's home, foster home, school, tent in which they are temporarily residing, shelter, or other community-based setting. These services are provided in a flexible manner with duration, intensity, and frequency based on treatment planning. Services are often provided by a team of professionals, but may be provided by an individual provider. It is important to recognize that many consumers are in temporary living situations that bring them out of their natural home environment; community-based services can also be provided in these environments (e.g., group homes, detention centers, shelters).

Restrictive Settings Are Not the Best Option for Most Behavioral Disorders

At times, inpatient psychiatric hospitals are the best fit for the severity of the presenting behavioral health issue. Inpatient facilities are designed to be safe settings for intensive behavioral health and substance abuse treatment that includes a component of observation, diagnosis, individual and group psychotherapy, and medication management. When a consumer goes into inpatient care, however, there is no question that the consumer experiences an interruption to daily life. Inpatient care is also an expensive solution and should be reserved for situations when safety is needed around-the-clock and direct observation and care are required. Most inpatient stays are designed to be only a few days to weeks, just enough time to resolve the most critical and urgent presenting problems. Alternatives can relieve the need for inpatient hospital care or serve as part of the discharge process. Depending on local availability, alternatives may include short-term crisis stabilization units, psychiatric emergency rooms, intensive outpatient treatment, partial hospitalization, residential treatment, or intensive home- and natural community-based treatment.

Currently, inpatient hospitals are used as well as PRTFs (Psychiatric Residential Treatment Facilities)[3] for higher levels of psychiatric and behavioral health intervention. From this level of care, individuals can step-down to less restrictive service environments. Consider for a moment a consumer with behavioral health needs severe enough to warrant placement in a higher level of care. This individual is removed from his or her home and community and any connection the individual has with family, friends, and informal support systems. This has to be a frightening experience for any individual. While some consumers are removed from their homes and communities due to safety reasons, many are removed because there may not be other intensive service and supports available to them in their local community. Many of these consumers could be able to achieve better outcomes if they were able to receive services in their own communities and homes. For others in residential treatment, their length of stay could be greatly reduced if viable intensive home- and natural community-based services were available. While many consumers are afforded, and do benefit from residential treatment, some consumers end up in a more restrictive service setting than is warranted because other (less restrictive) intensive services are not available to them in their local communities. Removing individuals from their homes and communities is not only disruptive to their lives, but may also cause the loss of a valuable link to the social, support, and communal connections in their home, community, and school. When this connection is severed, not only are consumers losing some of their immediate supports, but they are being transported to an environment that is very different and unfamiliar from their natural living environment. In fact, not every community has available placements for residential care, and many consumers must go out of state to receive these services. The end effect is that the consumers are even further removed from their families and communities. The difficulty not only lies in leaving their familiar settings, but in going to a new, different setting when they may very well be in the most vulnerable positions they have experienced in their lives. It is without this familiarity of home, without supports in their natural environment, and during this difficult time filled with fear and vulnerability, that the consumer is then expected to move through a crisis and begin to absorb skill-building and support services. Then, when they have graduated from this higher level of care, they are often moved to a lower level of care and must deal with the new issues of transitioning back. To add complication, upon discharge, not all consumers are given adequate transition and family support services and this only serves to compound the difficult transition.

We know that home- and natural community-based settings are more familiar for the consumer, but an important piece of the puzzle is whether providing behavioral health services in these natural settings is effective for the consumer. The Centers for Medicare and Medicaid Services (CMS) Psychiatric Residential Treatment Facility (PRTF) Demonstration Program was designed to determine just how effective community-based services are for youth who are at risk for entering a PRTF. They wanted to measure how well these services worked for high-risk youth. Results from this program showed that the implementation of home- and community-based services made a significant improvement in quality of life for this demonstration population. The PRTF Demonstration Program also showed that Medicaid agencies reduced the overall cost of care by utilizing home- and community-based services versus PRTF placements. Additionally, the demonstration program showed that 44 percent of children and youth improved their school attendance and 41 percent improved their grades after 12 months in home- and community-based services. Additionally, 33 percent of youth improved their behavioral strengths (ability to form interpersonal relationships, positive connections with family members, positive functioning at school, and ability to demonstrate self-confidence) after 12 months of service and 40 percent after 24 months (SAMHSA and CMCS, 2013).

Similarly, the Center for Mental Health Services (CMHS) of the Substance Abuse and Mental Health Services Administration (SAMHSA) funded a program to look at the effectiveness of home- and community-based services. The program was called the Comprehensive Community Mental Health Services for Children and Their Families Program (CCMHS). CCMHS provided cooperative agreements to communities to help build and recognize the importance of home- and community-based services to keep consumers in their homes, schools, communities, and close to their community links in an integral way. This project produced several positive outcomes related to the provision of home- and natural community-based behavioral health services. The positive outcomes reported (shown below; SAMHSA, 2008) are derived from data based on a comparison of how youth (ages 14 to 18) improved from the time they began these systems of care to 18 months following entry into services and included:

- Increased school attendance with 81 percent of consumers regularly attending school after six months of service;
- 20 percent reduction in school absences for youth whose attendance was affected by their behavioral and emotional problems;
- 44 percent reduction in the percentage of youth suspended or expelled from school;
- 31 percent of youth improved their school grades;
- Youth arrests dropped by more than half;
- Youth showed improved behavior and improved mental and emotional health by 48 percent;
- Youth became less depressed and anxious; and
- Suicide attempts and ideation decreased.

We know that home-, school-, and natural community-based services provide a more familiar environment for the consumer during what can be an extremely vulnerable time in his or her life. Research has also shown some promising outcomes from provision of behavioral health services in natural environments with specific populations. Research has indicated that these services, within certain populations, can be provided at a reduced cost of care (SAMHSA and CMCS, 2013). Given this data, it is a logical step to look at where we, as providers, legislatures, consumer advocates, and consumers, can advocate expanding service provision into these natural settings. Restrictive service settings are a needed part of the service continuum, but they are simply not the best option for most consumers.

Notes

1. Civil commitment is a legal process where a consumer with symptoms that constitute severe mental illness is court-ordered into inpatient hospital (or other treatment setting) for treatment.
2. A commitment order is an order issued by a judge when he or she finds that a consumer's mental illness presents a current danger to that person or those around him or her.
3. PRTF (Psychiatric Residential Treatment Facility) is any non-hospital facility with a provider agreement with a state Medicaid agency to provide inpatient services for consumers under the age of 21.

References

Community Care Division, Health Department, Scotland. (2013). *Short Breaks and Respite Care Services for Adults*. Retrieved November 2, 2013, from National Care Standards: www.nationalcarestandards.org/191.html

Department of Behavioral Health and Developmental Disabilities (DBHDD). (2013). *Georgia Crisis Response System for Individulals with Developmental Disabilities*. Retrieved October 22, 2013, from DBHDD: http://dbhdd.georgia. gov/sites/dbhdd.georgia.gov/files/imported/DBHDD/DD/Formatted%20 fact%20sheet_English_Final.pdf

National Alliance on Mental Health (NAMI). (2009). *Reinvesting in the Community: A Family Guide to Expanding Home and Community-Based Mental Health Services and Supports*. Retrieved November 1, 2013, from http://nami. org/Template.cfm?Section=Research_Services_and_Treatment&template=/ ContentManagement/ContentDisplay.cfm&ContentID=76200: (p. 11).

Substance Abuse and Mental Health Services Administration (SAMHSA). (2008, May 8). *Helping Youth Thrive in the Community*. Rockville, MD: Author. Retrieved October 31, 2013, from SAMHSA: http://digitallibraries.macrointer national.com/gsdl/collect/cmhssoci/index/assoc/HASH01f0.dir/doc.pdf

Substance Abuse and Mental Health Services Administration (SAMHSA) and Center for Medicaid and CHIP Services (CMCS). (2013, May 7). *Coverage of Behavioral Health Services for Children, Youth, and Young Adults with Significant Mental Health Conditions*. Retrieved November 5, 2013, from Medicaid: http://medicaid.gov/Federal-Policy-Guidance/Downloads/CIB-05-07-2013.pdf

3

BEHAVIORAL HEALTH TREATMENT IN THE HOME, SCHOOL, AND NATURAL COMMUNITY

Why Treatment Setting Is Important

Long ongoing has been a discussion between providers, researchers, consumer rights advocates, and legislators regarding the comparison of hospital-based versus community-based behavioral health treatment. Community-based mental health, as an initial concept, referred to services offered in non-hospital and non-institutional settings. While the term encompasses any non-hospital or non-institution setting, the current use of home- and community-based behavioral health treatment refers primarily to services provided in the least restrictive service environments—such as the consumer's domicile, school, and natural community. When looking at this issue, behavioral health care providers, consumers, and consumers' families tend to favor one treatment setting over the other. It is important to assert that each location of service provision and intensity of services occupies a needed position on the spectrum of behavioral health care provision. If hospital stays are accessed on an as-needed basis, only then can other community treatment programs be utilized (when consumers are not hospitalized) to give those consumers with more severe behavioral health issues the opportunity to receive therapeutic services, skill building, and resource coordination in a more familiar community environment.

In examining treatment settings, it is significant to assess how and why the setting itself may contribute to the number of consumers who choose not to seek care for their behavioral health issues. In its 2010 National Survey on Drug Use and Health, the Substance Abuse and Mental Health Services Administration (SAMHSA) examined why adult consumers did not receive behavioral health services when they had an unmet need in this area. Several major areas were identified as reasons why these survey participants did not receive services. Of the individuals in the survey, 43.7 percent stated they could not afford the cost of obtaining treatment; 32.3 percent of those surveyed felt they could handle their behavioral health problem without treatment; and 20.5 percent of the consumers in the survey stated they did not know where to go for services. Another 14.6 percent of those surveyed felt they could not find the time to devote to getting treatment; 10 percent did not want others to find out that they were seeking treatment for behavioral health issues. Of the remainder of the survey participants: 9.9 percent did not want their neighbors or community to have a negative opinion about them; 9.8 percent felt treatment would not help; 9.4 percent were concerned about confidentiality; 9.4 percent said health insurance did not cover enough treatment; 9.4 percent did not feel the need for treatment; 8.3 percent felt seeking treatment would have a negative effect on their job; 7.8 percent stated that health insurance would not cover any treatment; and 7.6 percent had a fear of being committed or having to take medication (Substance Abuse and Mental Health Services Administration, 2012). When we look at this data, it is worth noting that several of these barriers to obtaining behavioral health services could be ameliorated by the usage of home-, school-, and natural community-based services. As identified by the survey results, cost of services was one of the major barriers to seeking services. Since the most restrictive services usually require around-the-clock care, they typically are the most costly and serve the fewest consumers. The Psychiatric Residential Treatment Facility (PRTF) Demonstration Program conducted by the Center for Medicare and Medicaid Services (CMS) showed that state Medicaid agencies were able to reduce the overall cost of care for service by changing the treatment setting. In this study, intensive home- and community-based services provided to children and youth cost only 25 percent of what it would have cost to have served the same consumer in a PRTF (an average savings of $40,000 per year per child) (SAMHSA and CMCS, 2013, p. 2). This data resulted in Medicaid, as a payer, adding more home- and community-based services to its plans. While not all insurance plans have made this change, many Care Management Organizations (CMOs) and other payer sources have followed this trend.

Other barriers to seeking treatment identified in the National Survey on Drug Use and Health were that more than 20 percent of individuals in the survey did not know where to go for services, and almost 15 percent did not have time to get to service programs. Provisioning of services in the home, school, and natural community addresses both of these barriers. When services come to the consumer, both the eliminated logistical challenges of finding services and the reduced travel time may be enough to address known barriers to treatment for some consumers. Services in the home and natural community allow consumers to save time in the traditional commute to an office or facility. Many individuals with behavioral health issues may also find it difficult to hold a job or succeed in school, but service provision in their home environment and school environment, during non-academic class times, may allow them to reduce absenteeism resulting from attending traditional behavioral health appointments during the day. Employment and school issues often add even more complexity to the challenges consumers face in their everyday life. Keeping appointments during the day, that require the consumer to take time off from work or school, can interfere further with these two functions and often cause the issues to worsen. Service provision in the home, school, and natural community can remove this potential stressor from the consumer's daily living.

Other potential consumers still have difficulty navigating the behavioral health system in their community, and are able to receive services in the home and community that reduce time spent trying to find a match for services, and allow services in geographic areas that may not have traditional resources. Traditional treatment clinics, offices, and facilities provide the service at a particular location and the consumer must travel to them even if they do not live nearby. Service provision in the natural community is usually conducted by a provider who serves a general area around his or her clinic or home office. This allows companies to hire therapists and paraprofessionals in more remote or rural areas to service those outlier populations. This practice of being able to hire outside of a traditional radius of a central office, clinic, or facility can provide much needed enhancement to other service settings.

Box 3.1. Behavioral Health Consumer in Southern California: Consumer Experience

Academically, we can discuss what it means to lack necessary behavioral health services in a community. However, the words of another human being, a consumer who has experienced this paucity of available resources, speak volumes:

"There is a lack of mental health services in the community that are voluntary, friendly, competent and accessible. A number of years ago I was on the streets delusional and hearing voices for nine months in xxxx, California. You might have seen people like me . . . ragged hair and beard, very dirty and loudly talking to oneself. I asked for services at the shelter and the sheriff's station and was turned away. There was a missing person's report my conservator placed on me and when the police checked my ID they failed to connect. I sat in the waiting room of the county hospital for three days and was turned away. I stood in front of a bus and refused to move hoping that I would be taken to the hospital or the jail, but even that didn't work since I was physically removed by two passengers on the bus. This went on for nine months until someone took me and called my parents; who had me admitted to the hospital where

I received medicine that got rid of the voices. I would like to say this changed with the years, but it hasn't. In affluent xxxx, there are still no services for the homeless mentally ill."
Behavioral Health Consumer in Southern California
(New Freedom Commission on Mental Health, 2003, p. 19)

Another large group of individuals in the study seemed to be concerned about confidentiality, that is, how others in the community would view their mental disorder, and even the possibility that others would find out they were seeking treatment. These concerns can also be addressed, to some degree, with service provision in the home or natural community environment. While those living with the consumer may be aware of the treatment, the professionals that go to the home should honor the discretion required by HIPAA in the field (just as in their base office/institution). Providers going into the community should have a badge available to show their identification; however, this badge is not displayed in non-mandatory public settings, in order to protect the privacy of the consumer. When the consumer does not travel to a traditional treatment setting, he or she does not have to go to a parking lot, enter a building with signage that advertises the type of services he or she is seeking, or wait in a waiting room with others in the community. This reduced exposure can result in less inadvertent identification as a consumer of services by those not involved in their direct care.

Finally, one of the last areas individuals in the survey identified as a barrier to seeking behavioral health services was the fear of being committed or having to take medication. Home-, school-, and natural community-based services are provided in a familiar environment and a major aspiration of treatment is to prevent an inpatient hospitalization. All efforts are made by the provider to ensure the consumer has the tools he or she needs to be successful in his or her natural community. The use of formal supports and informal supports, already located in the natural community, can bolster the consumer's ability to succeed in that environment. In home-, school-, and community-based treatment, the consumer and the parent/caregiver/guardian should be informed participants in any applicable decision-making processes. Medication considerations are determined on a case-by-case basis, and should be based upon the individualized needs of the consumer. The prescribing psychiatrist can discuss options, and the consumer will be given the opportunity to talk about the potential benefits and risks associated with any proposed medication. In fact, the consumer should participate in a medication informed consent discussion that is fully documented. Consumers should be fully aware of any medication indications, dosage ranges, known potential

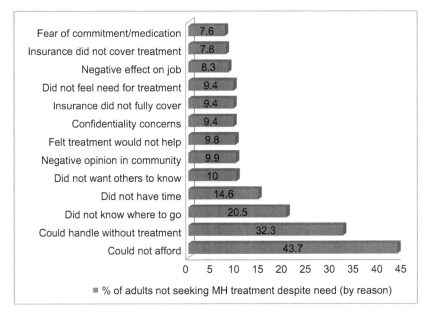

Figure 3.1 SAMHSA's Findings Regarding Reasons Adults Needing Behavioral Health Services Did Not Seek Treatment

Source: SAMHSA (2012)

side effects, and so on, via provision of a medication instruction sheet and/or oral explanation of the prescribed medication. Risks and benefits of medication, the possibility of side effects not currently reported, and alternative treatments should be discussed. The consumer completing this process is then able to make an informed decision as to whether he or she consents to take the proposed pharmaceutical intervention. The consumer has the right to withdraw consent at any time. See Figure 3.1 for a graphic summarization of the findings of the SAMHSA 2010 National Survey on Drug Use and Health regarding adult consumers who did not receive needed behavioral health services.

Coverage Considerations

Rural

Let's look at examples of geographic areas where traditional hospital- and clinic-based services may not exist or may exist, but that do not have the capacity to serve all of those in need in the surrounding community. If you are lucky enough to live in an area in a country with adequate behavioral health programs and policy, you are among the fortunate few.

There is not always adequate behavioral health service provision across the U.S. and elsewhere worldwide. The U.S. Health Resources and Services Administration (2013) conducted research to determine where there were Health Professional Shortage Areas (HPSA) and underserved areas or populations. In 2013, it determined that there are approximately 3,700 mental health HPSAs (based on a psychiatrist to population ratio of 1:30,000) (HRSA, 2013). Earlier studies reflected that up to 85 percent of federally designated HPSAs are in rural areas (New Freedom Commission on Mental Health, 2004). People who live in rural areas often experience stress associated with cyclical farm crises, natural disasters, and social isolation. These stressors have a bearing on behavioral health. This was demonstrated by the Farm Crisis Response Council of Interchurch Ministries of Nebraska. The council operated a hotline to serve rural individuals negatively affected by rural crisis. Between July 2008 and March 2009, the hotline reported that nearly 50 percent of its calls were related to mental health issues (Interchurch Ministries of Nebraska, 2009). To compound the situation, when a rural consumer has to travel a long distance to obtain treatment and lacks public transportation to reach care, the person often forgoes treatment.

> Rural Americans should be provided the same access to mental health emergency response, early identification and screening, diagnosis, treatment and recovery services as their non-rural peers.
> (New Freedom Commission on Mental Health, 2004)

Cultural

There are additional considerations regarding behavioral health service provision in rural areas as it pertains to tribal governments and cultural considerations. American Indian and Alaska Native Tribal governments, for example, are sovereign governmental entities. These groups may have unique behavioral health and substance use therapy needs stemming from entrenched poverty, historical trauma, small populations, and remote locations. In addition to needing more services for cultures that are more isolated and consequently have less access to services, there are additional cultural considerations to contemplate. In any group that is historically underserved, or inappropriately served, by behavioral health services, culturally appropriate services and provider representation is crucial. Outside providers, when utilized, need to incorporate into their treatment a respect for, and understanding of, the many elements that make up the culture of the consumer they are treating. Some considerations are an understanding of the histories, traditions, language, beliefs, politics, religious views, thoughts about behavioral health and treatment, and unique diverse racial and ethnic populations present in the culture. Some, but not all, cultural minority communities experience higher rates of risk for some behavioral and emotional issues. The risk factors for this increased rate may include poverty, domestic violence, childhood and historical trauma, and involvement in foster care and criminal justice systems. In these high service need areas, often there are not enough available providers to choose from, utilize, or recruit. That means that there may not always be exact cultural matches between providers and the community they serve. Regardless of the paucity of services and providers, however, attempts should be made to utilize culturally literate providers in targeted work with indigenous tribes, Asian Americans and Pacific Islanders, African Americans, Hispanic, and immigrant and refugee communities. It is within these groups that home- and natural community-based providers can most effectively meet the needs of a community. An agency can hire a practitioner that lives in close proximity to the need area to serve the population, and ensure that provider receives appropriate culturally based training. Additionally, in geographic areas where there simply are no available professionals in the area, paraprofessional and peer staff can be developed to meet behavioral health and substance use needs. Paraprofessionals that currently live in the community can receive targeted training to enable them to then work within the cultural community. Trained paraprofessionals can provide much needed skill building, training, and resource coordination. Additionally, peer supports, who are in recovery from mental and substance use disorders themselves, and that live in the community, can also receive additional training and/or certification to enable them to better serve their own community.

Commonly, there are individuals who, though unlicensed, are already recognized within the community as healers. Providers from outside the community and within can recognize these folk healers and thoughtfully consider the possibility of involving them in partnerships and collaborative care. It is relevant for behavioral health providers to be aware of folk healing practices in the communities they serve. In many cultural traditions, there is an element of spirituality that plays a role in cultural development. Many of these traditions are not practiced by the majority culture, but have been a base in certain therapies and activities that have developed within those cultures. The provider need not share the same belief system to show respect to the elements of culture that are personally significant to the consumer. Learning about the consumer's culture and beliefs as they pertain to health (both behavioral and physical) simply allows the provider to incorporate informal supports that may be vital to the consumer's full participation in treatment. The information available regarding folk healers is considerable and covers many cultures and practices; far too extensive to reference individually in this chapter. In recognition of this fact, the focus here will be on some of the more representative folk practices. Table 3.1 gives an overview of some of the

Table 3.1 Behavioral Health Collaboration With Traditional Folk Healers

Cultural Group	Tradition in Healing	Behavioral Health Applications
American Indians and Alaskan Natives	There are hundreds of tribes and almost as many healing traditions for American Indians and Alaskan Natives. Native American healing is usually a combination of herbal remedies, spirituality, and rituals to treat behavioral health and medical problems. Generally the underlying concept in most spiritual and healing practices is reverence for nature and for the earth. In most traditional indigenous healing practices, there is a medicine man, or shaman, that conducts his practices to bring about a cure. Native Americans also believe physical illness is a result of poor emotional health. This is often believed to be caused by not being in tune to the world around them, their family, or being respectful of self through moral behavior. The medicine man attempts to restore the person to his or her whole self and balance with nature in order to heal. Part of this process includes prayer and imploring Spirit, herbal remedies, and ceremony. (NIH, 2012)	Behavioral health providers can incorporate the concept of balance into their interventions. The shaman can be included in the treatment planning process and identified as an informal support within the community.
Caribbean	Santeria is practiced primarily in the Caribbean and merges the traditional religion of the Yoruba people of Africa with Catholicism. Although Santeria is magical in nature, it is the guiding force for those that follow it, as they turn to the *orisha* (go-betweens between divine powers and people). Those that practice Santeria believe the orishas require praise, food, and animal sacrifices in order to act as their go-between. Orishas are believed to rule over the forces of nature and human enterprise. Followers believe they can come face-to-face with orishas during trance possession. Believers turn to orishas for help with their daily problems in all areas: love, work, physical and emotional health. (BBC, 2013)	Behavioral health providers can acknowledge the importance of the consumer's central belief systems in overall treatment planning and goals.

(Continued)

Table 3.1 (Continued)

Cultural Group	Tradition in Healing	Behavioral Health Applications
Haiti and Parts of U.S. (New Orleans)	Religion plays a critical role in Haitian life and health. Vodou (also spelled Voodoo, Voudou, or Vodon) is practiced by the majority in Haiti, including those who identify as Catholic. Vodou is not only a religion, but is part of a health practice in that it includes healing practices, promotion of health, and prevention of illness. The levels of health, or illness, are based on a harmonious relationship with ancestors and the role of magic or sorcery attacks. The health or illness of a person is believed to be related to his or her connection with tradition and place in the social and moral order and a wider universe that includes ancestors and gods. Disturbances in health, including behavioral health, are seen as a sign that relationships among the dead and living are disrupted. It is believed that rituals can heal the participant by mending broken relationships. (WHO/PAHO, 2010)	Behavioral health providers can use spiritual leaders as allies to encourage consumers to adhere to recommendations and treatment. Spiritual leaders are trusted in the community and can serve as consultants and informal supports.
India	There are many different practices throughout India, but one folk healing tradition is that of the hereditary healer. These healers specialize in specific maladies. A healer who works with diseases of the mind is called a *manasika chikitsa*. These tribal healers utilize regional medicinal plants. The healing practices also include rituals, chants, and song therapy—which are considered sacred and specifically for diseases of the mind. Some medicinal selections overlap with more classic pharmacology used in Ayurvedic[iii] remedies. (NIH, 2013)	Behavioral health providers can incorporate healers into the informal support system for the consumer. Psychiatrists may find that some populations are hesitant to utilize traditional medication as they prefer natural prescriptions.
Japanese: Naikan and Morita Therapies	Mental illness is considered a stigma in Japan and therefore many consumers describe their behavioral health symptoms by the physical symptoms that accompany them. They seek treatment for these disorders from medical doctors. Modern Morita Therapy (Dr. Shoma Morita)[i] incorporates the Japanese philosophy of mindfulness while Naikan (Yoshimoto Ishin)[ii] involves self-reflection and a focus on how primary relationships have shaped the consumer's life.	Behavioral health providers can incorporate high regard for harmony, peace, and reciprocity into their interventions.

Mexican Descendants, Southwest U.S. and Mexico	*Curanderismo* is a healing method used by some people of Mexican decent in the Southwest U.S. and Mexico. The name is derived from the Spanish word *curar,* meaning to heal. Curanderismo is practiced by the shaman of the culture. The curandero/curandera, or shaman, treats both physical and emotional ailments and may be either a generalist or have a specialty (e.g., herbal medicine, massage, or midwivery). The curandero deals with all aspects of the client's life, including material, spiritual, and mental. Most treatment consists of herbal therapy in combination with ritual and counsel. (NIH, 2012)	As behavioral health providers in home and natural community settings, it is important to include respected healers, such as the curandero, in treatment planning and as resources for informal supports in the community.
South American Native Traditions	Healing traditions in South and Central America are numerous as there are large numbers of regional tribes and groups. An example is among the Andean people and traditions of Peru and Bolivia. Andean philosophy has a foundation of the Divine Feminine, the Divine Masculine, and that which is beyond the classification of gender. Lake Titicaca is known to the Andeans as Mamacota (Mother Lake) and is a strong natural center of feminine energies. Pachamama is known as the Earth Mother. The Andean people are well versed in herbalism and other native healing traditions.	As behavioral health providers in home and natural community settings, it is important to include respected healers, such as the *Kallawaya, hechiceros,* and *yatiris,* in treatment planning and as resources for informal supports in the community.
	In Bolivia, much of the population turns to natural prescriptions before going to a modern physician. In this culture traditional healers, called *hechiceros* and *yatiris,* deal primarily with mental disease and with the environmental, psychological, social, and cultural causes of disease. Villagers across the Andean area have a deep respect for natural healers, including the traveling *Kallawaya.*[iv] Kallawayas use different kinds of medicines and rituals to restore balance to the individual and his or her environment. This balancing is intended to ensure harmony between the two. (NIH, 2012)	Psychiatrists may find that some populations are hesitant to utilize medication as they prefer natural prescriptions.

(*Continued*)

Table 3.1 (Continued)

Cultural Group	Tradition in Healing	Behavioral Health Applications
The Tainos of Puerto Rico	The Taino are the native people of Puerto Rico. They share the same earth-based spirituality and reverence for nature as the American Indians. They revere Mother Earth and all inhabitants of the earth, including animals. Taino worship Father Sun. It is believed that one needs balance in order to maintain good physical and emotional health.	Behavioral health providers can incorporate the concept of balance into their interventions.
Traditional Chinese Medicine	The heart of traditional Chinese medicine is the balance of yin and yang. It is believed that if there is imbalance in someone's life that person can lack harmony and disease can result. Traditional Chinese medicine uses acupuncture, herbs, and Qi-Gong (energy cultivation). This combination approach is used to alleviate physical problems, bring about harmony, and eliminate bad habits. Tai Chi, a meditative exercise, is often used in conjunction with the prior approaches. (NIH, 2010)	Traditional Chinese medicine can be recognized by behavioral health providers in treatment planning and as an ongoing resource by including the medical practitioner in the planning process.
Vietnamese	Indigenous healing in Vietnam utilizes herbs, spices, and naturally occurring substances to heal. They consider physical health and emotional health to go hand-in-hand. Therefore, when someone is unwell, it is believed that the whole self needs to heal. The religion most frequently practiced in Vietnam is Buddhism. This religion teaches that man is born into this world to learn and stay on a spiritual path. It is assumed that life includes suffering to bring about wisdom. Therefore when Buddhists are in need of behavioral health support they are most likely to turn to their religion to explain their suffering and to seek healing.	Treatment planning for this population should include a holistic approach. Consumers may be most comfortable when the provider recognizes the importance of utilizing naturally occurring substances to heal.

*Several more prevalent folk healing traditions have been presented in the table above. This sampling is not, however, intended to be inclusive of all indigenous healing practices worldwide.

[i] Morita Therapy was developed by Dr. Shoma Morita of Jikei University School of Medicine.

[ii] Naikan was developed by Yoshimoto Ishin. This model is used in behavioral health counseling, addiction treatment, criminal rehabilitation, schools, and business.

[iii] Ayurvedic healing is a natural method of treating illness that has its origins in the Vedic culture of India.

[iv] *Kallawaya* means "he who carries medicines on his shoulders."

folk healers that home- and community-based behavioral health service providers may interact with and partner to provide holistic coverage to their consumers.

International

Mental and substance use disorders are common in all areas around the world. Those individuals that are affected by behavioral health or substance use issues cross every socioeconomic, cultural, gender, and age group. These issues do not respect geographic boundaries either. The World Health Organization (WHO) estimates that 14 percent of all global disease burden is attributed to these disorders. It is also relevant to note that 75 percent of the individuals affected are in low-income countries (WHO, 2011).

WHO, in fact, noted that resources are either unavailable or insufficient to provide equitably distributed and efficiently used health services across much of the world. This paucity of services, in some areas, has resulted in a large majority of people simply receiving no care for their disorders. As a result, WHO launched the Mental Health Gap Programme (mhGAP) to address the lack of mental health care, especially in low- and middle-income countries. In the WHO mhGAP Intervention Guide, the misconception that improvements in behavioral health systems require expensive technologies and solutions is rebuffed. The reality that many worldwide behavioral health and substance use issues can be addressed and managed by non-specialists is discussed. The initial mhGAP intervention guidelines were developed in 2008 and updated in 2013. mhGAP is a brief guide to facilitate interventions by non-specialists in low- and middle-income countries. The intervention guidelines even include the mhGAP Evidence Resource Center (updated in 2012). This area is intended to provide evidence-based guidelines for use in working with mental health, neurological, and substance use disorders in non-specialized settings. More details of these identified evidence-based recommendations are included in Appendix B. The mhGAP Intervention Guide provides a guideline for service development and unites well with home- and community-based settings to allow services to be provided in many geographic areas that may not have established treatment locations. It also provides information about integration of behavioral health services into primary care (WHO, 2011).

Blend of Services

Many geographic areas offer a large selection of services and settings to address the behavioral health challenges of the consumer. This diversity of services gives the consumer a chance to explore a mixed blend of available resources. It is important to note that services will vary by country, state, and community. Some regions have more access to resources than others. Consequently, some consumer treatment plans utilize a combination of these settings and approaches to provide well-balanced treatment.

Some mental and substance use disorder presentations are severe and require psychiatric hospitalization as the best option to ensure safety of the consumer. Community-based treatment programs geared toward severe mental illnesses, however, can reduce the need for acute inpatient hospitalization and reduce the length of stay. These community-based treatment services may be offered in office or facility (ideally with a component incorporating some home- and natural community-based service provision), or in the home, school, and natural community in which the consumer lives. In some circumstances, it may require a combination of models to successfully provide high-quality behavioral health treatment. The availability of resources also has a strong impact on the development of well-balanced behavioral health care services.

Home-, School-, and Natural Community-Based Services

Home-, school-, and natural community-based services provision allows the consumer to remain in a familiar environment and learn skills and new approaches in the very environment where the consumer may be experiencing difficulty. In-home services allow the consumer to feel more at ease in a familiar environment, while the behavioral health professional is afforded a unique glimpse into the consumer's everyday stressors, supports, and living conditions.

In this author's opinion, home and natural community-based services work because the behavioral health professional is able take a more holistic view as to what has contributed to the consumer's issues. The provider is also able to see and identify more of the environmental challenges and barriers and find ways to address them. When someone is part of an environment on a day-to-day basis, some of the challenges the person faces and strengths at his or her disposal to bring to bear upon those challenges, may not be obvious to that person. The person may have lost his or her perspective as to what is a proximal resource and what challenges are unique to him or her or his or her environment. By being part of the consumer's environment, a provider is able to gain a different perspective in this area. Home, school, and natural community environments can present challenges and struggles that are not readily identified without direct observation. When the behavioral health provider is present in the very environment where most issues present, he or she can provide insight into the catalysts for behaviors, stressors, or disorders.

During my years providing in-clinic therapeutic intervention, I was able to work with many consumers and help them reach the goals identified on their treatment plans. During those early sessions with consumers, I believed I often developed a skewed perception of the presenting issues. This is a risk in any practice, whether a practitioner treats a consumer in an inpatient, emergency department, residential facility, outpatient treatment center, or community-based setting. During early interactions, consumers may be in crisis and present with exaggerated symptomology or, conversely, with understated portrayals of their current situation. Also, during crisis, consumers may be experiencing extreme stressors, and present with one primary issue that is later identified as one of several presenting and relevant issues. Additionally, consumers may want to present in their best light if they are referred by the court or the Department of Family and Children Services.[1] So, as a provider, you are left to filter out how a crisis, situational stressor, outside assessment, substance use issue, physical health issue is affecting the presentation of the consumer in front of you. While home- and natural community-based behavioral health provision is certainly no magic hat of filtering through all of these issues, it undoubtedly affords the provider the luxury of observing the microcosm that is the consumer's world. This world, its inherent stressors and challenges, the supports that are built into this world, and the causal and curative factors become more visible when the provider is able to experience pieces of them firsthand. In my years of providing services in the home environment, I feel I gained a more intact picture of presenting issues, strengths, and challenges to consumers by assessing them in their home environments. Certainly, some of the same stressors and issues are present in any treatment setting, but the provider and consumer seem to build rapport and let go of pretenses much more quickly in an environment that represents more of the true stressors and challenges of everyday living.

Consumer Case Examples (Home-, School-, and Natural Community-Based)

Perhaps the best way to illustrate my assertion that home and natural community-based services provide a level of insight that is difficult to otherwise obtain is to provide examples of how this author has seen success in these very environments. These examples are drawn from real people and circumstances and their names and identifying information have been changed to protect their identity. The intent of these scenarios is to use real-life cases to illustrate how home- and natural community-based behavioral health services may provide a deeper level of observation and understanding of consumer's daily lives, symptoms, and environmental challenges.

Anna

Anna is an eight-year-old child who is referred for assessment and possible medication management for ADHD. Anna's grandparents brought her into the clinic for an assessment and medication evaluation for ADHD as they felt her behavior was vastly more active than typical for her age. They also felt she was less attentive than her peers and than their own children had been. Anna's parents had been in and out of jail and her grandparents had temporary custody during these periods of instability. When a rating scale was sent to the school it was returned without any flags for ADHD indicators. The parental/guardian assessment (given to the grandparents), however, showed positive identification of many behaviors typical of ADHD on the rating scale, particularly of those of ADHD-Hyperactivity-Impulsivity. Upon an interview with the grandparents, they reported being overwhelmed by Anna's constant movement, excessive talking, and interruptions.

An in-home counselor and community support individual[2] were able to go to Anna's home and talk with her and gain additional insight. Additionally, they were able to visit Anna's school and talk with her teacher to gain a more rounded viewpoint of her behavior in different environments. The in-home counselor and community support individual were able to observe Anna's behavior in the home and compare their observation to parental, teacher, and self-reports. The conclusions drawn were strongly influenced by the behavioral observations in the home. During the sessions, it was observed that the grandparents were highly agitated at Anna for behaviors which appeared to be typical of an eight-year-old child. When she was excited about her day at school and began to tell them the details, oftentimes she would be met with a strong negative reaction from her grandparents. When she asked to go out and play, she was often told to go read quietly or go to her room. Over the course of several sessions, it became apparent that Anna was not exhibiting behaviors atypical for her age. Her behavior appeared to be on level with other children her age and was not marked by any notable inattentive, distractible, or hyper behaviors. The variable that was identified during these sessions, however, was that the grandparents were resentful of being put in the position to parent a young child many years after their original child-rearing years. Both grandparents had previously developed their own social networks, had social outings that had been established, and were truly enjoying their Golden Years. Although they loved Anna dearly and wanted to be available for her, they simply were not prepared for the perceived disruptions it brought to their established and cherished daily life. They had lost connection with many of their friends and activities as they now were working around bath times, homework, and childhood activities. The resentment over the loss of their support networks had left them feeling tired, overwhelmed, and resentful of the changes. Through therapeutic intervention, the family was able to make some internal changes and have dialogue that allowed them to move forward in a positive direction. The grandparents set aside one night a week to reconnect with their friends and set up a babysitter. Family Meetings allowed the family to discuss daily happenings so that Anna was not always trying so hard to get her grandparents' attention. These changes, established through in-home meetings, helped this family successfully navigate many of their concerns.

In this case some of the observations made in the home and school environments during varied times of the day afforded the treatment duo the opportunity to both observe Anna in varied settings and her caregivers during typical daily stressors. These observations in a natural environment under natural stressors provided clarifying insight into the presenting issues.

John

John is a 51-year-old male who had been living under an interstate bridge and had a past diagnosis of schizophrenia. John had been in and out of inpatient treatment for the last 30 years of his life and is considered to have severe and persistent mental illness. He stabilized when in inpatient care and under medication. However, when he returned to the community, he was unable to be compliant with clinic-based services because he was unable to navigate the system, obtain transportation consistently, and have all of his health needs met. John has been a high utilizer of costly psychiatric services over the years as he has cycled in and out of inpatient hospitalization and emergency department treatment. An Assertive Community Treatment (ACT) Team responded to a referral for John and located him where he currently resided under an interstate bridge. He was usually able to be found in this location because he was vested in keeping this "home" as it provided shelter from the weather, allowed some compartmented areas where he was able to keep his belongings, and was not frequented by other homeless individuals due to its remote location.

The Assertive Community Treatment team comprised behavioral health and substance abuse professionals who provided 24-hour coverage and responded to all behavioral health emergencies for John. They had been able to provide services to John in his natural community surroundings, whereas he may not have gone back to a clinic-based service environment due to logistical challenges. His ACT team not only worked with his behavioral health and substance use issues, but they also assisted John in resource coordination, a much needed piece of his treatment. His physical health had deteriorated as a result of his behavioral health challenges and harsh living environment. There was an MD that was on the ACT team who attended to John's physical health and medication management issues. Therapists on the team worked with John's behavioral health and substance use issues and coping skills development. Paraprofessionals on the ACT team worked with John to make sure he was able to navigate and coordinate all needed services and identify any additional resources that were necessary. Oftentimes, they transported John to any clinic-based appointments to overcome his transportation challenges, and to ensure that he was prompted to comply with those aspects of his treatment. Additionally, the ACT team had members who specialized in housing and vocational support.

The ACT team was able to provide services to John in the very environment where he resided, they brought services to him where he was unable to consistently seek and coordinate these services himself. Over the course of eight months of ACT Team intervention, John was able to move to Supported Housing to allow him to move toward housing stability and supported services. Over time, John was able to move into his own apartment and gain employment through Supported Employment services. John still has some ongoing community-based resource coordination, group therapy, and medication management to support his independent living. With these supports in place, John is proud of his accomplishments in working and having his own apartment and has made great strides in his progress.

Providers Working Together

We have discussed the concept of behavioral health service provision in the home, school, and natural community, but it is important to look at ways that all providers can work together to minimize consumer length of stay in more restrictive service environments. These efforts do not have to be just reserved for the provider who can dedicate the practice to provision of services in the home and natural community. Instead, these efforts can be made by providers across the continuum of environments in which services can be rendered. An initial step for providers in inpatient hospitals would be to ensure that the hospital or PRTF has intensive case management to ensure that connections are made; appointments are kept; and follow-up services are provided to those diverted or discharged from short-term inpatient psychiatric care. When consumers have had an interruption to their daily lives and schedules, they may not be in a frame of mind conducive to making the decisions necessary to secure their next appointment or to implement other next steps to protect their behavioral health. Having someone to help consumers coordinate this journey can make a major difference for those trying to navigate their next steps. Emergency room providers can also be part of the community-based solution. Often, emergency rooms become holding placements[3] for consumers that are in severe psychiatric distress. Administration, however, can allocate additional staff strategically located in hospital emergency rooms to facilitate triage assessment and possible referral to community services. Both of these steps can help make the process smoother for consumers who are transitioning and help to ensure that they receive follow-up or step-down services in an expedient manner so that return visits to higher levels of care can be minimized.

Specific Services

It is essential to look more in depth at what specific services can be utilized in home-, school-, and natural community-based settings. Providers can offer the services, to follow, in home-, school-, and natural community-based settings entirely, or as augmentation of clinic-based or more restrictive service provision settings with an *à la carte*[4] model. While research in support of home-, school-, and natural community-based service provision may be based on service provision entirely in those settings, there are some providers who operate in traditional clinic settings who are able to use some of these services to bring additional perspective to their existing work. These providers, for example, may elect to use home- and natural community-based service provision for part of their treatment plan with a consumer. A specific example of this approach could be the provider who conducts the initial comprehensive assessment in the consumer's home and provides family therapy services in the consumer's home to ensure that all family members are able to participate. Individual therapy, group therapy, and medication management services may take place in a clinic. It is important for the provider to utilize the methodology that works best for him or her and the consumer. No two cases are the same, no two histories are the same, and therefore no two approaches should ever be exactly the same.

The home, school, and natural community services identified in the following paragraphs are representative of services that are available in many geographic areas. Of course, every state and country has different designations of these programs and variations of the concepts presented. This overview, however, is intended to show some of the ways to integrate services into home, school, and natural community settings. Many of the services listed may be called by a different name in other geographic areas and some of the program set-up parameters may vary as well. All of the services are listed as currently reimbursed services in the United States either under Medicaid/Medicare, Care Management Organizations, state payers, private payers, private insurance, or waivers. These services, or a variant thereof, may be reimbursed in your locale. Where they are not presently reimbursed, consumers, providers, and community advocates can promote inclusion of these services into their payer formats.

Early Identification and Intervention

Early identification is mentioned as part of the continuum of home-, school-, and natural community-based services because when behavioral health issues are identified early for a consumer, it is easier to treat the issue. Early identification leads to early intervention and can avoid more restrictive and severe treatments for the consumer in the future. Comprehensive assessment services are a route to early identification of issues. An assessor in the home environment has the added benefit of viewing some of the stressors and challenges the consumer is experiencing daily, as well as the supports in that environment. Issues may be identified earlier because the assessor will see the consumer's real life reactions to stressors as they develop in their natural environment.

Prevention and Early Intervention

Prevention and early intervention programs provide psychoeducation, early intervention treatment, and coping skills development for individuals who are at risk for mental illness. Support and education are also provided to family members. The goal of prevention and early intervention is to encourage positive behaviors and develop coping skills in individuals identified as at risk, prior to the point where more intensive services are needed and/or they enter into treatment. These services can be provided in individual or group format in many settings. Prevention services in the home can be provided to an individual or family that has risk indicators for mental illness. School-based prevention programs may be provided in group or individual formats and may focus on relevant student issues such as bullying prevention, violence prevention, underage drinking awareness, and teen pregnancy prevention. In 2010, the National Prevention Council published its National Prevention Strategy in support of implementation of community-based preventative services and enhanced linkages with clinical care. This strategy paper speaks directly to provision of prevention services in communities, worksites, schools, residential treatment centers, and homes (HHS: National Prevention Council, 2010).

Comprehensive Home-Based Assessments

The comprehensive home-based assessment is an extensive assessment (usually conducted for child/adolescent consumers) that traditionally utilizes information gathered from the consumer, family, caregivers, teachers, providers, and other involved entities. These assessments should include a visit to the consumer's home and visits or interviews with those individuals involved in the consumer's life. Traditionally, they will also include a complete treatment history, diagnostic assessment, and in-depth information on the consumer's strengths, skills, needs, and challenges.

Virtual Residential Services

Some organizations have come up with unique ways to serve consumers with more severe services needs in the home and community. Providence Service Corporation created the Virtual Residential Program (VRP) to meet the needs of children and adolescents with severe emotional disturbances that were at risk for out-of-home placement. It combined the structure of a residential placement with the effectiveness of providing services in the consumer's own home. Virtual Residential Program is composed of a team of professionals that include the consumer and the caregiver. VRP has a lead therapist, a home-based counselor, and a behavioral interventionist or coach. VRP has a two- to six-month length of stay that is characterized by a phased approach to treatment (with an average length of treatment of 4.3 months). This phased approach includes an orientation phase during which VRP staff may be in the consumer home up to 30 hours per week to set up structure and to make sure the presenting situation is stabilized. This phase offers the structure of a formal residential setting within the consumer's own home. After this point, the intensity of the services is individualized to meet the specific needs of the youth and the family. During the course of services, the family will progress toward less intensive intervention, toward greater self-reliance, and toward usage of natural support systems in their own communities. This natural phasing allows the consumer to move away from dependence on the VRP team. An outcome study on Virtual Residential Program revealed a shorter length of stay than that of residential placements, and 72 percent of participants successfully remaining in the community (Providence Service Corporation, 2013).

Case Management and Intensive Case Management (ICM)

A professional case manager is someone who can work closely with the consumer with serious mental illness to develop a comprehensive treatment plan. The case manager is able to coordinate the services and resources needed to keep the consumer in the home and community and receiving the services needed. The key components of case management and intensive case management include engagement, reviewing assessment information, treatment and resource planning, coordination of care, resource linkage and referral, monitoring of symptoms and follow-up, and discharge planning. ICM services range from intensive coordination and involvement with a singular case manager to a team approach that can involve frequent home and community visits that provide instruction; education; coping skills development; resource and care coordination; psychoeducational aspects; and assistance with housing, income, and vocational concerns.

Clubhouses

Clubhouses are community-based centers designed for individuals suffering from mental illness. They are utilized around the world. Clubhouses provide an opportunity for many consumers to belong to a group in their community. Services provided include assistance with employment, education, social development, access to needed services, and housing. Clubhouses also offer practical support opportunities such as working with staff to run the clubhouse, and learning job skills in the process. The membership is voluntary and members can choose when they want to participate. Members usually live in the surrounding community and go to the clubhouse for support services and even for evening and weekend social programs. Although the services are not offered in the home, they are offered in the clubhouses, which are located in natural community settings across rural, urban, and suburban areas that span a wide variety of ethnic, culture, and socioeconomic groups. The ICCD (International Center for Clubhouse Development) Clubhouse Model is listed on the National Registry of Evidence-Based Programs and Practices (SAMHSA, 2010).

Wraparound Services/Intensive Care Coordination

Intensive care coordination is an approach to collaborative care that includes assessment and treatment planning. This care coordination includes triaging for service needs and arranging for those services and supports. Many of these services are offered in the home and natural community.

> The wraparound approach is a form of intensive care coordination for children with significant mental health conditions. It is a team-based, collaborative process for developing and implementing individualized care plans for children and youth with complex needs and their families. This approach focuses on all life domains and includes clinical interventions and formal and informal supports. The wraparound "facilitator" is the intensive care coordinator who organizes, convenes, and coordinates this process. The wraparound approach is done by a child and family

team for each youth that includes the child, family members, involved providers, and key members of the child's formal and informal support network, including members from the child serving agencies. The child and family team develops, implements, and monitors the service plan.

(SAMHSA and CMCS, 2013, p. 3)

Therapeutic Foster Care

In therapeutic foster care, therapeutically trained foster parents work with youth in their own foster home. This placement option is for youth placed outside of the family home, but still within a family setting. Therapeutic foster care allows a child or adolescent with severe emotional and behavioral challenges to remain in a home environment rather than undergo a residential placement. The trained therapeutic foster care provider assumes the duties of the caregiver for the length of time the consumer is in the program. Additional community-based services, supports, and training are provided to help maintain the consumer in the community placement. The Surgeon General's report (U.S. Department of Health and Human Services, 1999) stated that "youth in therapeutic foster care made significant improvements in adjustment, self-esteem, sense of identity, and aggressive behavior. In addition, gains were sustained for some time after leaving the therapeutic foster home" (p. 177). Multidimensional Treatment Foster Care (MTFC) is a particularly effective service for youth with severe emotional disturbance, anti-social behavior, delinquency, and who are in need of out-of-home placement. MTFC foster parents receive training and supervision in behavior management and other therapeutic methods.

Paraprofessional Services

Paraprofessional services are provided by a paraprofessional who works with the consumer to develop and improve skills. These care providers may work with anger management, social skills, coping skills development, problem-solving skills, daily living, communication needs, vocational support, educational support, housing support, and resource coordination. Paraprofessional workers may be referred to as Behavior Aides, Community Support Individuals, Family Development Specialists, Mentors, or Resource Specialists. Different organizations and areas of the country have preferences as to the title they utilize to refer to an individual who works with skill building and resource coordination for consumers. Paraprofessional services are a crucial piece of behavioral health service provision, and working in the home, school, and natural community is the ideal place to offer these services as resource needs are more easily identifiable when the paraprofessional is in the consumer's own living environment. Additionally, paraprofessional staff can help consumers practice skills and learned positive behaviors in the home and school environments to provide real time feedback and opportunities for revision and review.

Mobile Treatment Teams/Crisis Stabilization

Crisis stabilization services provide assertive outreach, assessment, crisis intervention, and resource linkage necessary to support the consumer's services in his or her own environment. This level of intervention can be utilized to resolve an immediate crisis until a more appropriate and routine service can be put into place. Most teams have some combination of a crisis line and mobile crisis team. Services are also typically provided 24 hours a day and seven days a week in the home, school, emergency shelters, and natural community settings. In some cases, a two-person crisis team is on-call and available to respond in a crisis situation. Some Mobile Crisis Teams, however, may utilize a full team structure that includes professionals and paraprofessionals who are trained in crisis intervention skills. The team works with the consumer and family to identify any triggers to the crisis, to resolve the crisis, and to learn strategies to deal with the triggers and crises as they occur in the future.

Respite

Respite is a family support approach that provides relief for those caring for a consumer in the home. A caregiver may be placed into the consumer's home to provide services or the consumer may be placed in another setting for a brief time. This type of respite care allows families and caregivers of consumers with serious behavioral health needs to have a break from the day-to-day responsibilities associated with care. This break helps to reduce stress levels in the home and possible escalation of issues. Trained respite care providers assume the duties of the caregiver for a brief time to give parents and guardians a break from the strain of caring for a child or adult with serious emotional and behavioral problems.

Clinical Intervention and Supports

Psychosocial interventions are provided in the home, school, or other community settings in the form of individual or family therapy. Traditionally, the provider will utilize interventions from an evidence-based practice model. Clinical interventions and supports may be provided by professional counselors, social workers, marriage and family therapists, psychologists, psychiatrists, and substance abuse professionals. The regulations around who can provide therapy vary from state to country and even within payer panels. Most therapeutic intervention, however, is conducted by fully licensed, associate-licensed, and master's level behavioral health clinicians; and certified substance abuse professionals.

Assertive Community Treatment (ACT)

Assertive Community Treatment (ACT) started with a group of behavioral health professionals at the Mendota Mental Health Institute in Wisconsin (Arnold Marx, MD, Leonard Stein, MD, and Mary Ann Test, PhD) who recognized that consumers discharged from inpatient care in stable condition were often readmitted soon thereafter. This group wanted to find out how they could treat these consumers in their own communities and give them the opportunity to obtain a life not driven purely by their illness (SAMHSA, 2008). An ACT team is a multidisciplinary team-based model of providing comprehensive and flexible treatment and support to consumers who live with serious mental illness. The goals of the ACT Team are to let the consumer live in the community, avoid residential and hospital placements, and to assist the consumer with mental and substance abuse disorders. Teams can include peer support specialists and practitioners with expertise in psychiatry and medication management, nursing, counseling, social work, substance abuse treatment, housing, and employment who work closely together to provide services that are based on outreach. These teams are available for crisis seven days a week and 24 hours a day. ACT services are provided primarily in the community in which the consumer resides. Sometimes that living environment is in a residential family home, and sometimes in an apartment, shelter, transitional living, or perhaps even under a bridge. ACT services come to consumers who need intensive community-based treatment in their own surroundings.

Intensive Family Intervention (IFI)

Intensive Family Intervention (IFI) is an intensive service to children and adolescents who have severe emotional disturbances or substance abuse issues. These consumers are at high risk for out-of-home placement. The services are provided in a team approach and provided primarily in the home of the consumer. Services can also be provided in school, natural communities, community agencies, and courts as needed. IFI serves to assist consumers in stabilizing crisis, connecting with resources, obtaining appropriate clinical services, increasing ability for self-care, and reducing risk of placement outside of the home. Services usually include a team of three to four individuals including a fully licensed Team Leader and paraprofessional with additional master's degree level clinicians and paraprofessionals within the team design. IFI services are intended to prevent out-of-home placement and involve a higher frequency and intensity of services at the onset of services to mitigate crisis and a gradual step down in intensity of services provision (DBHDD, 2013).

Supported Living

Consumers with more severe mental illness may need the support of community behavioral health to be able to maintain housing in the community. The consumer with supported living supports is able to live in his or her own home and receive personalized supports to maintain that private home. Some services the consumer many receive include coaching, supported employment, transportation, companion services, and in-home supports.

Supported Employment

In supported employment, employment specialists work with consumers to help them gain the supports necessary to achieve competitive work. The employment specialist traditionally works with both the consumer and the behavioral health providers to identify and work toward specific vocational goals and objectives. Supported employment programs recognize that paid employment is an important part of the recovery and resiliency process for many consumers. Therefore, they traditionally provide ongoing support to the consumers to help them overcome challenges they may have in the workplace and to help them retain employment and succeed in their placement. These services can be provided in-clinic and as part of home- and natural community-based intervention. "Studies of supported employment show that 60 percent to 80 percent of people with serious mental illness obtain at least one competitive job—a clear success rate" (New Freedom Commission on Mental Health, 2003, p. 41).

Family Support Services

Family support services are traditionally community-based services that assist and support parents in their role as caregivers. The principle behind these services is that all families can benefit from support in some way, and the goal is to help caregivers enhance their skills and resolve issues so that optimal child development can be promoted. Family support programs may be generalized or may target particular groups such as minorities, kinship caregivers, substance abuse issues, behavioral health issues, or teen parenting. These services focus on skill development and/or resource coordination.

Peer Support

The role of the peer support approach is to help consumers understand and manage their illness, follow through on goals and action plans, re-establish social networks, decrease their social isolation, and access community resources. Additionally, the peer support approach includes providing emotional support and advocacy to consumers. Peer Support Specialists are a group of individuals who have learned through their own experiences as someone with behavioral health or substance abuse issues. As mentioned earlier, some peer providers may also undergo additional training and go through a certification process prior to providing support services. Peer providers can be used in traditional behavioral health programs as part of a service delivery team, as well as in home-, school-, and natural community-based services. Peer services can also take on the form of peer education, peer support groups, and peer-run services such as peer mentoring, peer case management, and peer support centers.

School-Based Services

School-based behavioral health services can be provided by the school and through community partnerships on the school campus. Many schools employ a school psychologist and/or school counselor/social worker to remain on campus and address behavioral health issues that arise in the course of daily school functioning. Some schools have created these positions to allow the school psychologist or school counselor/social worker to have outreach capabilities. This enables the professional to conduct home visits, when applicable, to better assist a student or family with a behavioral health, safety, or resource issue. These professionals are specially trained in school system functioning and learning in addition to behavioral health. Consequently, their focus may be primarily on how the student's behavior and behavioral health impacts the ability to succeed academically. Some school districts have made the decision to also partner with professionals employed in the community, versus school. These providers may focus on more global behavioral health functioning in how it affects the subsets of home, family, work, and school functioning. Many of these services can be provided in both the home environment or during carefully selected school attendance times. A provider generally will attempt to meet with a child/adolescent at school during non-academic class periods, whenever possible, to minimize disruption to the learning environment.

Medical Services

Although the majority of psychiatry and nursing services are provided in clinic and hospital settings, there is a growing number of medical providers who work with behavioral health teams to provide services in the home and natural community. ACT teams, for example, have a psychiatrist who is part of the multidisciplinary team and can respond to crisis or psychiatric emergencies in the community. While not all medical professionals can provide services in homes and communities, the advent of telemedicine[5] has allowed some medical professionals to provide services in the community even when they are not physically present. An example of this would be the professional counselor working with a consumer providing in-home counseling. The consumer in this example has been unable to leave his home for years due to anxiety of being in open places. His agoraphobia has made it nearly impossible for him to go to a traditional office setting. His in-home counselor has arranged for his psychiatrist, however, to be able to talk to him about medication management issues and monitor his behavior via video calls when the need arises. Telemedicine advances such as two-way video, applications that allow video calls, and video conferencing have been helpful tools in providing these needed medical services in non-traditional situations. Several payer plans have recognized the applicability of telemedicine and have included it in their reimbursement schedules. It is important, however, to know the regulations on types, bandwidth requirements, and quality of telemedicine technology mandated by certain payers.

Applying Skills in the Real World Environment

When the provider is in the consumer's home and natural community setting, the consumer is given the opportunity to practice learned coping skills and techniques in a real living environment. It may be much easier to practice skills in a hospital or office setting because the environmental and family stressors are not present. By allowing a consumer to practice skills in the true environment, the consumer is able to gain confidence for application of those skills in real world settings.

This chapter has provided examples of how home-, school-, and natural community-based services can be integrated into traditional office-based services as additional augmented community-based services, provided in their entirety in the home and natural community, provided as part of a blend of services, and finally, provided as part of a plan to offer services via the use of both professional and paraprofessional staff to bring services to underserved geographic areas. In looking at a more diverse description of how home-, school-, and natural community-based services can be used and integrated into existing practice, this author has attempted to demonstrate available options for a full range of providers and existing service models.

Notes

1. Department of Family and Children Services represents the generalized concept of state divisions working with child welfare. Different geographic regions or states use different terms, such as Department of Child Services, Division of Family and Children, or Division of Child Welfare.
2. Community support individual, as a title, represents a paraprofessional staff member that works with the consumer to provide training to develop needed coping skills, assist with resource development, and provide psychoeducation. Terminology for paraprofessional staff varies according to payer, treatment model, state, and country.
3. Holding placement refers to a temporary holding area for a consumer when appropriate-level mental health services are not immediately available.
4. À la carte is a French language phrase meaning "according to the menu" that is used more generally to denote selecting pieces of the whole of an item.
5. Telemedicine is the use of medical information exchanged from one site to another via electronic communications to improve a consumer's clinical health status.

References

BBC. (2013). *Santeria*. Retrieved December 1, 2013, from BBC Religions: www.bbc.co.uk/religion/religions/santeria/

Department of Behavioral Health and Developmental Disabilities (DBHDD). (2013). *Provider Manual for Community Behavioral Health Providers*. Retrieved October 22, 2013, from Georgia Department of DBHDD: https://gadbhdd.policystat.com/policy/648736/latest/

Health Resources and Services Administration (HRSA). (2013, November 14). *Shortage Designation: Health Professional Shortage Areas and Medically Underserved Areas/Populations*. Retrieved November 28, 2013, from U.S. Department of Health and Human Services: Health Resources and Services Administration: www.hrsa.gov/shortage/index.html

Interchurch Ministries of Nebraska. (2009). *Rural Response Hotline Report: 1-800-464-0258*. Lincoln, NE: Interchurch Ministries of Nebraska.

National Institutes of Health (NIH). (2010, June). *Traditional Chinese Medicine: An Introduction*. Retrieved December 1, 2013, from National Center for Complementary and Alternative Medicine (NCCAM): http://nccam.nih.gov/health/whatiscam/chinesemed.htm?nav=gsa

National Institutes of Health (NIH). (2012, February 7). *Terms Related to Complementary and Alternative Medicine*. Retrieved December 1, 2013, from National Center for Complementary and Alternative Medicine (NCCAM): http://nccam.nih.gov/health/providers/camterms.htm?nav=gsa

National Institutes of Health (NIH). (2013, August). *Ayurvedic Medicine: An Introduction*. Retrieved December 1, 2013, from National Center for Complementary and Alternative Medicine (NCCAM): http://nccam.nih.gov/health/ayurveda/introduction.htm

New Freedom Commision on Mental Health. (2003, July 22). *The President's New Freedom Commission on Mental Health Report.* Retrieved November 15, 2013, from New Freedom Commision on Mental Health: http://govinfo. library.unt.edu/mentalhealthcommission/reports/FinalReport/downloads/ FinalReport.pdf

New Freedom Commission on Mental Health. (2004). *Subcommittee on Rural Issues: Background Paper.* Rockville, MD: Author.

Providence Service Corporation. (2013, September). *Virtual Residential Program.* Retrieved November 16, 2013, from Providence Service Corporation: www. providencehumanservices.com/images/Providence-Virtual-Residential-Program-Overview-and-Outcome-Summary.pdf

Substance Abuse and Mental Health Services Administration (SAMHSA). (2008). *Evidence Based Practices: ACT.* Retrieved November 1, 2013, from SAMHSA Publications: http://store.samhsa.gov/shin/content//SMA08-4345/UsingMultimedia-ACT.pdf

Substance Abuse and Mental Health Services Administration (SAMHSA). (2010). *ICCD Clubhouse Model.* Retrieved November 15, 2013, from NREPP: SAMHSA's National Registry of Evidence-Based Programs and Practices: http://nrepp. samhsa.gov/ViewIntervention.aspx?id=189

Substance Abuse and Mental Health Services Administration (SAMHSA). (2012). *Results from the 2010 National Survey on Drug Use and Health: Mental Health Findings.* NSDUH Series H-42, HHS Publication No. (SMA) 11-4667. Rockville, MD: Author.

Substance Abuse and Mental Health Services Administration (SAMHSA) and Center for Medicaid and CHIP Services (CMCS). (2013). *Coverage of Behavioral Health Services for Children, Youth, and Young Adults with Significant Mental Health Conditions.* Rockville, MD: SAMHSA.

U.S. Department of Health and Human Services. (1999). *Mental Health: A Report of the Surgeon General.* Rockville, MD: U.S. Department of Health and Human Services, Substance Abuse and Mental Health Services Administration, Center for Health Services, National Institutes of Health, National Institute of Mental Health.

U.S. Department of Health and Human Services (HHS): National Prevention Council. (2010). *National Prevention Strategy: Clinical and Community Prevention Services.* Retrieved November 17, 2013, from Surgeon General: www. surgeongeneral.gov/initiatives/prevention/strategy/preventive-services.pdf

World Health Organization (WHO). (2011). *WHO Mental Health Gap Action Programme (mhGAP).* Retrieved November 15, 2013, from WHO: www.who. int/mental_health/mhgap/en/index.html

World Health Organization (WHO)/PAHO. (2010). *Culture and Mental Health in Haiti: A Literature Review.* Retrieved December 1, 2013, from World Health Organization: www.who.int/mental_health/emergencies/culture_mental_health_ haiti_eng.pdf

4

EVIDENCE-BASED
INTERVENTION

Evidence-Based Practice

As each provider seeks to find the best approach to treat the individualized needs of the consumer and/or family, there are myriad treatment approaches that are available to utilize. This chapter will focus on an overview of those interventions that are rooted in research and have been proven to be effective with specific populations. While popularity and selection of evidence-based practice can be heavily influenced by the state, regulatory bodies, and the payer of services, this chapter will focus on an in-depth overview of several approaches. This overview will include what works best in home- and natural community-based settings.

When we review the myriad of information available regarding evidence-based interventions there are a lot of acronyms present that can require clarification. Empirically Supported Treatments (ESTs) and Evidence-Based Treatments (EBTs) refer to empirically[1] developed interventions that are based on trials using a control group and an experimental group to prove they are valid and effective approaches. The term Evidence-Based Practice (EBP) has more recently replaced the uses of EST and EBT in behavioral health jargon. EBP is used primarily as the acronym for Evidence-Based Practice, but is also used interchangeably to denote Evidence-Based Programs.

Evidence-Based Practices (EBPs) refer to those approaches to treatment that have been validated by some type of research or documented scientific evidence. A broader definition of EBPs refers to a set of practices, other interventions or supports, and services that contribute to successful outcomes for children, youth, families, adults, and consumers. In other words, EBPs usually refer to sets of practices and not just a singular intervention or treatment approach. Generally speaking, but not in all cases, treatment and practices need to produce positive outcomes in two or more studies to qualify as an EBP. Typically EBPs have shown positive outcomes in the areas of symptom reduction, functional improvement, and prevention/reduction of higher levels of care (i.e., decreased hospital

Figure 4.1 Evidence-Based Practice Integration Model

Evidence-Based Practice is the central concept that structurally overlaps with four areas that contribute to the whole. Research and scientific evidence are needed to validate the practice and the outcomes of the intervention(s). Second, the provider brings a crucial component of expertise and the clinical resources necessary to successfully address the identified need. The identified need is the third component. That need may actually be the presenting issue or identified area of challenge. Finally, the circle is not complete without the preferences and input of the consumer. This input is a crucial component in identifying the goals of treatment and directionality of the plan. Together, these four contributing areas assist in merging the concept of EBP.

admissions, institutional care, and other out-of-home placements). See Figure 4.1 regarding the four contributing areas that play a part in merging the concept of EBP.

In the last decade there has been a lot we have learned about EBPs. However, not every EBP has been studied in every community. Some studies may not have included some populations, cultural groups, or settings for treatment. It is important to realize that just because a consumer is receiving treatment that has not been recognized as an EBP, that does not mean the intervention will not be successful with that particular consumer. There are many EBPs worldwide, and beginning consumer treatment with a proven method is a great place to start. After all, treatments that have been shown to be effective in several studies provide an excellent base and structure to service provision. As a provider, however, you may find that you augment existing preferred practices with those interventions that you know work best with your particular consumers.

An EBP Starting Point for Providers

Providers may choose particular EBPs or types of treatment that they prefer and in which they specialize. This specialization allows them to delve deeper into the intricacies and proficiencies of particular practices and models. There are times, however, when a consumer with a particular disorder does not respond optimally to the selected approach. In those cases, it is important for the provider to utilize the arsenal of information that is available regarding alternatives to treatment and other EBPs that may be a better fit for the consumer or treatment of the specified disorder. Many EBPs are listed by their outcome areas or populations with whom they have been most effective. An EBP search by disorder or challenge will yield targeted intervention results for the provider.

There are many resources available for providers to further their knowledge in the area of EBP identification and keep abreast of the most recent supporting research and data. One such source is the Substance Abuse and Mental Health Services Administration (SAMHSA) National Registry of Evidence-Based Programs and Practices (NREPP). NREPP is a searchable online registry of hundreds of interventions in the areas of prevention, behavioral health, and substance abuse treatment. While the NREPP is not an exhaustive list, it is quite comprehensive and will assist providers in determining when a particular intervention may meet their needs. The NREPP registry includes interventions that are reviewed and rated by independent reviewers. The intent of the registry is to reduce the time between the creation of interventions and when they are ready for practical application in the field. NREPP has already been implemented in 50 U.S. states, seven territories, and in 110 countries (SAMHSA, 2013).

Many other state, county, organizational, and international websites also publish lists of preferred EBPs used primarily in that locale or by that specialty of practice. An example is the California Evidence-Based Clearinghouse for Child Welfare (CEBC). The CEBC for Child Welfare supplies providers of service with information about selected child welfare related programs. The primary task of CEBC is to inform the public about research-based programs being marketed or used in California (California Evidence-Based Clearinghouse for Child Welfare, 2013). Not all EBPs are a fit for every specialty or service type and it takes some time to find the best principal one to use for your practice. It may take some experimentation to find the alternate practice methods you use with consumers that are not responsive to the primary EBP you have selected. Providers within a larger company may have a preferred organizational EBP that they should follow for most cases. Individual providers or those in private practice may also have one EBP that they prefer above others. In selecting a preferred EBP, the provider can ensure that he or she receives in-depth training in the implementation of that model and how it best works. Then, as needed, the provider can choose to bring in additional EBPs to meet the needs of particular consumers. SAMHSA, in fact, offers EBP Kits that provide tools for developing behavioral health services within your own practice. Appendix A of this book also offers more EBP resources that are accessible on the World Wide Web.

In the sections to follow several EBPs will be explored by general treatment type. Only a small sample of EBPs will be presented and the highlights provided are intended to bring deeper knowledge in common types of treatment focus versus being comprehensive of all available EBPs in each treatment area.

Types of Evidence-Based Practice

Psychosocial treatments provide education, support, and guidance to consumers living with behavioral health and substance abuse issues. Psychosocial EBPs can encompass several areas of intervention. Psychosocial treatments can include therapy, social supports, vocational training, and the like. Treatments that are considered to be psychosocial usually assist the consumer with developing the skills and coping mechanisms the consumer will need to better manage the challenges and symptoms associated with the behavioral health or substance use issues. A psychiatrist, psychologist, professional counselor, social worker, marriage and family therapist, psychiatric nurse, peer specialist, or other trained paraprofessional typically provides these psychosocial treatments.

Since no two cases are ever the same, there are times when two providers of different disciplines may work together to most effectively treat the consumer. One example of this merging of disciplines would be with therapeutic interventions and medication management services. In more complicated clinical cases, these two treatments may need to be combined. In these situations, the consumer may meet with the psychiatrist for medication management and the individual counselor will work with the consumer on therapeutic issues and make observations regarding the consumer's response to medication treatments. Both disciplines can work together to share information and coordinate services. Another example may be when a social worker and paraprofessional support work together to provide therapeutic and vocational support services to an adult struggling with depression and the emotional toll of job loss. The social worker can assist the consumer in working through his depression while the vocational support can walk the consumer through the practical steps of regaining competitive employment. By working together, two disciplines can often quite effectively meet the individual consumer's complete set of needs in a more holistic manner.

Psychoeducation

Psychoeducation is a form of psychosocial intervention that involves teaching consumers about their disorder or challenges and about how they can best manage these issues. Education allows consumers and their familial support structures to recognize the signs of the disorder, the consumers' triggers, and the signs of relapse so that they can get necessary treatment when it is needed versus waiting for the condition to worsen. Family Psychoeducation (FPE), is an EBP that includes teaching needed problem-solving skills and ways of coping to families, and support structures, of consumers with behavioral health issues. Families often do not have access to the resources and information they need to be able to best work with their family member with behavioral health issues. When the consumer's family and other identified informal support systems learn these skills, they are better able to interact more effectively with the consumer. FPE is different from some other types of family intervention. In FPE, the family itself is not the object of treatment, but rather the illness is the object of treatment. The FPE's focus primarily is on the consumer, but family well-being is also an identified essential outcome. FPE allows individuals to support their loved ones through the treatment process in a way that can surround the consumer with much-needed support during a difficult time. The critical components of any FPE include education about serious mental illness, identified resources to use during stressful situations, ongoing education and skills training regarding managing mental illness, problem solving, and social support. FPE has been shown to have the following outcomes: fewer consumer relapses and hospitalizations, improved family well-being, increased family knowledge of serious mental illness, increased consumer participation in vocational rehabilitation programs, reduced feelings of stress and isolation, and reduced medical illness of families. There is a variety of FPE programs that are offered as a part of overall clinical treatment for the consumer. These programs can last nine months to five years and are usually diagnosis specific. FPE can take place in any setting where the family is comfortable and lends itself well to home-based treatment. One model of family psychoeduction that has been well researched is the Multifamily Psychoeducation Group (MFPG) program. It is specifically targeted to support families of consumers with mood disorders, particularly bipolar disorder and major depressive disorder. Consumers and families who attend these multifamily group formats benefit by connecting with others who have had similar circumstances. Currently, SAMHSA offers an evidence-based practice kit for Family Psychoeducation Evidence-Based Practice to develop this EBP (SAMHSA, 2013, March).

The National Alliance on Mental Illness (NAMI) Family-to-Family Education Program is another family psychoeducational program intended for family members of consumers living with serious mental illness. This 12-session (2.5 hours each) course covers current education on disorders, current research related to the science of brain disorders, information on EBPs, and family member's responses to the impact the consumer's mental illness has on their lives. Trained family members of consumers living with mental illness are the teachers for this course. The trainer must participate in an intensive training workshop to learn how to deliver this structured curriculum. The NAMI Family-to-Family education program has been implemented in 49 U.S. states, as well as several international locations. The NAMI Family-to-Family Education Program materials have been translated into Spanish (NAMI de Familia a Familia) and are culturally adapted for use in Mexico and Puerto Rico. Materials have also been translated, but not culturally adapted, into Arabic, French, Italian, Mandarin Chinese, and Vietnamese (NAMI, 2013a).

Evidence-Based Individual Therapy

Individual therapy (sometimes referred to as psychotherapy and/or counseling) is a psychosocial process where consumers work with a therapist to explore their feelings, behaviors, and belief systems. The consumers in individual therapy may also identify areas of their life they would like to change or where they want to work toward an identified goal. Individual therapy typically includes sessions at pre-scheduled intervals. The frequency of services is determined by the consumer's treatment plan and current needs. The goal of individual therapy is usually to allow consumers with behavioral health issues to gradually gain a greater understanding of themselves and the problems they are experiencing, through working with a trained provider. It is important to note that individual states and countries have different regulations around who can perform individual therapy. While this varies from geographic area to payer source, most standards require a minimum of a master's degree in a helping field, that is, counseling, social work, psychology, or the like. Some standards also require licensure within the field in the state, county, or province where services take place. Each of those geographic areas will have licensure boards and traditionally the master's level clinician is required to demonstrate clinical knowledge by completing a licensure exam. In addition to education and examination, the therapist may be required to demonstrate years of supervision under a qualified licensure supervisor in the field.

Generally speaking, no one type of therapy is better than another. There are, however, certain EBP therapy approaches that have been shown to be effective with certain populations. Some of the approaches used in individual therapy (psychotherapy or counseling) include, but are not limited to, those discussed below.

Cognitive Behavioral Therapy

Cognitive behavioral therapy (CBT) was developed by Dr. Aaron Beck in the 1960s. It was created as a time-limited, problem-focused, and collaborative approach to treatment. CBT can be utilized with a wide range of consumers: children, adolescents, adults, and older adults in individual and group settings. Sessions can take place in a variety of locations, including home and natural community settings. A typical treatment episode can last 8 to 14 sessions and is dependent on treatment planning goals. CBT is a type of psychotherapeutic treatment that integrates two schools of psychotherapy, behavioral therapy and cognitive therapy. The CBT therapist helps the consumer understand the thoughts and feelings that influence behavior. A CBT therapist will try to explore the connection between the thoughts and emotions a consumer experiences prior to disruptive behaviors. A goal of CBT is to have the therapist teach consumers that they can take control of how they deal with and interpret the components of the environment. In CBT a therapist works with consumers to help them realize that they are able to choose positive thoughts, expectations, and behaviors as replacements for negative and/or inaccurate thoughts. CBT utilizes numerous techniques including, but not limited to, cognitive restructuring, physiologic techniques, and behavior modification. CBT is often used as a first line of treatment for many anxiety disorders such as Panic Disorder and Obsessive-Compulsive Disorder. There are currently several recognized approaches to cognitive behavioral therapy, including Rational Emotive Behavior Therapy, Rational Behavior Therapy, Rational Living Therapy, Cognitive Therapy, and Dialectical Behavior Therapy.

Trauma-Focused Cognitive Behavioral Therapy (TF-CBT) is a well-researched psychosocial treatment model that is specifically designed to treat post-traumatic stress disorder (PTSD) and related emotional and behavioral problems in consumers. It was developed to address the psychological trauma associated with childhood sexual abuse, but has been adapted for use with a wide array of traumatic experiences. Today it is used to treat domestic violence, traumatic loss, and multiple traumas. This EBP is generally delivered in 12 to 16 sessions. It can also be provided in the context of longer-term treatment or in group format. TF-CBT can be provided in traditional treatment settings as well as home- and natural community-based settings. Some other variants of CBT that are

EBPs include Cognitive Behavioral Social Skills Training (CBSST); CBT for Adolescent Depression; CBT for Late-Life Depression; Combined Parent-Child Cognitive Behavioral Therapy (CPC-CBT): Empowering Families Who Are At Risk for Physical Abuse; Computer-Based Cognitive Behavioral Therapy: Beating the Blues; Cultural Adaptation of Cognitive Behavioral Therapy (CBT) for Puerto Rican Youth; and Mindfulness-Based Cognitive Therapy (MBCT) (SAMHSA, 2008).

Dialectical Behavior Therapy

Dialectical Behavior Therapy (DBT) is a cognitive behavioral treatment approach developed by Dr. Marsha Linehan. DBT blends the modalities of Family Skills Training and Individual Dialectical Behavior Therapy. The two key and interwoven characteristics of DBT are a behavioral, problem-solving focus and an emphasis on dialectical processes. Dialectical refers to the multiple issues that result when a provider is working with a consumer that has more than one disorder. DBT has been shown to produce significant improvement in the areas of emotional dysregulation, suicidality, and depression. When DBT was introduced in 1993, it was originally used to treat consumers with Borderline Personality Disorder (BPD), but was adapted for suicidal adolescents in 2007. It is now used for consumers with multiple, different disorders. It has been adapted for use with consumers with suicidal ideation (adolescents), addiction disorders, eating disorders, comorbid HIV and substance use disorders, developmental delays (adults), depression (older adults), schizophrenia, domestic violence issues (women), and stalking behaviors. In standard DBT, different types of psychosocial therapies are utilized. These interventions may include traditional individual psychotherapy, group skills training, and phone consultation as part of the process. DBT takes the approach that consumers have previously developed ineffective ways of regulating their emotions and cognitions and the ways they cope with distress. DBT assists the consumer with learning new skills that are more effective. The four major skills areas are mindfulness, regulation of emotions, interpersonal effectiveness, and tolerance for distress. DBT can be used in a variety of treatment settings, including home- and natural community-based settings. DBT has been implemented in the following geographic areas since 1993: Argentina, Australia, Canada, Germany, Japan, New Zealand, the Netherlands, Norway, Spain, Sweden, Switzerland, the United Kingdom; and the United States (Behavioral Research and Therapy Clinics, 2013).

Exposure Therapy

Exposure therapy is used to educate and teach consumers about how to manage their worries, fears, and anxieties and to reduce their distress level around these stressors. It is often used to treat OCD and PTSD.

During exposure therapy the provider will help the consumer identify the triggers that bring about increasing anxiety. The therapist will then gradually expose the consumer to whatever triggers the obsessive thoughts or reaction. This exposure is accomplished in a controlled manner to allow the consumer to safety experience these fears in small steps. The therapist will work with the consumer to teach skills and strategies to minimize fear and anxiety. Some of these skills may include deep breathing; expressing fears to another person; or replacing the behavior or thought with a healthier alternative, such as exercise. Exposure and Response Prevention (ERP) is a type of CBT that is usually the first type of treatment selected for PTSD and OCD, but is also often used to treat generalized anxiety disorders and phobias. ERP involves the consumer facing that which he or she fears in order to learn how to handle it versus using avoidance or re-assurance seeking to cope with fears. In more complicated cases, exposure therapy may be used along with medications to reduce symptoms. Prolonged Exposure (PE) Therapy for PTSD is a cognitive behavioral treatment program for consumers who have experienced single or multiple traumas and consequently have developed PTSD. The program includes individual therapy to help the consumer process traumatic events and reduce the problematic symptoms of PTSD that may be interfering with daily functioning. There are several variants of exposure therapy that are evidence-based. The EBPs include Prolonged Exposure Therapy for Posttraumatic Stress Disorder (PE) (SAMHSA, 2013) and Prolonged Exposure Therapy for Adolescents (PE-A) used for adolescents who have experienced significant trauma. The PE manuals have been applied internationally through use of translations to Hebrew, Spanish, and Japanese languages (California Evidence-Based Clearinghouse for Child Welfare, 2013).

Interpersonal Therapy

Interpersonal Therapy (IPT) is a time-limited psychotherapy developed in the 1970s at Yale University by Dr. Gerald Klerman, Dr. Myrna Weissman, and Dr. Eugene Paykel. IPT focuses on the relationships a consumer has with other individuals. The IPT provider assists the consumer in looking at what may be causing the behavioral health issues and concerns. The provider is an active teacher who assesses the consumer's interactions with others to help the consumer develop awareness of where he or she has relationship issues. The basic assumption behind IPT is that there is a relationship between the onset of depression, and similar disorders, and the consumer's interpersonal relationships at the time. Interpersonal therapy is expected to last three to four months and target specific symptoms associated with depression, bipolar disorders, eating disorders, ADHD, postpartum depression, and Generalized Anxiety Disorder (GAD). ITP is used in a broad range of consumers from children and adolescents to the elderly.

One EBP variant is Interpersonal Therapy for Depressed Adolescents (IPT-A). IPT-A is a short-term treatment that focuses on current relationship issues for the consumer (age 12 to 18 years) that has mild to moderate depression. The typical length of treatment is 12 weeks. IPT-A attempts to help adolescents improve communication and social problem-solving skill use in their current relationships. IPT-A can be conducted in a range of settings, including hospital-based settings, school-based settings, outpatient settings, and community-based settings. IPT-A has been adapted for use with Puerto Rican adolescents with depression (SAMHSA, 2013).

Motivational Interviewing

Motivational Interviewing (MI) is a counseling approach, first described by Dr. William Miller in 1983, that is person-centered and directed toward a goal. Motivational Interviewing helps to bring about behavioral change by assisting the consumer in an exploration of ambivalence and resistance to the process. The primary assumption in MI is that resistance, ambivalent attitudes, and lack of resolve are the primary obstacles to behavioral change. The primary goal of MI is therefore to examine that ambivalence and attempt to resolve it. The principles of MI include the provider's expression of empathy. The process of expressing empathy relies on the consumer experiencing the provider as able to see the world as the consumer sees it. Another key principle of MI is the support of self-efficacy. In MI, providers support self-efficacy by focusing on the consumer's previous successes and highlighting strengths and abilities. A hallmark of MI is responding to resistance without confrontation. The provider simply uses resistance as a signal to adjust the approach. This principle is referred to as "rolling with the resistance." A final principle of MI deals with developing discrepancy. The provider helps consumers see areas where their current behaviors put them in conflict with their future goals and values. When consumers realize this discrepancy, they are more likely to develop motivation to make important life changes. MI has been applied to a wide range of problem behaviors related to alcohol and substance abuse, as well as health promotion, medication compliance, and behavioral health issues. MI can be used in traditional outpatient settings as well as school, home, and natural community settings. Motivational Enhancement Therapy (MET) is an adaptation of MI. In MET the provider facilitates one or more consumer feedback sessions in which the provider gives feedback in a non-confrontational manner. MET uses an empathic, but direct, approach to give this feedback. It is intended to strengthen the consumer's commitment to treatment and elicit intrinsic motivation for change (SAMHSA, 2013).

Evidence-Based Family Interventions—Family Therapy, Parent Training, and Family Education and Support

Family Therapy (sometimes referred to as psychotherapy and/or counseling) is a psychosocial therapy process where family members work with a therapist to improve communication and resolve conflicts. Family therapy is often short-term and may include all family members or just those that are able to participate. Family therapy is usually provided by a psychologist, professional counselor, social worker, or marriage and family therapist. These services can take place in traditional outpatient offices as well as home- and community-based settings.

Parent training is another form of evidence-based family intervention. Parent training is a service to help parents improve communication with their children and learn additional parenting techniques. These services traditionally focus on skill-building intended to help parents improve their performance around necessary parenting functions. Parent training is typically performed by the same providers that conduct family therapy, as well as paraprofessional staff specifically trained in parenting techniques. Parent training can be delivered in several different formats: individual, group, parent-child dyads, online courses, and video. These services can take place in traditional outpatient offices as well as home- and community-based settings.

Family education and support services refer to community-based psychosocial services that are provided to ensure the safety and well-being of children and families. Family education and support services provide education to families to increase parents' confidence in their parenting abilities, strengthen the relationship between parents, and enhance child development. Support services refer to supports provided to address family needs related to emotional well-being, health, finances, parenting, and family interactions. Family education and support services are primarily provided by trained paraprofessional staff, but can also be provided by counselors, social workers, and marriage and family therapists to augment therapeutic services.

In general, no one type of family intervention is superior to another. There are, however, certain EBP intervention approaches that have been shown to be effective with families. Some of the approaches used in family intervention (family therapy, parent training, and family education and support) include, but are not limited to, those discussed below.

Brief Strategic Family Therapy

Brief Strategic Family Therapy (BSFT) is intended to prevent, reduce, and/or treat specific adolescent behaviors such as aggressive/violent behavior, anti-social behaviors, conduct disorders, use of illegal substances, delinquency, and/or sexually risky behavior. At the same time, the program is set up to improve pro-social behaviors. BSFT considers adolescent symptomology to be rooted in interactions with their family that are maladaptive; family alliances that are inappropriate; inappropriate family boundaries; and parents' blaming behavior (usually on the consumer). BSFT operates on the premise that improving how the family functions will improve the adolescent's issues. BSFT is typically conducted in 12 to 16 family sessions and frequency is dependent on the severity of management and communication issues within the family system. BSFT was developed by Dr. Jose Szapocznik at the Spanish Family Guidance Center in the Center for Family Studies at the University of Miami. There it was shown to be effective with Latino and African American youth and their families. Sessions can be conducted in locations that are convenient to the family, including the family's home. BSFT has been used across the United States, as well as in Chile, Germany, and Sweden (Miller School of Medicine, 2009).

Functional Family Therapy

Functional Family Therapy (FFT) is a research-based family therapy technique developed by Dr. James F. Alexander. It is used principally with adolescents, ages 12 to 18 years, that are at risk for delinquent behavior. FFT is a type of family therapy that focuses on the areas of communication, parenting skills, solving problems, reducing problem behaviors, and aligning the family. FFT has been successfully proven to decrease violence, drug abuse and use, conduct disorders, family conflict, residential treatment placement, and juvenile justice involvement. FFT has also been shown to prevent problem behaviors for younger siblings of FFT treated adolescents. Most FFT episodes of treatment occur over a three-month period with an average of 12 one-hour sessions. FFT can be used in a variety of treatment settings, including home- and natural community-based settings. Currently FFT sites can be found in almost all 50 United States and numerous sites in Europe and New Zealand (FFT, 2013).

Nurturing Parenting Program

Nurturing Parenting Programs (NPP) are family-based programs to help prevent child abuse and neglect. NPP instruction, developed by Dr. Stephen Bavolek, is based on educational and cognitive behavioral approaches to learning and focuses on helping parents learn new ways to parent to replace their existing, learned, abusive patterns. The nurturing philosophy of non-violent parenting focuses on several areas of development. Participants expand their knowledge of development in five areas: age-appropriate expectations; empathy, bonding, and attachment;

non-violent nurturing discipline; self-worth and awareness; and empowerment and autonomy. Additionally, the NPPs have been established according to the three standard levels of prevention: primary, secondary (intervention), and tertiary (treatment). Primary is designed to educate and provide the consumer and family with new skills and knowledge base. Secondary is designed for consumers and families experiencing moderate levels of dysfunction. Lastly, the tertiary level is centered around families referred by Mental Health/Social Services. Sessions are then based around the three standard levels and include meetings where the parents and children convene separately and then together during a lesson (one time per week for approximately 15 weeks). While NPP lends well to home-based interventions, it can be offered in group settings, home settings, or in a combination of group and home settings. NPP materials are used in many areas of the United States and have been translated into Arabic, Hmong, Haitian, and Spanish (Nurturing Parenting, 2013).

Parent Child Interaction Therapy

Parent Child Interaction Therapy (PCIT) is a behavioral intervention for children ages two to seven. The program, developed by Dr. Sheila Eyberg, works with parents and/or caregivers to decrease externalizing child behavioral problems (i.e., defiance and aggression). The program also works with the parent to increase children's social skills and cooperation. The treatment has two phases, each focusing on a different parent-child interactions. The two phases are Child-Directed Interaction (CDI) and Parent-Directed Interaction (PDI). In each phase the parent attends a session to learn skills and then a series of coaching sessions where they apply the skills with the child. Parents are taught play-therapy skills to utilize with their own children over the course of 15 weeks (average length of treatment). PCIT has been shown to be effective with families with a history of physical abuse, children who were exposed prenatally to drugs or alcohol, and children with developmental disabilities (PCIT, 2013). The PCIT program has been adapted for use internationally in Australia, Germany, Hong Kong, the Netherlands, Norway, Puerto Rico, Russia, and Taiwan (SAMHSA, 2013).

Parent Management Training

Parent Management Training (PMT) is a behavioral training program developed by Dr. Alan Kazdin that teaches parents some basic principles to help manage their child's behavioral problems at home and at school. Interventions are targeted for children and adolescents with oppositional, aggressive, and anti-social behavior. PMT is a short-term program that usually takes 4 to 6 sessions to see lasting results. An EBP variation is the Oregon Model, Parent Management Training (PMTO) that has been shown to be effective with children ages 2 to 18 years. PMTO refers to a set of parenting interventions developed over the course of 40 years (originating with work of Gerald Patterson and colleagues at the Oregon Social Learning Center). The target population is the parent of a child with disruptive behaviors (i.e., conduct disorder, oppositional defiant disorder, or anti-social behaviors). This program can be delivered in different formats, to include parent groups, individual family treatment, audio tapes, and video recordings. The average length of intervention, depending on the severity of presenting issues, is four to six months. Traditionally, there are parent group sessions each week in addition to weekly individual and family sessions. PMTO can be used in traditional settings such as outpatient clinics and community agencies, as well as home- (biological, adoptive, and foster) and natural community-based settings. PMTO materials are available in English, Danish, Dutch, Icelandic, Norwegian, and Spanish translations (California Evidence-Based Clearinghouse for Child Welfare, 2013).

Evidence-Based Intensive Home- and Community-Based Interventions

We have discussed several psychosocial EBPs in different treatment areas that work well in home- and community-based treatment settings. To follow are those EBPs that are intensive in nature and either delivered with a higher frequency/intensity by individual providers or by a team of practitioners. Some of the intensive EBPs used in home and community settings include, but are not limited to, those discussed below.

Assertive Community Treatment

Assertive Community Treatment (ACT) evolved out of the work of Dr. Arnold Marx, Dr. Leonard Stein, and Dr. Mary Ann Test in the late 1960s. ACT is a consumer-focused, recovery-oriented behavioral health service delivery model that has received substantial empirical support. ACT serves consumers that have severe and persistent mental illness. The typical ACT consumer may have gone without services for some time or been homeless or incarcerated. ACT, therefore, is mobile and is a team service delivery model in which several providers offer an individualized mix of services to a consumer for as long as they are needed. By providing these services in the natural community the consumer is often able to successfully make appointments that he or she was unable to make in the past, due to transportation or logistics challenges. Approximately 75 percent, or more, of ACT services are provided outside of the program offices in locations that are comfortable and convenient for the consumer. These services are available 24 hours per day, seven days a week. The ACT team teaches skills in-vivo, in the actual settings and context in which the problems arise. Team members work in collaboration to integrate various interventions to meet the consumer's needs and are equipped to make adjustments quickly when needed. Team models can vary, but a typical ACT teams may include 10 to 12 staff members that can represent the following professions: psychiatry, nursing, physician assistants, professional counselors, social workers, substance abuse providers, vocational specialists, peer specialists, housing specialists, and other similar type providers. A staff-to-consumer ratio of one to ten is usually recommended. The services provided by the ACT team are varied and often involve a rehabilitative approach to daily living skills, counseling, vocational and education liaison work, psychoeducation, health linkage, budgeting, housing assistance, medication management, and resource coordination. This EBP has shown positive outcomes in the areas of consumer and family satisfaction, reduction in psychiatric hospitalization, higher levels of housing stability, and improved quality of life. ACT has been widely implemented in the United States, Canada, and England (NC EBP Center, 2013).

Critical Time Intervention

Critical Time Intervention (CTI) is an intensive program, developed at Columbia University and New York State Psychiatric Institute, to prevent recurrent homelessness in consumers with severe mental illness. CTI involvement lasts approximately nine months following the release from an institutional setting (e.g., hospital, jail, shelter). CTI has two major components. The first component involves strengthening the consumer's supports such as long-term ties to services, friends, and family members. The second component involves providing the emotional and practical support the consumer needs when transitioning from the institutional setting to the community. CTI treatment is intended to be delivered in three phases: (1) transition to the community with intensive support and resource access; (2) trying out and adjusting to systems established in first phase; and (3) transfer of care to community resources. Although CTI was originally developed for male consumers, it has been adapted for use with women and families who are homeless. CTI has been implemented in approximately 25 U.S. sites as well as internationally in the United Kingdom and the Netherlands (SAMHSA, 2013).

HOMEBUILDERS

HOMEBUILDERS is an intensive family preservation services program designed to prevent out-of-home placement of children. Within 24 hours of a referral, the family begins receiving services from a master's level therapist who meets with the consumer and the family in the home and natural community. The therapist provides counseling, parenting skills development, extensive treatment planning, family advocacy, and social support (i.e., extensive resource identification and coordination). Therapists serve a very small caseload to allow them to work more intensively with the family. Moreover, therapists are on call 24 hours per day, seven days per week during the duration of the program. This is an intensive model given that the family receives more than 40 hours of face-to-face contact over a period of four to six weeks. Extensions can be granted from the initial time period and the fidelity model includes two booster sessions for after-care. Since its initial development in 1974, HOMEBUILDERS has been implemented in 23 U.S. states as well as internationally. HOMEBUILDERS has also been culturally adapted for use in Australia (Aboriginal and non-Aboriginal), Belgium, and the Netherlands (IFD, 2013).

Mentoring Programs

Mentoring programs typically involve an adult who works intensively with a child or adolescent over a period of time. The mentor's roll is to help the child or adolescent increase healthy activities and involvement in school and in the community. An example of a mentoring EBP is the Big Brothers Big Sisters of American Mentoring Program. It is designed for youth 6 to 18 years of age to have a supported match with an adult volunteer mentor. Volunteers are screened and undergo training. Their training includes developmental stages, communication and limit setting, building relationships, and how to best get along with their match. Big Brothers Big Sisters Mentoring Program has shown positive outcomes in reduction of drug use, reduction of aggressive behavior, improved family relationships, and increased school competence and achievement. The Big and Little agree to meet frequently for get-togethers that are typically three to four hours and consist of activities the two find mutually enjoyable. Services are typically conducted in the natural community. Big Brothers Big Sisters has been in existence since 1904 and since that time has established agencies in all United States, the District of Columbia, and Guam (SAMHSA, 2013).

Multi-Systemic Therapy

Multi-Systemic Therapy (MST) services are intended to be delivered in the natural environment (e.g., home, school, natural community). These intensive services typically last between three to five months and include multiple contacts each week. The MST team is available 24 hours a day, seven days a week. MST recognizes the parents and families as valuable resources, even when they have some serious needs of their own. MST therapists work to empower families by strengthening their informal support systems (family, neighbors, clergy, designated community contacts, and school). Research has shown that MST is effective in reducing antisocial behavior, substance use, and contact with law enforcement. EBT variants of MST include Multi-Systemic Therapy for Juvenile Offenders—used to address behavior problems with troubled youth; Multi-Systemic Therapy for Youth with Problem Sexual Behaviors (MST-PSB)—which is a clinical adaptation of MST targeted at adolescents who have committed sexual offenses; and Multi-Systemic Therapy with Psychiatric Supports (MST-Psychiatric)—designed to treat adolescents who are at risk of out-of-home placement due to their problem behaviors. MST for Juvenile Offenders has been implemented across most of the United States and 12 international sites (SAMHSA, 2013).

Peer Support

Peer support services are an evidence-based behavioral health model of care. Peer support providers, sometimes called peer support specialists, are individuals who have experienced mental and/or substance abuse disorders and advanced enough in their recovery to help others with recovery challenges. Peer services may include support groups, peer psychoeduction, peer mentoring, peer-run programs, skill building, and resource support services in hospital-, residential-, outpatient-, home-, and natural community-based settings. Some peer supports have simply learned through their own experiences, while others undergo training and certification to qualify. In addition to direct service provision, peer supports may advocate to improve opportunities for people recovering from mental illnesses (SAMHSA, 2011).

Peer recovery education is structured instruction taught by someone who has experienced mental illness. Peer education can include information on the recovery process, self-care, symptoms and diagnoses of behavioral health issues, and what to expect from professional behavioral health services. Peer case management involves a peer support specialist helping to plan a consumer's recovery and identify supports. Peer mentors teach coping skills as well as emphasize self-care through attention to sleep, good nutrition, stress management, and social support. Peer mentoring can occur at a center or in the community.

Peer support is gaining acceptance as a valuable part of service delivery in a variety of settings from inpatient to community-based, and home-based services. Medicaid and public mental health systems will often pay for services provided by certified peer support specialists as part of an intensive service delivery team (e.g., as a part of ACT team). Peer support can be particularly useful for consumers who lack trust in professionally delivered services (NAMI, 2013b).

Virtual Residential Program

Virtual Residential Program (VRP) was created to meet the needs of children and adolescents with severe emotional disturbances that were at risk for out-of-home placement. VRP combines the structure of a residential placement with the effectiveness of providing services in the consumer's own home. VRP is a strengths-based and family-centered intervention with a primary goal of keeping families intact. The VRP team is composed of professionals, the consumer, and the caregiver. VRP structure includes a lead therapist, a home-based counselor, and a behavioral interventionist or coach. VRP has a two- to six-month length of stay that is characterized by a phased approach to treatment (with an average length of treatment of 4.3 months). This phased approach includes an orientation phase where VRP staff may be in the consumer home up to 30 hours per week to set up structure and make sure the presenting situation is stabilized. This phase offers the structure of a formal residential setting within the consumer's own home. After this point, the intensity of the services is individualized to meet the specific needs of the youth and the family as they progress through the remaining phases of acceptance, working, consistency, and graduation. During the course of services, the family will progress toward less intensive intervention, toward greater self-reliance, and toward usage of natural support systems in their own communities. This natural phasing allows the consumer to move away from dependence on the VRP team. An outcome study on Virtual Residential Program showed a shorter length of stay than in residential placements and 72 percent of participants successfully remaining in the community (Providence Service Corporation, 2013).

Wraparound Services

Wraparound is a philosophy of care that includes a unique set of community services and natural supports that are individualized to assist the consumer in achieving positive outcomes. This intensive strengths-based approach has four phases intended to engage individuals with complex needs so that they can continue to live in their homes and communities. The first phase includes family meetings with the facilitator to identify strengths and needs and determine what other team members may be involved. The second phase involves the development of the initial treatment plan. During the third phase, the plan is underway and the team begins to review accomplishments and make any needed adjustments to the treatment plan. The last phase involves the transition out of wrap-around and into establishing any needed supports. Wraparound services are provided by both professional and paraprofessional staff to include therapists (counselors, social workers, marriage and family therapists); in-home behavioral support specialists; facilitators; coaches; and resource coordinators. The wraparound approach has been implemented across the United States and internationally (National Wraparound Initiative, 2013).

Integrated Dual Disorder Treatment and Integrated Treatment of Mental Illness and Substance Abuse Disorder

Integrated Dual Diagnosis Treatment (IDDT) services are treatments for people who live with the co-occurring disorders of substance abuse and mental illness. Research has strongly indicated that, to recover fully, a consumer with co-occurring disorders needs treatment for both problems. While there are different schools of thought on this approach, we know that simply focusing on one issue at the very least does not provide any assurances the other issue will go away. IDDT integrates behavioral health and substance abuse interventions at the clinical interaction level. That means that services that address both issues are provided in a coordinated fashion. IDDT includes the critical components of staged interventions; motivational interventions; counseling services; social support interventions; cultural sensitivity and competence; long-term, community-based perspective; rehabilitation activities to prevent relapses; and assertive outreach. Assertive outreach refers to engagement of consumers by providing outreach through intensive case management and home-based meetings. Research on integrated dual disorder treatment indicates that fidelity models have the following outcomes: stable remission of substance abuse, reduction in hospitalization, stability in housing, decreased psychiatric symptoms, increased quality of life, and increased functional status. IDDT can take place in a variety of treatment settings. The IDDT model includes more traditional treatment settings as well as those accessed in assertive community outreach (natural community and home) (NC EBP Center, 2013).

Other Community-Based Evidence-Based Practices

Wellness (Illness) Management and Recovery

Wellness (Illness) Management and Recovery (WMR) is a broad base of strategies whereby a consumer with behavioral health issues is given information and taught skills by either professionals or peers to help the consumer learn ways to better manage his or her illness. WMR is intended to utilize psychoeducation to improve the consumer's knowledge of mental illness. It also serves to empower the consumer with coping skills to reduce the severity and distress of the symptoms. Moreover, WMR uses behavioral tailoring to ensure medication compliance and relapse prevention to reduce symptom relapses. The WMR program can be provided in an individual or group format and generally is provided in weekly sessions over the course of three to six months of treatment (NC EBP Center, 2013).

Intensive Case Management

In intensive case management, specially trained individuals coordinate or provide individualized services to help the consumer live successfully at home and in the community. These services include psychiatric, financial, legal, resource coordination, and medical services. The foundation of case management is an ongoing, person-centered treatment plan that is based on strengths and needs assessment. This person-centered plan is developed by the consumer and the case manager, as a team, and is updated at regular intervals. In partnership with the consumer, the case manager makes needed links to benefits, supports, and services. Once in those services, the case manager should monitor the quality of care provided and the consumer's progress toward his or her goals. Children's case management is a similar service that works primarily with parents and caregivers to support healthy growth and development for children (NAMI, 2013b).

Permanent Supported Housing

Permanent Supported Housing is an evidence-based practice model that supports the goals implied in the name: permanence, support, and housing. Permanent means that tenants can remain in their homes as long as they meet the basic tenant obligations (i.e., paying rent). Supported means that tenants have access to support services they need to ensure they can retain their housing. Housing means that the tenant has the right to a private and secure home. Lack of safe and affordable housing is one of the most significant barriers to recovery for people living with mental illness; a safe place to live is essential to recovery. Without options to meet this basic need, too many consumers are caught in a cycle in and out of homelessness, jails, shelters, emergency departments, or institutionalization. Supported permanent housing, as an EBP, attempts to break this cycle and offers several key elements to reach this goal. One element is that tenants have the lease in their own name and there are no provisions in the lease that would not be found in a similar lease for someone without a psychiatric disability. Another important element is that participation in services is voluntary and therefore a tenant can't be evicted for rejecting services. Additionally, house rules are not restrictive. The tenant has the same rights as someone else without an illness in that he or she can have visitors. In fact, many neighbors do not have psychiatric disabilities, as this model includes integrated housing. Another distinguishing factor is that housing services and support services are distinct. They are not provided by the same individuals and therefore there are no issues resulting from conflicting roles. Permanent supported housing can provide a stable base for recovery and is particularly useful for those consumers that have been homeless, are living in unnecessarily restrictive settings, are at risk for losing housing, are living with others in strained circumstances, or are living in substandard living situations. The Substance Abuse and Mental Health Services Administration offers a Permanent Supported Housing Evidence-Based Practice Kit to develop this EBP (SAMHSA, 2010).

One such supported housing EBP is Pathways' Housing First Program. Housing First was developed by Pathways to Housing as an effort to end homelessness and support recovery for those with serious mental illness or substance use disorders. The program is consumer-perspective driven and provides immediate housing (apartments) without any prerequisites for sobriety or psychiatric treatment. Treatment and support services are provided through ACT teams and recognize that consumers are in different recovery stages, therefore interventions are tailored to the consumer's individualized needs. The team works with a consumer through challenges such as housing loss, hospitalization, or incarceration and helps obtain housing following these upsets. While consumers can refuse therapeutic services, the program does require that consumers meet with a team member frequently to ensure their well-being and safety (SAMHSA, 2013).

Supported Employment

Supported Employment (SE) is a well-defined approach to helping consumers with severe mental illness and/or co-occurring substance use disorders participate, as much as possible, in the competitive job market. Most consumers want to work and feel that work is an important goal in their recovery. Competitive work is in integrated settings and consistent with the identified strengths, needs, preferences, and abilities of the consumer. First introduced in the psychiatric rehabilitation field in the 1980s, supported employment programs are now found in a variety of service settings including community treatment centers, psychosocial rehabilitation settings, and in community-based settings. Supported employment outcomes are better when integrated with a behavioral health treatment team. These behavioral health services can be provided in the home and natural community (NAMI, 2013b). SE programs are based on a core set of principles that form the foundation of the program. One principle is the eligibility in SE is an individual choice. That means that no one is excluded from participating due to mental illness, work history, or other impairments. Another driving principle of SE is that services are integrated with comprehensive behavioral health treatment (i.e., case management, ACT services, etc.). It is believed that coordinating SE services with other clinical treatment allows consumers to better meet their goals. A third principle of SE is the belief that competitive employment is the goal. Competitive work is valued because it allows consumers to integrate into the community with normalized activities that reduce the stigma of mental illness. An additional principle involves personalized benefits counseling. Many consumers are fearful they will lose their benefits when they become employed and a benefits counselor can assist the consumer in getting accurate information to guide employment decisions. Rapid job search is another driving principle of SE. Job searches start soon after the consumer expresses a desire to work. This is done to support the desire to work, to overcome job search fears, and to act on the current consumer motivation. One more SE principle states that follow-along supports for SE are continuous. The last principle identifies the importance of individual preference. Consumer preference drives the type of job search, the nature of support provided, and whether or not the consumer discloses the behavioral health or substance abuse issues to an employer.

The evidence for the effectiveness of SE comes mainly from two types of research. The first showed that when day treatment programs are replaced with a SE program there was a substantial increase in employment rates. A second source of evidence has been with controlled experimental studies comparing SE to traditional vocational approaches (e.g., skills training preparation, sheltered workshops, transitional employment). All studies showed better employment outcomes for consumers receiving SE. Additionally, these studies suggest that SE is superior to other vocational approaches in both urban and rural areas (NC EBP Center, 2013).

Therapeutic Foster Care

Therapeutic Foster Care (TFC), also called Treatment Foster Care in some areas, is an evidence-based practice placement outside of the family home for children and adolescents with more serious behavioral health needs. TFC is included in this overview of EBPs that apply well to home- and natural community-based treatment because it does allow treatment in the community and in the treatment home under a structured format.

Trained treatment parents work with youth in the home to provide a therapeutic and structured environment and living situation. Youth are placed in therapeutic foster care because of more intensive needs and to allow them to receive a higher level of treatment in the community with ongoing contact with their biological families, when applicable. The core components of TFC include structure, monitoring, close supervision, and support. The average length of stay is about 22 months. TFC is the least restrictive treatment-based out-of-home option for youth with serious behavioral health problems (NC EBP Center, 2013).

Multidimensional Treatment Foster Care (MTFC) is another similar EBP community-based intervention for adolescents (12 to 17 years of age), and their families, that have had severe and chronic delinquency. MTFC was developed as a viable alternative to placing an adolescent in a group home or state facility. These adolescents had been removed from their homes due to conduct and delinquency problems, substance use, and/or involvement with the juvenile justice system. Youth are typically referred to MTFC after previous efforts at family preservation or other out-of-home placements have failed. Juvenile courts and probation, mental health, and child welfare agencies typically are the ones who make referrals to MTFC. MTFC aims to help youth live successfully in their communities while also preparing their biological parents (or adoptive parents or other after-care family), relatives, and community-based agencies to provide effective support, parenting, and skill development so that the adolescent and family have the skill base to attempt a positive reunification. MTFC typically lasts for six to nine months and is reliant on interventions between the foster home, the youth's biological or after-care family, and the youth. Involvement with the youth's family is emphasized from the beginning of services in order to help the youth return successfully to their families in a supported manner. MTFC can utilize home- and natural community-based service provision to provide needed services to support the reunification process. MTFC programs have been set up across the United States as well as in Denmark, Ireland, New Zealand, the Netherlands, Norway, Sweden, and the United Kingdom. Additionally, the manuals have been translated into Dutch and Swedish (SAMHSA, 2013).

Psychotropic Medications

Research and information about the brain's function and relation to behavioral health is updated frequently. Consequently, new medications are developed every day to treat behavioral health issues. It is important to clarify that not everyone responds to medications in the same way and consumers and families should be fully informed on all the risks and benefits associated with medications. In fact, a psychiatrist, physician's assistant, nurse practitioner, or nurse should explain the medications, their side effects, potential gains, and risks associated with use on all new medications prescribed. By making an informed choice, the consumer, in conjunction with the provider, can determine if psychotropic medications are the best option. Consumers and their families can learn more about psychotropic medications through information provided by the National Institute of Mental Health (NIMH). NIMH provides detailed information for the public on mental health medications, medications used to treat mental disorders, and medications used in specific disorders. In addition, it has provided pubic educational resources and guides for consumers in knowing what questions to ask their doctor about prescribed psychiatric medications (NIH, 2008).

Psychotropic medications can be a crucial part of a treatment plan for a consumer with mental illness. They can be an effective part of treatment, especially when combined with therapy and other psychosocial interventions. It is not uncommon for a consumer to have to use multiple medications to determine which one is effective. Additionally, some medications take longer to show an initial clinically discernible effect than others. The consumer's psychiatrist, physician assistant (PA), nurse practitioner (NP), or psychiatric nurse can work closely with the consumer to monitor how each medication affects the individual consumer.

Long-Acting Injectable (LAI) Antipsychotic Medications are an alternative to the oral administration route for some medications. Consumers who elect for treatment with LAI antipsychotic medications are more likely to continue their medications than consumers who take their medications daily by mouth. Primarily, this is due to the fact that many consumers find it easier to remember to go to an appointment to receive a shot (once or twice each month) than remembering to take a pill (once or twice each day). LAI medications are available for consumers suffering from schizophrenia, schizoaffective disorders, and other serious mental illnesses such as major depression and bipolar disorder. Some studies have shown that people who elect for treatment with long-acting injectable antipsychotic medications are less likely to need to be hospitalized due to symptoms associated with their mental illness. This result may be primarily because consumers who are on a stable medication regimen are less likely to experience symptom relapse. Additionally, consumers who take their medication by injection are unable to overdose on their medication. This is a valid risk area for consumers living with chronic mental illness or that are at risk for suicide.

Many consumers can gain some control over their behavioral health issues by actively following their individualized treatment plan. There are numerous approaches and EBPs available and a combination of treatment and services, or a single approach, may be utilized. The method used depends in most cases on the behavioral health issues, the severity of symptoms, and the consumer's preference. Regardless of which approach or EBP is selected, the individualization of the process can be a key determinant in the success of the consumer.

Cultural Considerations

There has been much discussion around EBPs, but we also know that culture can play a role in the selection of treatment or practices, as well as the effectiveness of those selections. One way to further assess for and incorporate culture is through the selection of treatment setting. Home- and natural community-based services allow the provider to have a different viewpoint of the consumer's culture, traditions, customs, and way of life. When a consumer selects a race or ethnicity on assessment paperwork or tells a provider what his or her background is and what is important to him or her, that is a big step in beginning to understand how this consumer's unique life experiences have contributed to who the person is and what types of approaches will work best. When the provider, however, conducts a session in the consumer's natural environment, the provider gets a very different perspective of how culture plays into so many areas of the consumer's life. The provider gains access to natural community cultural intermediaries that know the culture, experience it, and can help to interpret it. The approach that a provider takes will very quickly be endorsed and show as relevant to the consumer or very rapidly be rejected by the consumer or those in his or her support group.

Providers of services also need to be aware that while particular EBPs may work well with identified consumers and disorders, the variable of culture can also have an effect on service provision. In consideration of this issue, EBP cultural adaptations have been developed. These adaptations include modifications to an EBP that involves a change in the service delivery approach to consider cultural beliefs, attitudes, and/or behaviors. These cultural adaptations can fundamentally adapt the practice to better represent the consumer's cultural traditions, beliefs, spiritual perspective, values, and practices. There are many examples of these adaptations in the communities around us. While each of these cultural adaptations may not have been researched empirically, they have a value to the community and, in some cases, have met the community's needs for years or centuries. It is also important to realize that while not all of these cultural adaptations may be generalizable or transferable, they may work very well for one specific population.

Note

1. Empirical evidence or knowledge is acquired by means of observation or experimentation.

References

Behavioral Research and Therapy Clinics. (2013). *Dialectical Behavioral Therapy*. Retrieved December 1, 2013, from University of Washington: Behavioral Research and Therapy Clinics: http://blogs.uw.edu/brtc/dialectical-behavior-therapy/

California Evidence-Based Clearinghouse for Child Welfare. (2013). *Program Search*. Retrieved November 16, 2013, from CEBC: www.cebc4cw.org/

Functional Family Therapy (FFT). (2013). *Functional Family Therapy*. Retrieved December 2, 2013, from FFT: www.fftinc.com/

Institute for Family Development (IFD). (2013). *Welcome to the IFD: Developers of the HOMEBUILDERS Program*. Retrieved December 1, 2013, from Institute for Family Development: www.institutefamily.org/

Miller School of Medicine. (2009). *BSFT*. Retrieved December 1, 2013, from University of Miami: Miller School of Medicine: www.bsft.org/

National Alliance on Mental Illness (NAMI). (2013a). *NAMI Family-to-Family*. Retrieved December 2, 2013, from NAMI: www.nami.org/Template.cfm?Section=Family-to-Family&Template=/TaggedPage/TaggedPageDisplay.cfm&TPLID=4&ContentID=32973

National Alliance on Mental Illness (NAMI). (2013b). *Treatment and Services*. Retrieved November 20, 2013, from NAMI: www.nami.org/template.cfm?section=About_Treatments_and_Supports

National Institutes of Health (NIH). (2008). *Mental Health Medications*. Retrieved November 15, 2013, from NIH: National Institute of Mental Health: www.nimh.nih.gov/health/publications/mental-health-medications/index.shtml

National Wraparound Initiative. (2013). *The National Wraparound Initiative*. Retrieved December 1, 2013, from NWI: www.nwi.pdx.edu/

North Carolina Evidence Based Practices Center. (2013). *NC EBP Center*. Retrieved November 15, 2013, from Assertive Community Treatment: www.ncebpcenter.org/index.php?option=com_content&view=category&id=28&Itemid=54

Nurturing Parenting. (2013). *What Are Nurturing Programs?* Retrieved December 1, 2013, from Nurturing Parenting: http://nurturingparenting.com/NPLevelsPrevent.html

Parent Child Interaction Therapy (PCIT). (2013). *About PCIT*. Retrieved December 1, 2013, from PCIT International: www.pcit.org/

Providence Service Corporation. (2013, September). *Virtual Residential Program*. Retrieved November 16, 2013, from Providence Service Corporation: www.providencehumanservices.com/images/Providence-Virtual-Residential-Program-Overview-and-Outcome-Summary.pdf

Substance Abuse and Mental Health Services Administration (SAMHSA). (2008, June). *Trauma-Focused Cognitive Behavioral Therapy*. Retrieved November 20, 2013, from NREPP: http://nrepp.samhsa.gov/ViewIntervention.aspx?id=135

Substance Abuse and Mental Health Services Administration (SAMHSA). (2010, July). *Permanent Supported Housing Evidence-Based Practices (EBT) Kit*. Retrieved November 15, 2013, from SAMHSA Publications Ordering: http://store.samhsa.gov/product/Permanent-Supportive-Housing-Evidence-Based-Practices-EBP-KIT/SMA10-4510

Substance Abuse and Mental Health Services Administration (SAMHSA). (2011). *Consumer-Operated Services EBP Kit*. Retrieved December 2, 2013, from SAMHSA Store: http://store.samhsa.gov/shin/content/SMA11-4633CD-DVD/ HowToUseEBPKITS-COSP.pdf

Substance Abuse and Mental Health Services Administration (SAMHSA). (2013, March). *Family Psychoeducation Evidence-Based Practices (EBP) Kit*. Retrieved November 15, 2013, from SAMHSA Publications Ordering: http:// store.samhsa.gov/product/Family-Psychoeducation-Evidence-Based-Practices-EBP-KIT/SMA09-4423

Substance Abuse and Mental Health Services Administration (SAMHSA). (2013). *Find an Intervention*. Retrieved November 15, 2013, from NREPP: SAMHSA's National Registry of Evidence Based Programs and Practices: http://nrepp. samhsa.gov/Index.aspx

5

ASSESSMENT AND TREATMENT PLANNING

Building Rapport in Home- and Natural Community-Based Settings

When you are going somewhere you have never been before, you need a map, directions, or GPS (Global Positioning System) to help you get to a new location in the most expedient manner. Sure, you can try to get there by guessing which road to take, but planning helps avoid roadblocks, construction, and paths that take you off the intended route. Planning in behavioral health treatment is not dissimilar; you need to plan treatment and take several variables into account. Without a plan, the consumer's treatment can deviate off course and take longer than it should because there is no purposeful directionality. This chapter will explore developing rapport, gathering the best information for assessment purposes, and how all of that information fits together into the consumer's "road map" or treatment plan.

A crucial piece of the rapport building and assessment process begins the moment the provider meets the consumer. At this very moment, there are perceptions being formed on both sides about the other individual. One of the important aspects of the rapport-building process begins with establishing a relationship between the consumer and provider. The rapport-building step is where home- and natural community-based services can really be a game changer. As a professional counselor treating consumers in my office environment, commonly much of the initial sessions were spent in an interesting exchange I like to refer to as "the dance." During this period the consumer spends a large amount of time observing the provider and trying to determine if he or she feels a level of comfort that enables the consumer to open up and expose some of his or her most vulnerable feelings and innermost thoughts. Providers often take this process for granted and begin to quickly ask direct questions about the consumer's past, about the person's innermost thoughts and feelings, about how the person feels currently, along with a myriad of other personal questions to determine the consumer's status. While it is important to get to the place as providers where we have the information necessary to move forward with an accurate impression or diagnosis, there are moments in these first sessions that must be reserved for the rapport-building process. If this process is aggressively pursued, the bond between the consumer and provider may never reach the potential it has if the first few sessions are handled with more restraint. When a consumer would come into my office, the person would spend several sessions gathering information about me as a professional, about my degrees on my wall and inquiring about how I felt regarding certain issues. In essence, the consumers were triaging me to see if I was trustworthy, if I would have pre-conceived biases about their condition or lifestyle, and if I would be able to see them as the persons they were past the banner of their diagnosis. Meeting one time a week for one hour, this process was often a lengthy course of action that could be wrought with misconceptions. As a professional, I am not just a degree or certification on a wall, am not always a well-put-together package of authority, and am not always what I appear to be on the outside. Not only could I, as a provider, be impaired by this short and somewhat artificial interaction, but so could the consumer. Both of us were "dancing" in this clinical environment trying desperately to understand the other.

As an in-home provider, I saw an improved dynamic when I walked into a consumer's home for the first few sessions. Invariably, there were some of the same triage behaviors on the part of the consumer; however, this process or "dance" seemed to go much faster and the focus had to shift more quickly by the simple fact that the physical surroundings had changed. Now, the focus had shifted to the consumer's surroundings versus that of the provider. Those physical surroundings make a difference!

> Home is a name, a word, it is a strong one; stronger than magician
> ever spoke, or spirit ever answered to, in the strongest conjuration.
> (Charles Dickens)

Let's think about the comfort of the home for a moment. Just the word *home* summons up many emotions and thoughts. Each of us has strong feelings and emotions attached to our home environment. Not all of these feelings and emotions are positive or healthy connections, but, nonetheless they are quite powerful. Some consumers attribute positive feelings, emotions, and associations to their home environment when it may be difficult for someone else, from outside of that milieu, to even see the same assets or evaluate them in the same way. That is why home is an important concept; it is often based on perception and individual perception is an essential feature in how we view the world. The definition of home, itself, can be different from person to person. For many people, home means four walls where they live on a permanent basis. That home is personalized and belongs to them. For others, home has four walls, but lacks a personalized touch as these individuals may be living with others and following the rules of their home. Still for others, those traditional walls of home are non-existent; they may dwell in a hut, tent, or lean-to[1] with open doors and windows. For yet another group of people, home is not permanent, but changes with seasons, employment, and financial conditions. As a behavioral health professional, I have seen living conditions that challenged my own preconceived concept of what a domicile was, with abusive situations and substandard living conditions (by societal standards). Many of these very homes, however, were earnestly sought after and desired by the children I was treating that currently resided in an out-of-home placement. Similarly, these homes were also craved by the adults I was treating that currently were placed in a correctional institution. Regardless of societal perceptions of someone else's home environment, for someone that home environment is very valuable. There is a connection and a level of comfort for most individuals in their home despite any outside perception of that home. For many homeless individuals, their lack of home can actually define their living space. Their living space may be under a bridge, an abandoned building, or a particular spot in the park; but that is their home, the place where they live. At times leaving that living space to come into an office or institution may be quite stressful on the individual. All we have to do to see the importance of home is to take a literary inventory of quotes and statements over time about home. There is a veritable plethora of notions and opinions on the concept of home over the centuries. The reason the concept is commented on throughout history is because it is a fundamental element in how humans have lived in society, their lifestyle, and the social interactions and status of each inhabitant. Home has defined so many aspects of being a human being and of who we are as individuals as well as a part of a larger group.

> People would rather live in homes regardless of its grayness. There is no place like home.
>
> (L. Frank Baum, *The Wonderful Wizard of Oz*, 1900)

Imagine the possibilities of community-based behavioral health service provision given the previous descriptors of home and comfort. Services can be provided in the home, in the school environment where a child is experiencing the majority of his or her challenges, or under a bridge where a homeless consumer resides. What a difference location makes! Now, the provider can spend those first few sessions in the very environment where the consumer spends much of his or her time and see, first-hand, the challenges the consumer experiences on a day-to-day basis.

Some of my first home-based sessions were eye openers for me as a new counselor. When I arrived at the door of my consumer's home, I knocked or rang the bell and waited for a response. Was this what consumers felt when they walked across the threshold of my office door? Often I sat in the living room or at the kitchen table waiting for the consumer to come out to join me. Was this what consumers felt when they sat in my waiting room? I was in someone else's home, on their turf, in their everyday living environment. Perhaps even more valuable, I was a guest in the consumer's home. I could immediately see some of the strengths and challenges of the everyday environment directly in front of me. For me, this cut out a lot of the "dance" concept introduced earlier and helped both the consumer and myself, as the provider, focus directly on the issues at hand. A beautiful side effect of working in the consumer's environment is that the consumer very quickly views the provider as a vested professional working with him or her toward a solution and taking the consumer's particular life circumstances into consideration. While there are certainly "templates" for treatment, just as there are in any field, it is more difficult to give generic direction to a consumer when you can see the many facets and circumstances that can contribute to the success of the plan and that can serve as a stumbling block to the plan. I can recall many times developing a vastly different diagnostic impression based on initial sessions in the consumer's home than I would have based upon a similar number of sessions in the office. This can best be demonstrated with an actual case example where an organization received a referral for a consumer that appeared to have some unambiguous issues and treatment history. Through services in the natural community and changes made as a result of these services, the topography of this consumer's map of the future changed dramatically for the better.

Box 5.1. Assessment Case Study*

Rosalyn

Behavioral Health History and Profile: Rosalyn is a 12-year-old female referred to the agency and reported to be in need of a higher level of care due to daily anger outbursts, without any identifiable trigger, and oppositional and physically aggressive behavior (exhibited by biting, hitting, kicking, throwing items, and destroying property). The consumer's symptoms were able to be maintained with medication in the past; however, she has developed an allergy to her primary medication. Rosalyn exhibits aggressive behaviors in both the home and school environment and she received individual therapy on an outpatient basis for five years prior to referral.

The consumer has been hospitalized for crisis intervention on two occasions. Additionally, she has also been evaluated by a developmental delay team, but the team determined that her behavioral health issues were primary to secondary developmental delay issues.

Medical and Health Issues: Chromosome Duplication, Asthma, Chronic Constipation, and Bicuspid Aortic Valve Disease.

Family History: There were allegations of neglect and abuse (possibly sexual and physical), by biological mother, prior to current placement with the consumer's biological father and extended family members.

Strengths: Rosalyn loves to draw and wants to help others. She is described by others as sweet and happy when she is not in a period of escalation (of negative behaviors). She was able to identify her grandparents as informal support systems within the family and the school psychiatrist as a natural support in her educational environment.

Goals for Treatment: When Rosalyn was asked her goals, she stated, "I want to be a nurse because they take care of people." When asked her expectations of treatment, she stated "I need to not get angry. When I get angry I kick. I get angry when people tell me what to do."

Previous Psychiatric Evaluation (sent with intake referral):

> Axis I: Asperger's[2] D/O, Mood Disorder NOS Chronic,[3] Post-Traumatic Stress Disorder,[4] Oppositional Defiant Disorder,[5] Borderline Intellectual Functioning, R/O Bipolar 1 Disorder,[6] Most Recent Episode Mixed, Chronic
> Axis II: R/O Mild Mental Retardation
> Axis III: Chromosome Duplication
> Axis IV: Severe history of trauma, conflict with caregivers, conflict with peers
> Axis V: GAF (Global Assessment of Functioning):[7] 40[8]

Psychological Recommendations: Many of Rosalyn's psychological deficits appear to be developmental and neurological in nature. As such, individual psychotherapy will be very difficult and any progress made is likely to be incremental and prone to reversals. However, with such limitations understood, one of the more fertile areas for psychotherapeutic interventions will be in teaching Rosalyn interpersonal skills and assisting her in interpreting social behaviors. Furthermore, behavioral therapy aimed at providing her with an environment which reinforces positive behavior and punishes negative behavior may be beneficial. The use of specific rewards and punishments is encouraged.

Home-, School-, and Natural Community-Based Treatment: Given the intensity of Rosalyn's symptoms and the impact her behavior was having on the home and school environment, she was assessed at intake and it was determined that she would be best served with a more intense level of community-based intervention. She was assigned to an Intensive Family Intervention (IFI) Team. IFI is a team approach to community-based intensive service provision for a child/adolescent and his or her family. The services are provided by a team of fully licensed and paraprofessional behavioral health professionals in an effort to stabilize the consumer's living environment and prevent out-of-home placement (i.e., psychiatric hospital, therapeutic foster care, psychiatric residential treatment facilities, or therapeutic residential intervention services). Services are provided primarily in the consumer's current living arrangement and within the family system. The services are provided on a 24-hour per day and seven day a week basis. IFI services are provided to defuse current crisis situations, to ensure linkage to needed community services and resources, and to assist the consumer and family in being able to self-manage and recognize behavioral health issues. (While this service may not be recognized in all geographic areas or payer systems, it is an intensive service that is often authorized over a 90-day period for a higher amount of units than traditional therapy and support services on their own. An example of IFI regulations and parameters would be 72 hours of intervention authorized over a 90-day period. This would average about 6 hours of intervention per week versus one hour of individual therapy in most traditional settings.) (DBHDD: Georgia Department of Behavioral Health and Developmental Disabilities, 2013)

While Rosalyn previously had five years of traditional outpatient therapy, she had not been able to successfully apply those skills she had learned in the office to her home and school environment. Rosalyn had been unable to control her emotions and behavior once they began to escalate. When she reached a certain frustration level and when her triggers presented at home or school, her behaviors had quickly escalated to the point she was seen as a threat to others' safety. While she conceptually understood some of the skills she had been taught previously, she was not able to retrieve the information and use the skills when under stress. While receiving IFI services, Rosalyn was given the opportunity to practice newly learned skills in her home and school environments with her therapist and/or resource support present. IFI Therapists were also able to work with the parents to help them to identify some of the triggers to Rosalyn's oppositional behavior. Additionally, they were able to work together to help determine what her early escalation behaviors looked like. By preventing the early steps from progressing, Rosalyn was able to be successful in many situations in the home environment. Similarly, an IFI paraprofessional went to the school environment with Rosalyn to help her identify her own triggers and behaviors in that environment. The IFI staff were able to educate her teachers, as well, on early recognition of escalation behaviors and how to best work with Rosalyn.

After three months of services with an IFI team, the providers were able to reduce the level and intensity of Rosalyn's treatment to meet her current needs. Rosalyn's current therapist works with her on a much lower level of care and lower frequency of service provision. Rosalyn's current provider has very rarely seen Rosalyn's behavior escalate to any advanced level and stated that the consumer currently even endeavors to teach other people the same skills she learned because she is so proud of her accomplishments. The key to success for Rosalyn was being able to practice her learned skills while experiencing an authentic stressor versus a simulated one. By doing so, she could more readily access these skills in situations where the IFI team was not present, because she could draw from other actual situations in which she had been successful with those learned techniques.

*Based upon an actual case; names and identifiers have been changed to protect consumer identity.

Early Identification and Strengths-Based Assessment

One of the key components of treatment and service planning is accurate identification of symptoms and assessment of issues. Each and every consumer brings a unique package of past experiences, current fears, symptoms, hopes, dreams, triggers, strengths, and challenges with them. Although each package may look similar on the outside, to those of other consumers, each consumer contributes different variables to the process. Part of the responsibility of the provider is to fully understand the presenting issues and how history and current stressors affect the demonstration of these issues. It is also important to make strides to identify issues early for a consumer so that treatment can begin before symptoms degenerate.

For consumers of all ages, early detection, assessment, and links with treatment and supports will help prevent mental health problems from worsening.

(New Freedom Commision on
Mental Health, 2003, p. 11)

84

A strengths-based approach to this process is one way for the provider to focus on the positive, affirming ways to find resources within the consumer's own arsenal and make a diagnosis or identification as early as possible. A strengths-based assessment focuses on measurement of behavioral and emotional skills, characteristics, and abilities that serve to create a sense of personal pride and accomplishment for the consumer. It is important, as a provider, to try to assess for those characteristics and skills that will help the consumers navigate some of the more difficult times in their lives and help them develop the connections they need socially, personally, and often academically and vocationally. The belief system behind using a strengths-based approach is founded in the belief that all consumers have strengths. Oftentimes, the strengths are difficult for them, their families, and those around them to immediately identify. That does not mean, however, that the strengths are not there. Additionally, failure of a consumer to demonstrate an identified strength during a stressful situation does not necessarily mean that it does not exist, but could simply mean that it has not been utilized during all applicable scenarios. There are many advantages to using a strengths-based approach to assessment. When the provider begins with focusing on the problem in the first conversations, for example, the consumer may be left feeling disconnected, defensive, and resistant to the process. Simply by focusing on questions like "What would you like to see change?" or "How can I help you meet your goals?" the provider helps to build an alliance that is a central part of rapport building and trust in moving forward toward positive change. These approach changes can help the provider or intake assessor to engage positively with the consumer that is making those crucial steps to come for treatment. The provider and consumer can work as a team to identify what is going well in the consumer's life. Together, they can document the strengths or competencies that the consumer has mastered. This evaluative process also highlights what support or resources may need to be put in place to assist the consumer in reaching his or her goals.

Using a strengths-based assessment approach is quite purposeful. It helps the consumer, and in some cases the family, as well, to create a vision for moving forward. It also helps to identify the goals of services. When consumers are actively involved in identifying these goals, they become more vested in how the goals can come to fruition and are more unambiguous in their own role in the process. This strengths-based process also helps to identify clear strengths to be used for planning purposes. There are several ways to identify consumer strengths in the assessment process. One such method is to utilize an established outcome measure that specifically measures identified strengths in a somewhat objective manner. There are many outcome measures available for this purpose and the choice of instrument is dependent on the provider's preference as well as those recommended by certain payer systems. Some of the outcome measures currently in use to assess consumer's strengths include, but are certainly not limited to, Strengths and Difficulties Questionnaire (Goodman, 1997); Child and Adolescent Needs and Strengths (CANS-MH) developed by Lyons and published as an open domain tool (The Praed Foundation, 2013); Profiles of Student Life: Attitudes and Behaviors (PSL-AB) (Search Institute, 1996); Behavioral and Emotional Rating Scale (BERS-2) (Epstein & Sharma, 2004); Scales for Predicting Successful Inclusion (SPSI) (Gilliam & McConnell, 1997); and the Adult Needs and Strengths Assessment (ANSA) developed as an open domain tool (The Praed Foundation, 2013).

The second method of identifying consumer strengths, however, is the one preferred by this author. While much more informal, simply talking with the consumer and observing allows the provider and/or assessor to get to know the consumer better and to identify known and hidden strengths. For many assessors and providers, fully evaluating the strengths the consumer brings to the process can be difficult and requires some practice in asking the right questions to identify obvious and hidden consumer and familial strengths. There is no such thing as the perfect question or method to find out strengths, but a seasoned provider and/or assessor will be able to tell what methods are working best with the consumer, as well as which methods are a dead end. In identifying strengths, the consumer is usually much more willing and available to participate than in simply responding to a series of questions based on problem behaviors. The Strength Identification Dialogue text box in this chapter suggests some questions and discussion topics that can be useful in getting a strengths-based assessment underway. It is the strength identification methodology results that help the provider develop a list of SNAPS (strengths, needs, abilities, and preferences) for the consumer. Person-centered care heavily focuses on the consumer's personal input in the process leading to identification of the consumer's own unique strengths, identified needs, preferences for treatment, and abilities and talents that may assist in reaching the treatment goals. Information to develop the SNAPS is gathered in the assessment, and is a critical piece of establishing the foundation of treatment goals and objectives listed on the treatment plan. See Figure 5.1 regarding SNAPS use in person-centered treatment.

Box 5.2. Strength Identification Dialogue

Questions and Discussion Points for Children and Adolescents:

- If you could tell me one good thing about yourself, what would it be?
- Name two good things about your parents (family, school, etc.).
- Who is your favorite adult? Why do you like him/her?
- What is your favorite thing to do (hobby, sport, reading, etc.)?
- What would your friends say is the best thing about you?
- My life would be better six months from now if _____.
- I am most proud of _____.
- What have you learned about yourself and your world when times have been tough?

Questions and Discussion Points for Adults:

- Who has been the biggest influence in your life?
- What was the best vacation or period of relaxation you ever took?
- Tell me what the best things are about you (your family)?
- The most important thing I have ever done is _____.
- The thing I want others to remember about me is _____.
- My best qualities as a parent (friend, worker, etc.) are _____.
- What are the things you value the most?
- How have you managed to survive so far, given all the challenges you have had to deal with?

Questions and Discussion Points for Family/Extended Supports:

- The thing I like most about (consumer) is _____.
- Does your family belong to the faith community? In what capacity?
- Were there some special family beliefs or values passed down to you from your parents or grandparents that have been important to your family?
- What family traditions or important cultural events do you value?
- What is something special about (consumer) that you wish others could see like you are able to?
- Who are special people on whom you can depend?
- In the past when things were better (more stable) what do you think was different?
- What seems to be working for (consumer)?

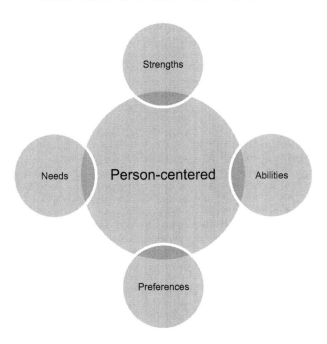

Figure 5.1 SNAPS (Strengths, Needs, Abilities, and Preferences) Used in Person-Centered Treatment

Strengths and *Abilities* refer to consumer characteristics or elements in their past or present that they have used to help them cope with stressful situations. Examples of *Strengths* could be employment, supportive family, principles, religious beliefs, hope, desire for change, commitment to education, and supportive friends. Examples of *Abilities* could be asks for help, learns from errors, saves money, follows directions, recognizes triggers to behaviors, recognizes medication side effects, and researches self-care. *Needs* refer to problems, issues, or concerns identified by the consumer. Examples of needs include learn about my illness, vocational support, resources for learning, skills to recognize triggers, and companionship. *Preferences* refer to what the consumer wants in terms of treatment. There are some things that may be easily accommodated, such as a preference for a provider of a specific gender, culture, ethnicity, or belief system. Consumers may also express preferences for particular program type, service, and time of day for appointment purposes.

Person-Centered Treatment Planning

Person-centered behavioral health treatment planning is based upon the initial assessment of the consumer's strengths, needs, abilities, and preferences. That treatment plan then serves to define the direction of treatment. The days of a professional briefly meeting with a consumer and diagnosing the consumer based on the assessments and observations of previous providers have passed for most organizations and providers. It is important for the individual being diagnosed to be a part of the assessment process and be able to help identify the concerns and issues in the person's own words and with his or her own descriptions of experiences.

Following the premise of consumer participation in assessment, consumers can also best contribute to their own treatment plan by being part of the process of identifying needs and goals. After all, when individuals are part of the process, they can begin to see themselves as active contributors to the steps, goals, and final outcomes of intervention. Would you want to be dictated a plan for yourself in which you were not part of the planning process? This question is best answered when we are able to think of how we would feel in a similar situation. If your Primary Care Physician (PCP) dictated a health plan to you that did not take all variables of your lifestyle and situations into account, you may attempt to follow the plan, but may not feel vested in the process. Similarly, if you were experiencing financial problems and had student loans, family loans, job change issues, and medical bills that were all requiring attention, but you received a financial re-payment plan that only took some of those variables and paybacks into account, the plan would not be solid. It would not be effective because it would only serve to address portions of the problem. If your financial planner, however, sat down with you, sought your input, and made sure all unique areas were addressed, the plan would be stronger and easier to follow for you. Behavioral health plans are no different. Often, our consumers have been in and out of treatment and are given a plan to follow that is just missing pieces of the puzzle. While they may work on the plan and make some progress, they are far more likely to actively participate if they feel they were part of each step of the process and the plan reflects the unique components of their life situations and goals.

In the past, treatment plans traditionally would focus on the problems the consumer was experiencing in his or her life and often looked like a list of all the things that were wrong with the consumer. Understandably, some people find it less than motivating to see all of their problem issues listed out in written format. For some consumers, this format did not motivate them to change, but rather became a roadblock and source of frustration. Many providers and programs today, however, embrace a strengths-based approach to assessment and treatment planning which shares a core belief that every consumer has strengths, abilities to help cope with difficulties, resiliency in the face of trauma, and/or skills to help the consumer function when faced with significant stressors. The degree and effectiveness of these strengths may vary from individual to individual, but all consumers do have strengths that should be taken into account when developing a treatment plan that will guide the process of their treatment. Earlier, strengths-based assessment was introduced as a way to establish positive expectations for the consumer and to empower the consumer in the process of contributing to treatment decisions and goals. A strengths-based and person-centered approach to treatment planning serves to fortify the rapport between the provider and consumer and bring the consumer's input to the process. This approach is a logical complement to services provided in the home and natural community where the consumer's experience is also highly valued. See Table 5.1 for a

Table 5.1 Treatment Planning Comparison for Home and Natural Community Service Provision

	Traditional Treatment Planning	Strengths-Based Treatment Planning
Function of Treatment Plan	Traditionally a listing of all problem areas that must be addressed.	A way to frame treatment and guide the provider and consumer through the process. This plan is living and can be updated to reflect current needs and changes.
Role of Consumer in Planning	Traditionally the consumer gives very little input to this process. Often treatment plans include input from previous diagnoses and treatment plans.	Consumer is fully involved in the assessment and treatment planning pieces. The plan is really centered on consumer input and requires his or her signature acknowledging participation.
Location of Planning	Usually in an office or meeting room and may follow a prescribed format.	Planning can take place anywhere—in the consumer's home, in a coffee shop, the library, or any place the consumer is most comfortable.
Community-Based and Information Supports	May be utilized in traditional planning, but not a mandatory component.	Viewed as an important piece to the strengths-based treatment plan, the extended family, informal supports, and community resources serve to augment the plan and give needed supports for success in the natural community. Informal supports are more easily identified and accessed in the home, school, and natural community service environments.
Presenting Issues	Problems may be viewed as a pathology and the plan is based on addressing these problems.	While problems are addressed in the treatment plan, they are viewed as challenges to the consumer that may have caused unsuccessful attempts to manage the illness or issues. A strengths-based approach looks at the consumer's own strengths as tools to work through these challenges.

Strengths	Either not listed or not prominently listed.	Since the strengths-based assessment serves to identify positive attributes, these will be integrated into the treatment plan itself—usually in a prominent position. Planning will focus on the consumer's abilities and what the consumer or the natural/ informal supports have to contribute to the process.
Goals of Treatment	May be worded in terms of behaviors that consumer must stop and focus on problem issues.	Worded positively in terms of what a consumer will do more of (behavior). Goals integrate consumer's strengths and problems. Worded in such a way it is easy for all participants to understand.

comparison of traditional treatment planning and strengths-based treatment planning.

It is this strengths-based focus that is the basis for person-centered planning and care. The consumer is at the center of the entire treatment planning process. He or she is part of the assessment and planning, and even is a part of deciding when meetings take place, who is present, and where they take place. This change, where the consumer is an integral part of each process, is supported by multiple reports that have asked providers to re-examine how consumer participation and treatment planning is conducted. One such report, the Report of the President's New Freedom Mental Health Commission, stated the following (New Freedom Commission on Mental Health, 2003, p. 5):

Successfully transforming the mental health service delivery system rests on two principles:

1. First, services and treatments must be consumer and family-centered, geared to give consumers real and meaningful choices about treatment options and providers—not oriented to the requirements of bureaucracies.
2. Second, care must focus on increasing consumer's ability to successfully cope with life's challenges, on facilitating recovery, and on building resilience, not just on managing symptoms.

The New Freedom Commission also published six goals to transform the behavioral health system. The one that best addresses treatment planning is Goal Two. This goal calls for behavioral health care that is consumer- and family-driven and states:

> When a serious mental illness or a serious emotional disturbance is first diagnosed, the health care provider, in full partnership with consumers and families, will develop an individualized plan of care for managing the illness. The partnership of personalized care means basically choosing who, what, and how appropriate care will be provided:
>
> - Choosing which mental health care professionals are on the team,
> - Sharing in decision-making, and
> - Having the option to agree or disagree with the treatment plan.
>   (New Freedom Commission on Mental Health, 2003, p. 4)

The Commission goes further to make recommendations on how it believes the behavioral health system can be transformed. The report states: "The hope and the opportunity to regain control of their lives—often vital to recovery—will become real for consumers and families. Consumers will play a significant role in shifting the current system to a recovery-oriented one by participating in planning, evaluation, research, training, and service delivery." To aid in this transformation of the behavioral health system, the Commission makes five recommendations:

- Develop an individualized plan of care for every adult with a serious mental illness and child with a serious emotional disturbance.
- Involve consumers and families fully in orienting the mental health system toward recovery.
- Align relevant Federal programs to improve access and accountability for mental health services.
- Create a Comprehensive State Mental Health Plan.
- Protect and enhance the rights of people with mental illness.
  (New Freedom Commission on
  Mental Health, 2003, p. 9)

Treatment Planning Components

Treatment plans vary from provider to provider, but all have some components that are required by local entities, accreditation bodies, payers, and/or licensure bodies. Person-centered treatment planning also has variations in terms of facilitation and required planning tools in different states and regions. There are some components, however, that should be part of any plan that is person-centered. These include determination of strengths, needs, abilities, and preferences that may be ascertained in the assessment process, but are used as a foundation when developing goals and objectives listed on the treatment plan. Additionally, all treatment plans should include stated goals, objectives, and interventions.

Goals

Person-centered planning really encourages consumers to examine their lives. Consumers look at all parts of their lives, from the miniscule, to the more considerable components. This type of examination helps the consumers put all these components together in a way that is important or significant to them, and values their informal and peer supports systems. When consumers are able to put these pieces together, the end result is a direction or goal for treatment. Goals usually reflect the consumer's and family's primary reasons for seeking help and services. They are broad general statements that express the consumer's and family's desire for a change in a particular area of their life or functioning. A goal can be short- or long-term and written in a way that is positive. Ideally, the goal is captured in the consumer's own words. While goals may not be measurable, their achievement should be something that is easily observed.

> First build a proper goal. That proper goal will make it easy, almost automatic, to build a proper you.
> (Johann Wolfgang von Goethe, German
> writer and politician, born 1749)

In a person-centered approach, the provider can work with the consumer to help the consumer best identify and express the concerns and needs he or she has. The provider can also help frame the resolution of those needs as goals to be included in the treatment plan. In person-centered planning the provider's role is to be respectful of the consumer's and family's preferences and to assist them in reaching those goals. A treatment plan usually has several goals, but it may be appropriate, in some cases, to have only one goal that captures the fundamental vision of the consumer's and family's service needs.

It is often difficult for consumers to think in terms of what they would like to see happen in their life. This is particularly relevant when a consumer has a long-standing mental illness or life situation that is extremely challenging. That consumer may not have had the opportunity to experience life outside of the challenges or be able to identify what changes are needed to move away from the issues. The consumers may not even be in a place where they are able to articulate what would feel better for them because they are "comfortable in their discomfort." There are some questions the provider can utilize that help assist the consumer in identifying and formulating the goals. These questions include:

- If you no longer had (disorder/symptom) what would you want to do?
- Is there anything missing from your life as a result of (disorder/symptom) that you would like to have?
- Before you started to have (symptom/disorder), what did you want out of life?
- If you were not (condition/disorder), how would your life be different?

Another way to help develop goals is to think in terms of addressing targets that:

1. address treatment goals (often linked to identified issues that brought the consumer into treatment);
2. address goals for the consumer's overall improvement; and/or
3. address overall quality of life concerns (human needs).

An example of identified goals in these areas would be:

Treatment Goal: Demonstrate the needed skills to be able to live independently with minimal ongoing support. Note: treatment goals may not be written in the consumer's words, but may be the provider's elucidation of what is needed to reach a consumer's stated goal (e.g., overall improvement goal of living in own apartment).
Overall Improvement Goal: I want to live in my own apartment.
Quality of Life Goal: I want to have more friends.

We discussed how identifying and formulating goals can be a very difficult process for many consumers. There is a vulnerability to sharing hopes, desires, and innermost thoughts for change. It is particularly difficult for the individual who may have experienced rejection in the past and who is not confident in expressing his or her own desires or directionality. It is imperative that a provider of services show deference to the consumer's identified goals. The consumer may identify a goal that seems unrealistic, but the provider needs to exercise moderation in how to respond. There is usually a time for "reality testing" for unrealistic goals at a later time. The provider's initial acceptance of the consumer's efforts, however, can be a significant opportunity to empower the consumer.

Objectives

Objectives identify the changes that are necessary to help the consumer and family meet their goals. They help to identify the immediate focus of treatment. The objective also helps to break up tasks incrementally so that the consumers can focus on steps as they move toward their identified goal. Objectives are action-oriented and typically use action words to state desired changes in behavior. The attainment of the objective will typically require the consumers to master new skills and abilities that will support them in developing more effective responses to the challenges they face. The main characteristics of a strong objective are that they are able to be measured; able to be reached; reasonable given the consumer's age, level of development, and resources; written in language which is behaviorally specific; written in language that can be understood by everyone in the process; and time-limited. Objectives should describe positive change that builds on past accomplishments and existing resources. In a person-centered model, objectives usually reflect an increase in functioning and ability or mastering of new skills versus just a decrease in symptomology or problem behavior.

A properly written objective typically begins with "the consumer will" and then describes the desired change in behavior, function, or status as a step toward reaching the larger goal.

Example Format for Writing Objectives:

(Consumer's name) will _____ (what consumer needs to do and in what circumstances) _____ ("X" number of times per day/week/ month or target date).

Objectives are also characterized by a popular mnemonic[9] that states that objectives should be SMART:

- Simple/Specific/Straightforward

    The objective should be in language that is easy to understand for all involved. The steps involved in meeting the objective should be as simple and as specific as possible. The plan should also be easy to recall. If the consumer is part of the planning and the objectives are written simply, the consumer can easily recall the objectives. Additionally, person-centered planning uses words that the consumer can easily comprehend and avoids excessively clinical language.

- Measurable

    The change that is identified in the objective should be one that is easy to observe. This change should be easy for both the provider and the consumer to distinguish. There are many ways change can be measured, however, it is acceptable to measure change by such methods as consumer or family member self-report, assignment completion, drug screens, standardized testing, behavior charts, observation, and journal entries.

- Achievable/Attainable

  The stated objective should be appropriate to age, developmental abilities, cultural considerations, and reflective of the consumer's strengths and limitations. The consumer should have the capacity to be able to reach the designated objective. The concept of achievement also applies to the number of objectives for each goal; having too many objectives may not be attainable.

- Reasonable/Realistic/Relevant

  The objective should not only be achievable, but also reasonable for the consumer. Language on the treatment plan should convey realistic expectations for the consumer given his or her resources and abilities. Additionally, the objectives should have something to do with the presenting issue and/or something the consumer identifies as personally important.

- Target Date/Time Frame

  Dates for targeted completion should be relevant to the scope of the objective, the consumer's motivation, and the necessary resources available to support and facilitate the change. Target dates are specific to each objective and predict how long it will be before the consumer is able to reach the designated objective. Setting a time frame sends an important message to both the consumer and the provider that change is anticipated. The provider needs to be careful not to set extended target dates as this can convey low expectations for the consumer. A general rule is to set target dates in 90-day increments to allow for reasonable change within that set time period.

Interventions

Interventions are methods, approaches, actions, or strategies used by the provider to support the consumer's attainment of objectives. Typically, they will describe the specific activity, service, or treatment, identify the provider or other responsible person, and clarify the intended purpose or impact as it relates to the objectives. The intensity, frequency, and duration of treatment should also be specified. While the objective details desired changes for the consumer, the intervention details the steps the provider will take to help bring about the change desired in the objective.

All parts of the treatment plan should be easy to understand to anyone who may be reading them. This holds true of the intervention area, as well. The intervention area should be so specific that it can be easily interpreted by any other provider involved in the consumer's care. It should also have clear steps for any other provider that may need to supply services to the consumer during the assigned provider's absence (e.g., vacation, illness, or unexpected leave). Writing interventions such as "The therapist will conduct individual therapy for depression." may be too vague. The treatment plan should include specific interventions (specific types of therapy or activities) as well as the aforementioned frequency, duration, and provider assignment. When examining the topic of interventions, it is key to point out that person-centered planning does not mean simply giving the consumers whatever they want. Rather, it requires the provider to determine the services he or she provides in a collaborative decision-making process in which the consumer plays a central role. The emphasis is on the consumer's own preferences and identified goals. This process, however, is not in conflict with evidence-based practice. Evidence-based practices are preferred as the approaches used by the provider to help the consumer meet the goals. Ultimately, however, the provider wants to find the intervention that works best with the consumer to meet the identified goals. In many cases that intervention will be from an EBP. In some situations, however, the provider may personalize an approach to meet the individualized needs of a consumer without compromising the value and benefit of the service provision.

Use of Natural and Informal Supports

A person-centered approach to planning includes an expansion of the word *supports*. Supports are not simply paid providers and professionals that are working with the consumer and family to meet their goals. Informal, or natural, supports include other people in the consumer's life or resources in the consumer's natural community. Informal supports can include extended family, friends, neighbors, peers, religious leaders, and traditional healers (see Chapter 3, Table 3.1). The consumer is the one who is truly the expert in his or her own life and often is aware of informal supports that can assist in the recovery and healing process. Informal supports are not intended to replace the provider, but rather enhance the services being provided professionally. Additionally, informal and natural supports are beneficial in helping the consumer with transitions and ultimately helping to support the consumer in the community, when the consumer is discharged from services. These informal supports should be identified and utilized in the treatment planning as well as discharge planning details.

Early Discharge Planning

It may seem strange to focus on discharge when you are just beginning services with a consumer, but this is the optimal time to do so. After all, we talked about going on a destination trip and how there are several steps necessary in the planning. You want to determine why you are going somewhere and where you are going. By identifying where you are headed you can pick the best route. You also want to know what you have planned while you are there and when you will be leaving to return to your point of origin or next destination. Again, behavioral health planning is no different, as at the onset of services it is important to identify when you will know the consumer is ready for discharge or transition to the next stage. The early identification of discharge steps helps the consumer to be part of the process and to have awareness of what is needed to discharge or move to the next lower level of services. This process begins in the assessment phase and continues through treatment planning, treatment planning updates, and actual discharge from services.

Included within the treatment plan itself should be an identifiable and written transition/discharge plan. One should bear in mind several components and concepts when developing this area of the treatment plan. First is that it must be developed at the onset of treatment in collaboration with the consumer and (as applicable) with the family and informal supports. Additionally, it should be individualized and reference specific consumer symptoms, behaviors, and/or circumstances. A good way to look at this individualization is to ask yourself as a provider if the consumer could identify his or her own transfer/discharge plan if handed his or hers among a total of five such plans from your practice. If the transfer/discharge plans are so generic that this would not be possible, they need to be individualized further. The provider also wants to ensure that the goals on the treatment plan, and consequently the discharge/transition steps, are realistic. A statement such as: Consumer "will be discharged from services when he exhibits no symptoms for six months" may be unlikely for most consumers. For many consumers with more severe conditions, it may be that the transition/discharge area documents the consumer's likely transition to a lower level of care or independence when specific treatment goals are met. Providers should also remember that the treatment plan is a living document. The discharge/transition portion of the plan should also be updated according to the consumer's progress or lack of progress in treatment. With person-centered planning, the provider should be certain that the goal achievement statements in the transition/discharge portion reflect resolution of the issues or needs that initially led the consumer and family to seek services. That is, after all, why the consumer sought services in the first place. To meet those discharge/

planning requirements, therefore, the link between them and the treatment plan goals should be obvious and without ambiguity. This section of the transition/discharge plan should also include clear projections of dates for discharge or transition, as well as identify any anticipated step-down services specifically.

Deferred Issues

It is important to identify all goals and concerns for the consumer's treatment through the assessment process. There may be times, however, when the consumer is not ready to address an issue or has expressed a preference to defer an issue at the current time. Those need areas that are deferred can be listed in a deferral section to note that they have been discussed and deferred at this time. This documentation ensures that provider and consumer are aware of the issue, but either have deferred due to preference or lack of readiness at the present time.

Periodic Assessment of Consumer Progress

Periodically, it is clinically sound to assess and monitor the consumer's progress in reference to treatment goals and objectives. Revisions and updates to the treatment plan usually occur on a quarterly basis, but can be done every 30 to 60 days depending on the intensity of the services provided. This is a necessary step to re-assess how appropriate the treatment plan is for current needs, as well as evaluate the effectiveness of current interventions. Additionally, this update process can help identify new issues or needs that may have arisen during the course of services. Just as the initial treatment planning is completed collaboratively with the consumer, the family (as applicable), any other service providers, and relevant community supports, the re-assessment may also include these same contributors and serve as a formal process to re-access treatment needs.

Evaluating the Person-Centered Plan

We discussed the importance of centering service provision setting, assessment, and treatment planning around the consumer. Now that the plan has been developed, there are easy ways to re-evaluate to make sure that what was facilitated was, indeed, the development of a person-centered plan. When you look back over the treatment plan the following items should be apparent:

- The results of the initial assessment were discussed with the consumer and family members, as applicable.

- A planning meeting took place with the consumer, providers, and other identified informal, natural supports, to discuss and develop the plan.
- The goals determined on the treatment plan are in line with the initial assessment information.
- The goals on the treatment plan are linked to the Strengths, Needs, Abilities, and Preferences (SNAPS) identified in the assessment process.
- The treatment plan is written in words the consumer can easily understand.
- The objectives follow a SMART model.
- The consumer, and family members, as applicable, can verbalize their understanding of the plan and their role in the objectives.
- There is evidence of participation, usually in the form of consumer signature, on the plan itself.

Most providers will find that part of providing services includes developing a treatment plan. In fact, most providers are required by regulation and/or law to provide a treatment plan for each consumer as part of the process of being paid for the services they provide. Some payers may not require a treatment plan, but it is certainly more than just paperwork. Treatment plans are an important tool to put into writing: the specific goals, objectives, and interventions for service provision; the expectations for transition and discharge; and the identification of formal and informal supports. Finally, treatment planning is an essential process that documents the consumer's, provider's, family member's, and informal support's agreement and awareness of a step-by-step, individualized, guide for the consumer's movement toward recovery.

Notes

1. A lean-to is a rough shed or shelter with a lean-to roof (roof with single slope).
2. Asperger's syndrome is often considered a high functioning form of autism.
3. Mood disorder not otherwise specified (MD-NOS) is a mood disorder that is impairing but does not fit in with any of the officially specified diagnoses.
4. Post-traumatic stress disorder (PTSD) is a type of anxiety disorder. It can occur after an extreme emotional trauma that involved the threat of injury or death.
5. Oppositional defiant disorder is a pattern of disobedient, hostile, and defiant behavior toward authority figures.
6. Bipolar disorder is a condition in which a person has periods of depression and periods of being extremely happy or being cross or irritable.
7. The Global Assessment of Functioning (GAF) is a numeric scale (0 through 100) used by behavioral health professionals to subjectively rate the social, occupational, and psychological functioning of a consumer. Higher numbers indicate better functioning.

8. GAF of 40 indicates some impairment in reality testing or communication OR major impairment in several areas, such as work or school, family relations, judgment, thinking, or mood.
9. Mnemonics refer to something used to assist the memory.

References

DBHDD: Georgia Department of Behavioral Health and Developmental Disabilities. (2013, September 1). *Provider Manual for Community Behavioral Health Providers for DBHDD*. Retrieved October 29, 2013, from DBHDD: http://apsero.com/webx/.ee83019

Epstein, M. H., & Sharma, J. (2004). *Behavioral and Emotional Rating Scale: A Strength-Based Approach to Assessment*. Austin, TX: PRO-ED.

Gilliam, J. E., & McConnell, K. S. (1997). *Scales for Predicting Successful Inclusion*. Austin, TX: PRO-ED.

Goodman, R. (1997). The strengths and difficulties questionnaire: A research note. *Journal of Child Psychology and Psychiatry, 38*(5), 581–586.

New Freedom Commission on Mental Health. (2003, July 22). *Achieving the Promise: Transforming Mental Health Care in America*. Retrieved November 3, 2013, from http://govinfo.library.unt.edu/mentalhealthcommission/reports/FinalReport/downloads/downloads.html

The Praed Foundation. (2013). *About the CANS*. Retrieved November 15, 2013, from The Praed Foundation: www.praedfoundation.org/About%20the%20CANS.html

Search Institute. (1996). *Profiles of Student Life: Attitudes and Behavior*. Minneapolis, MN: Author.

6

RESOURCE SUPPORT
MEETINGS AND IDENTIFYING
INFORMAL SUPPORT SYSTEMS

Resource Support Meeting Process

While many traditional behavioral health services focus on the individual presenting for therapy or support services and those the person may bring for family therapy or intervention, usually there are those family members that are hesitant to come into a formalized office environment or be part of therapy. They may be cautious of contributing to the process because of fears or stigma surrounding the condition of their family member. An alternative, but very effective tool in garnering family support, when applicable, and identifying informal supports is the Resource Support Meeting. This type of meeting can be used by providers across the service location spectrum to obtain input and to identify informal and natural supports for the consumer. The Resource Support Meeting is an option for those providers who provide services in a clinic-based office, residential setting, or hospital-based setting to incorporate a component of the natural community behavioral health experience into their existing practice. It can be used to assist with treatment planning or, on an as-needed basis, to trouble-shoot problem issues that appear to be void of apparent solutions and supports. While person-centered treatment planning does have, as a key element, the identification and inclusion of natural supports throughout the process, not all providers utilize this same type of planning process. This process, however, gives options to providers, who are not conducting full fidelity person-centered planning, to incorporate a crucial element of natural community-based resource coordination.

With the permission of the individual in services (and identification of participants), family, extended family, and natural community supports are invited to a conference for the purpose of supporting the success of the individual and his or her treatment. Confidentiality and ground rules are established and as a group both strengths and needs are identified. The behavioral health professional serves as the facilitator to ensure efficacy of process. Those that fall outside of the ground rules may be asked to leave. The purpose of this conference is to show the individuals in treatment that they do have strengths and needs that can be addressed by themselves, as well as through identified formal and informal supports.

Box 6.1. Resource Support Meetings

Resource Support Meetings can be used by those providers working with consumers in traditional outpatient settings, residential settings, and across the service location spectrum. Any provider can bring in a component of the natural community behavioral health experience into his or her existing practice with this tool. The consumer must be a willing participant and is the key component in identifying participants, including formal supports, family and extended family members, clergy, friends, supportive neighbors, and identified community supports. The identified participants are invited to a conference for the purpose of supporting the success of the consumer and his or her treatment outcomes. The meeting helps to identify informal supports and is a useful tool in helping the consumer find support in both treatment and in the natural community once the consumer leaves a provider's office.

As a provider, I conducted many similar type meetings over the years and found them to be one of the most productive tools for coordination and resource identification that I have had at my disposal. Oftentimes, I would work with an individual consumer, either a child, adolescent, or adult, and focus entirely on the perspective and information that the person was bringing to each session. While this focus is crucial, usually an entirely new perspective and viewpoint can be identified through Resource Support Meetings. It is often in these alternate perspectives and viewpoints that untapped resources are identified that can serve to benefit the consumer.

In this chapter, I will provide details of the steps a provider should take in conducting a Resource Support Meeting. I have found these steps to be most effective in ensuring a respectful and productive meeting. The first crucial step is talking with your individual consumer about what a Resource Support Meeting is and what it entails. This critical step of informed consent will be the base of moving forward in a successful process. The consumer needs to know what a Resource Support Meeting involves and should be involved in identifying who the consumer would like to participate. If the consumer is uncomfortable with this step, you simply do not move forward with the meeting. It is important to remember that not all consumers have a supportive family of origin or group of active supporters in the past or current situation. Identifying informal supports, therefore, is not just about identifying relatives, but rather about looking beyond the obvious systems to those a few steps beyond. Sometimes, the most supportive community members for a consumer have been a dedicated teacher, a member of the clergy or his or her religious organization, a neighbor who has always been supportive, or a family friend. A provider can assist the consumer in looking beyond obvious support systems into these potential informal supports.

> Some individuals don't have the gift of a loving and supportive family. Identifying informal support systems is not just about identifying relatives, but rather someone or something that will be a stable and identifiable support in at least one area of identified need.

To begin the process of initiating the Resource Support Meeting, a formal letter should be sent to participants with the specific location, date, time, and expectation requirements. A typical letter should also include the implied expectation of positive planning. The facilitator should always ask participants to note any identified strengths of the consumer and his or her family, as applicable, and then notate any concerns and needs they may be aware of with the consumer. This step sets the expectation for all involved that this process will include a discussion of strengths as well as need identification. Simply by requesting that this step is conducted prior to the meeting, the participants are able to give time and thought to the subject and be prepared to speak about strengths and needs when addressed.

Location is also a key variable in this process. It is most effective to find a neutral community location to conduct the Resource Support Meeting. An office may feel too formalized, the home may feel too intrusive for the consumer, but often a neutral location within the community may help all participants enter with equal footing. Possible locations for meetings may include community centers, churches, libraries, or local colleges as long as the facilitator is able to secure a closed door meeting room to help ensure confidentiality. Prior to the meeting, the facilitator should make sure the room is welcoming and allows for dialogue without the potential for obvious breaches of the confidentiality of protected health information provided orally in the meeting. If the facilitator is unsure if the area is conducive to a confidential meeting, a white noise maker placed near the door is an additional protective measure that helps ensure conversations are not overheard when in a natural community setting.

Once families and community supports arrive the facilitator should initiate introductions and establish the concept of confidentiality. In the interest of informed consent, a provider should explain mandated reporting criteria and the expectations for those in the group in terms of keeping personal information regarding the consumer confidential. A written confidentiality agreement is a good tool to utilize to show those participants in the Resource Support Meeting that you are serious about this expectation.

Next the facilitator should introduce the purpose of the Resource Support Meeting. The Resource Support Meeting is a solution-based approach used to resolve issues for consumers. The main goals of the meeting are to ensure safety and identify solutions and supports for resiliency and/or recovery goals. After having a discussion on the purpose of the Resource Support Meeting, the concept of ground rules should also be introduced. The facilitator will want to create ground rules and state these clearly at the beginning of the meeting to set expectations of behavior that will be allowed and behavior that is destructive to the process and for which the offending individual may be asked to leave the meeting. Since the purpose of these meetings is to support the consumer and be solution-focused in approach, individual participants who are not willing to participate accordingly can be damaging to the process and lose the privilege of participating.

A printed format can also be utilized to keep some order in the meeting and allow steps to take place in intended sequence. It is often helpful for the consumers to tell their story in their own words and to the extent they feel comfortable. They can identify their needs and preferences for treatment and goals. This allows them to have more control in a process that they may have had little control over in past treatment. Each participant can also be given the opportunity to present the list of strengths he or she has identified for the consumer and family supports, and also to present goals. Needs can be addressed next and listed on a dry erase board or flip board so that each of the strengths and needs can be easily reviewed by all participants. Next it is appropriate to identify steps and time frames to meet the consumer's needs. There is a great deal of information that can be brought together to help an individual consumer. Additionally, a solution that a consumer and/or family generates is more likely to be successful, because it will respond to the consumer's unique strengths and needs. Consumers are more invested in a plan in which they are full partners in the decision-making process. Most consumers, families, and surrounding support systems have strengths. By focusing on the strengths first and identifying needs next, the problems can be addressed in a way that incorporates the unique formal and informal supports that are available to the consumer. This is *your* plan!

Identifying Informal Support Systems the Consumer Can Utilize in His or Her Own Community

Supports can be differentiated into formal supports and informal supports. Formal supports are those provided by organized networks and can include education, behavioral training, therapy, respite services, organized programs, and the like. Informal supports, on the other hand, are not provided by an organized network, but rather by family, friends, and faith connections. As a result of following the process outline for the Resource Support Meeting, informal supports are identified, as well as any formal supports that may have been overlooked. It is possible to delve further in exploring supports since the process allows strengths to be identified. Let's focus on this strength identification, as it is a critical piece of the entire process and perhaps the gilded treasure among the numerous beneficial products of this process. Imagine a room where there are identified individuals who care about the outcome of the consumer all gathered together for the purpose of coming up with identified supports to help that individual succeed with the treatment plan in the community where he or she resides. This group thinking allows solutions to develop that may not have been obvious, or may have been somewhat occult, in previous processes. See Figure 6.1 regarding the role of identified supports in the equation for consumer success.

Let's look at a traditional session to further elaborate on the necessity of identifying all needed formal and informal supports to ensure the consumer has the tools needed to successfully address the treatment plan. When a consumer sits in front of a provider in a session, he or she has a set amount of time and often is focusing on the most critical issues or events that have presented as a problem during the last week. This makes sense in that the consumer needs to process critical events and issues that are current to him or her. Therefore, in a traditional hour-long session, there is a look back at the previous week, an overview of current issues and events and how they tie into the diagnosis, and a look at the goals set out on the treatment plan for the particular session. Much must be covered during the

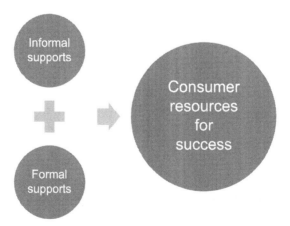

Figure 6.1 Equation for Consumer Success: Identification of Informal and Formal Supports

106

session, and often consumers may lack the perspective to see some of the more subtle issues or triggers that contribute to the current disorder or situation. When we have grown up in a particular environment or family style, it is difficult to see the patterns within those groups that contribute to current issues. Additionally, we are conditioned to the physical environments in which we live and may see them as normalized and static. In essence, it becomes difficult to see how some variables can be changed, removed, added, or modified to help create an environment that is more supportive of the behavioral health challenges being experienced. A community perspective often helps identify these unseen or unvoiced barriers to wellness. A Resource Support Meeting can help the consumer obtain a different perspective on his or her situation. Instead of a hopeless, immutable world, positive changes to the consumer's situation are likely possible with the help of others that live in the very environment from which the challenge springs. A solution to a problem is often available for discovery in our own backyards. The Resource Support Meeting helps uncover and make available those proximal solutions.

Box 6.2. Case Example for Resource Support Identification

Aaron

Aaron, a 13-year-old male, is suffering from depression. He presents with symptoms of irritability, anger, loss of interest in activities, and often has aches and pains that prevent him from going to school. In session with his individual therapist (clinic-based), Aaron is able to pinpoint some of the causes of his depression that include being bullied at school, pressure to smoke marijuana, and failing grades. Each of these external pressures serves to ostracize Aaron from everyday activities and cause him to further withdraw from his peer group and family. He is embarrassed he is being bullied at school and being picked on makes him feel he is out of control and weak. Some of his friends have been noticeably absent as they fear they may get picked on too if they stand up for Aaron and hang out with him. The bullying has also taken on the form of text harassment. Even when Aaron is away from his tormenters he still receives texts from an unidentified number and his self-esteem is plummeting. Add to that the feeling he is just not smart enough to make good grades (often because he is so distracted in class) and Aaron is having thoughts of just "ending it all."

Aaron's therapist has a solid treatment plan and has been working on many of the identified issues with Aaron, however, many of

---

the pressures he has identified are outside of his immediate control. His therapist has advised him to tell a teacher or authority figure at the school to bring awareness to the bullying behavior. Aaron said he would, but knows he does not intend to because he is fearful the bullying will get worse. His therapist has provided a strong psycho-educational groundwork on bullying and assisted him with developing some coping skills to deal with the bullying behavior. Additionally, his therapist has been utilizing cognitive behavioral therapy to address his depressive symptoms. His therapist, fearful that Aaron was expressing suicidal ideation, has also triaged him for suicidal thoughts and a plan and determined he did not have an immediate plan or intention. Nonetheless, the therapist and Aaron created a Safety Plan that addresses how he will deal with identified stressors or triggers to his depression and who he will notify if his suicidal ideation returns. While all of the provider's interventions resulted in some progress, the therapist felt Aaron's symptoms were not really improving and organized a Resource Support Meeting to see if any additional informal support systems could be identified to assist Aaron beyond the office setting.

A Resource Support Meeting took place, in the natural community, for Aaron and informal supports were able to step in and help support this young man in ways he did not even know were options. While his single mother worked late, Aaron took the bus home and was bullied while waiting for the bus, on the bus, and then pressured by drug dealers on the way home from his drop-off corner. A Family Support Meeting included some identified family members, Pastor Earl from his local church, and several family friends. During the course of the meeting, Pastor Earl contributed his identification of an afterschool program at a partner church that had a tutoring program. A family member volunteered to pick Aaron up from school (thus avoiding waiting for the bus, the bus ride itself, and the walk home from his bus stop) and take him to the church for the afterschool program. The afterschool program provided a safe environment and helped with his homework and study to address his academic challenges. Aaron's mother was able to then pick him up after her work shift. His mother was unaware of the text bullying and, once aware, was able to change his phone number. One of the family friends in the resource meeting had identified their cousin, a local police officer, as someone they could contact regarding tracing the offending texts.

It is important to realize that none of these informal supports took away from the original treatment plan or goals for treatment itself. Rather, the Resource Support Meeting served to help identify informal supports that Aaron did not realize were available to him. These informal supports were able to augment the formalized supports put in place by the original treatment plan and clinician. Together, these supports helped to create an environment that could allow Aaron to practice those very coping skills and educational base he had been exposed to in outpatient therapy.

Box 6.3. Resource Planning Guide

When consumers have profound behavioral health or substance use issues they may find themselves feeling like they do not belong anywhere. Consumers may lack a sense of self-worth and feel that they do not have choices in their lives or even the power to choose. To compound issues, often consumers spend much of their time in services and interact primarily with paid staff and others with mental illness or substance abuse disorders. This can leave the consumers without a sense of purpose or belief that there are other avenues available to them.

Behavioral health professionals can show the consumer how to utilize available resources (formal services) as well as how to identify informal supports in the natural community. This identification of resources often provides a redefined vision of hope, purpose, and a sense of community for the consumer. Successful resource planning may result in the consumer developing a new vision of the possibilities in front of him or her. The behavioral health professional can partner with the consumer to identify services and resources and suggest strategies for change that might help move the consumer beyond perceived and identified limitations.

Formal Supports

Formal supports are typically individuals from organizations or agencies that provide help or a service to the family. Some critical topic areas to consider when developing a list of formal supports include:

- Behavioral Health and/or Substance Abuse: These services may be accessed through the current provider or may include collaboration or referral to outside agencies.
- Medical, Dental, and Vision: These services can be provided via referral and linkage to local medical services, health departments, and low-income dental clinics. Kiwanis and Lions Club

are charitable organizations that help with securing hearing aids and eyeglasses.

- Income and Entitlements: Providers can help consumers apply for and successfully acquire all eligible income and entitlement benefits (SSI/SSDI, food stamps, VA benefits needed to reach income goals).

- Legal Resource Identification and Linkage: Local resources for legal assistance, such as Legal Aid that helps individuals with financial challenges, can be identified and consumers can become engaged in these services on an as-needed basis.

- Leisure Activities Resources: The provider can assist the consumer in identifying positive activities for exploring leisure activities (involvement in positive activities provided by local Parks and Recreation, libraries, gyms, YMCA, etc.).

- Housing Resources: Linkages can help maintain stable housing through local housing authorities, U.S. Department of Housing and Urban Development (HUD), rental assistance vouchers, and identified options through organizations such as the National Coalition for the Homeless.

- Daily Living Assistance: Providers can assist consumers with skill-building activities in the area of daily living.

- Support Networks: The provider can encourage consumers and families to become involved in organizations like NAMI (National Alliance on Mental Health) and other family support groups specific to behavioral health and substance abuse issues.

- Transportation: Providers can assist the consumer with identifying and accessing public transportation (which offers half-fare cards for individuals with disabilities in many larger urban areas), Medicaid Non-Emergency Transport (NET) for consumers with Medicaid (for medical and mental health appointments only), and other identified resources (e.g., Department of Community Health (DCH) provides some coordinated transport).

- Employment, Education, and Vocational Training: Assistance can be provided to the consumer in identifying available colleges, universities, trade schools, specialty schools in the community, and GED attainment options.

- Vocational Rehabilitation: Providers can help consumers begin to prepare, start, and maintain competitive employment. Some linkages may be through the local Department of Labor, employment websites, schools, government agencies, clubs, libraries, and hospitals.

Informal Supports

Informal supports are people who are part of a consumer's personal social network. They may be related to the consumer (e.g., sister, parent, uncle, grandparent) or they may be a neighbor, work colleague, friend, family friend, or someone from a faith-based community. One way to gather information about informal supports is to create an ecomap. First described by Hartman (1978), the ecomap is a graphic representation or visualization ("picture") of the people or support providers in a family's life. The ecomap also helps to illustrates how much support the family reports they receive from each identified support.

The provider can help consumers identify informal supports by asking questions that assist consumers in thoughtfully considering the people in their lives. It is also important to discuss perspectives about helpfulness and the strength of each informal support. Some pertinent questions to help the consumer identify these informal supports and their usefulness include:

- Who are the members of your family?
- What other people (related or otherwise) are connected to you and your family?
- Who is important to you and your family (or your child)?
- Who do you call on for help?
- Tell me about the people who help you? How do they help you?
- How helpful are each of these supports?
- Are there any of the people we identified that you find particularly unhelpful to you?

Reference

Hartman, A. (1978). Diagrammatic assessment of family relationships. *Social Casework*, *59*(8), 465–476.

7

DISCHARGE PLANNING

Nuts and Bolts of the Discharge Process

The process of discharging a consumer begins at admission and the length an individual is in services should be as short as possible. Movement goals should always be targeted toward the least restrictive setting feasible. To this goal, it is the provider's responsibility to begin aggressive discharge planning at the very onset of services. It is important for the provider to *begin* services with this road map and directionality of services.

When discharge planning is addressed at the onset of services and shared fully with the consumer, there are no surprises to the consumer regarding the course of the anticipated treatment. Discharge planning helps all parties have a clear understanding and expectation of the plan of action at discharge. This planning also helps providers keep in mind the ultimate goals of providing services to that particular consumer. Another way to look at the importance of this document is to attach the concept of treatment planning to something you may have experienced in your own life. Let's take the example of education. Think for a moment back to college and the course you had laid out for your study. When you first entered college, you may have known the exact route of your journey: from selecting your major and electives, to the exact degree you were seeking, to your expected graduation date. If you were like many students, however, you may have lacked clarity as to exactly where you were going and how you would get there, but hoped it all worked out. If you were lucky enough to have a good college advisor who sat down with you and explained your options and solicited your feedback as to your preferences and what was the best fit for you, you may have had a solid plan for college. This plan may have looked at your goals, where you wanted to be in your career in five to ten years, and the necessary steps for you to get there. The plan may have had steps and time frames that helped you anticipate the next steps in your journey. If, however, you "winged it" and tried an economics major and then changed your mind when you took Advanced Microeconomic Theory, then switched to pre-med and stayed on that course until you took Organic Chemistry, then finally decided on a psychology major your third year in college, your experience may have been vastly different. If your path was not planned, you may have taken courses not necessary for your ultimate goal and spent more time on your "four year" plan than anticipated. The same can be said for treatment planning. If the consumer's goals are taken into consideration at the onset and the consumers is aware of the goals, steps, and target dates of each, the consumer is an informed participant in his or her plan of treatment. Pre-planning, written goals and directions, and a plan and target date for each of the steps helps the process to have direction and minimizes time off track.

In this chapter, we will discuss the actual discharge and transfer from services, but would be remiss if the entire discharge process itself was not discussed. There are several stages involved in this process and some of the initial stages are discussed in detail in earlier chapters regarding assessment and treatment planning. Each step in the discharge process, however, will be further discussed as a sequence in steps toward discharge from services or transfer to another level or type of treatment. Additionally, we will explore areas where home-, school-, and natural community-based service provision further enhance this process.

Assessment

The assessment should be conducted by a qualified person at the beginning of the intake and/or admission process. While the assessment component is covered in more detail in Chapter 5, it is important to look at it as a starting point for the discharge itself. Assessment can take place in a formalized clinic, inpatient facility, office environment, or in the home and natural community. Regardless of the setting in which the assessment takes place, it is crucial to build a strong rapport with the consumer and to create a relaxed environment in which to effectively gather the information necessary for accurate diagnostics and to build a strengths-based intervention. Most organizations or providers will follow a specific format for the assessment, as may be required by licensing, letters of agreement or contracts, state or local regulations, accreditation standards, payer expectations, and as a way to provide uniformity in the intake process. Person-centered assessments include identification of consumer strengths, needs, abilities, and preferences (SNAPS), informal supports, and skills that can be used for initial discharge/transition planning and throughout the entire discharge process.

Sharing of Information

Another significant segment of the entire discharge process involves information sharing and having discussions about the SNAPS of the consumer. Identification of SNAPS should not be done just on paper from documentation received from a previous provider or referral source, but rather should be based on the participation of the provider and/or treatment team and active involvement of the consumer and his or her social support system. Strengths-based assessment and person-centered planning can be utilized in any treatment setting, but is particularly suited for home-, school-, and natural community-based services. In these environments, the provider is often able to go to the other professionals working with the consumer and ensure that more information is shared in a way that ensures the best care for the consumer. Certainly, this information sharing can be done electronically (with HIPAA regulations in place) or via phone. Meeting face-to-face with the consumer and/or social and professional support systems, though, in those matching environments, can lead to additional information not easily garnered otherwise. It is a reality that, in our modern world of instant communication and multitasking, most professionals are vested in finding the most expedient route to gather and transmit information. While efficient, from a time usage perspective, this type of succinct communication may not always be the most effective as relates to the best interest of the consumer. A summary of services faxed over to another provider may provide information needed for paperwork trails and to plug in dates into a template, but may not tell the critical information between the lines. When one provider takes the time to meet face-to-face with another provider, they may share information that is not on a summary, but that is nonetheless beneficial to structuring treatment for the consumer. The open dialogue between two professionals, both vested in helping the consumer, may lead to open-ended questions and clinical analysis that sheds new light on the consumer's strengths, issues, and/or disorder(s). The Resource Support Meetings and identification of informal support systems, discussed in Chapter 6, also serve to augment the goal of disclosing information needed for continuity of care or simply to make sure all variables are taken into account. This sharing of information, while a crucial part of the actual discharge or transfer, should be apparent throughout the provider's interactions with the consumer and identified supports. Sharing of information occurs during the referral process, assessment, treatment planning, throughout active treatment, and in coordinating discharge referrals and resource contacts.

One significant caveat, as it relates to information sharing, relates to permission to share information. HIPAA allows covered entities to use and disclose protected health information, without a consumer's authorization for the purposes of treatment, payment, and healthcare operations. That means that a provider can share information regarding the consumer's treatment as it pertains to continuity of services and treatment. This can be done without the consumer's permission, but it is always a good practice to make sure consumers are aware of all uses of their protected health information. When speaking to informal supports or those not directly involved in continuity of services or treatment coverage, the provider should always obtain an authorization to release information from the consumer. Release of information forms should be specific in terms of identifying who information is obtained from or released to. The specific type of information to be shared should be included on a release form. It is also best practice to include a time limitation on the length of time information can be released from the date release of information was signed (e.g., one-time release or 90 days).

Planning

The planning piece of the discharge process should include the overall direction in which the consumer will be headed. Chapter 5 goes into more detail regarding the treatment planning component of discharge planning; however, we will look at this piece as a part of the whole of discharge planning in this chapter. Person-centered treatment planning works well with home- and natural community-based service provision as both recognize the consumer as a crucial source for identifying his or her own strengths, challenges, and goals for treatment. The identified SNAPS, that are recognized initially in the assessment process, are further elaborated upon in this treatment planning state. Each goal, objective, and intervention should incorporate the strengths, needs, abilities, and preferences identified in assessment. The treatment plan should also include a specific area that identifies the precise plan for discharging from services or stepping down to a lower level of care. This area should detail the steps involved in recognizing when either discharge or transition should take place. This is a vital piece of treatment planning that is often overgeneralized. Providers need to recognize the criticality of this section of the treatment plan. This section is a written plan that gives both the provider and consumer the clarification of what needs to happen prior to moving from one level of care to another or in discharging from services. When this discharge/transfer criterion is not clearly established and put into written format, the process for discharge is ambiguous at best. Readiness for movement then becomes based on subjective assessment. Both the consumer and provider need to agree upon how to determine whether the consumer has met the goals on the treatment plan substantially and upon whether the consumer transitions to a lower level of care or instead is discharged from services. This written transfer/discharge planning area unambiguously establishes the specific steps and indicators for discharge or movement to another level of care. The placement considerations, in most circumstances, may include a step-down to lower level of services, or discharge to the home and/or natural community.

The treatment plan is a tangible format to accomplish goals, and allows both the consumer and the provider to be on the same level of understanding as to the direction of treatment and anticipated date of discharge. It is important to remember that the treatment plan is a living document, and as such, the goals, objectives, interventions, and discharge planning may be updated during the course of treatment. These changes can be preceded by new stressors or challenges, progression through previous goals, changes in life circumstances, or any change in variables affecting the course of treatment and/or discharge.

Needs Determination

Needs determination is both a critical part of establishing the treatment planning goals and an ongoing process for the consumer in treatment. Needs determination helps to put important structures in place. While person-centered planning focuses on the strengths and skills the consumer brings to the process, it is also crucial to identify the needs the consumer and family may have in meeting their goals. Consumer preferences and the initial assessment are used to determine goals and objectives that are measurable and attainable. In order for these goals to be attainable, however, all necessary resources needed to make steps toward reaching the goal should be identified. Identification of each need is critical, and resources coordination to support each need is imperative to make sure that this process can flow smoothly. The provider should consider the consumer's current capacity to identify and utilize resources. In the past, the consumer may have been given a treatment plan with goals that simply were not attainable because the consumer was unable to self-identify and utilize resources needed to reach the goal. Oftentimes, the challenge of identifying resources and utilizing them may have been a result of the consumer's disorder or behavioral health issues. Walking with the consumer through the process of finding resources that match needs can help ensure that the consumer is successful in reaching goals. This walk can also serve as a teaching tool to help the consumer go through the process himself or herself, with assistance, to see how resources can be identified and employed. The process provides the consumer with skills to help with identification of issues and how to seek future help if issues exacerbate. Part of the discharge process should also include discussions about how to request assistance from informal supports identified (e.g., pastor or aunt) and/or re-initiate assistance from formal supports.

Referral Source Identification

During the treatment process, the provider may also identify specific support organizations in the community to supplement work being done with the provider or to address issues that are outside of the practice of the current provider. Throughout treatment, this is a valuable step to ensuring all current treatment plan needs of the consumer are being addressed. An example where this outside referral may be used during treatment is the young consumer dealing with the challenges of OCD (obsessive compulsive disorder). The provider in this scenario may make a referral for a local support group for "Adolescents Living with OCD." Treatment issues can still be addressed with the consumer in individual therapy and through support services. Family issues (including psychoeducation, family therapy, and parenting skills specific to parenting an adolescent with OCD) can be addressed in family therapy and through resource supports. To the adolescent with OCD, however, who feels he or she is different and strange, a belief often supported by other school age children, it may mean the adolescent needs an additional support. Connecting the adolescent consumer to a weekly adolescent OCD support group will allow the youth to share stories with other youth in similar situations. When the consumer is able to talk to other youth experiencing some of the same social and school challenges that result from OCD, the consumer receives a support not easily emulated in traditional services. A provider should also make referrals for any issues outside the scope of practice.[1]

Hands-on Appointment Follow-up

During the last stages of treatment, the provider should be making specific linkages to resources and referral sources to allow the consumer to access needed contacts in the community after the consumer terminates from the current service level (step-down) or discharge from services. It is not enough for providers to identify that the consumer may need support groups or group therapy. Those are generic referrals that may be meaningless to someone who refers to the resource list when experiencing an emotional setback or stressor. During those times, the consumer may need very specific instructions as to how to access other resources.

Since the discharge process may be emotionally charged, it is important to have specific steps in place for the consumer moving from one treatment setting to another or discharging from services. To ensure better post-discharge care, it is essential to develop a written action plan or discharge summary to continue services, treatment, and care without interruption. This written plan should include specific referral sources, their contact information, and steps necessary to access the resources or services. Additionally, if it is known at discharge that a consumer will need a specific appointment within a certain window of time, that appointment should be set up with the consumer. An example may be the consumer discharged from therapeutic services, but that is still in need of medication management. The discharge plan should include the psychiatrist's contact information, address, and time and date of next session. The plan may also include what paperwork or items the consumer needs to bring to the follow-up appointment. If the referral is for a support group, it is often best for the provider to introduce this referral prior to discharge and perhaps go with the consumer to the first group to help alleviate any fears of transition and moving into a new group. This assisted transition can give the consumer the added confidence of returning to a known environment versus the more fear-inducing concept of going to a completely new environment sight unseen.

Step-Down in Services

A crucial piece of home- and community-based behavioral health services is the step down[2] of service provision. Services are slowly reduced according to goals being met on the treatment plan. As an individual shows progression on the treatment plan, the frequency and intensity of services in the home and community is reduced. The reduction in services is done in full partnership with the consumer so there are no surprises.

With behavioral health, and many other types of services, the consumer needs time to experience challenges one step at a time. If the consumer is pushed through a treatment plan quickly, and is not allowed to take the time to experience some mastery of the skills taught at each level of service provision, much of the progress may be lost when the consumer is put back into situations with the same stressors. Much as with learning progressively harder math levels quickly, the learner may become frustrated if not allowed to fully master one level before quickly progressing to the next level. For example, mastering differential equations, without fully feeling grounded in algebra, may leave the learner in a state of anxiety. Similarly, with a consumer that has multiple goals and objectives on the treatment plan, moving through the plan without fully experiencing the stepping stones leading to that next goal can lead to frustration and lack of successful completion.

Discharge Summary

In effective discharge planning, the process is documented in the assessment and treatment planning stages and is summed up in the final discharge summary. Discharge planning and documentation of this process is important in that it also provides for the physical safety of the consumer. One very important aspect of discharge planning is that it puts information into a written format. Oral information is more easily misinterpreted or later forgotten. It is vital to consider this fact when considering the consumer's well-being during times of change. Transfers to lower levels of care and discharges from treatment can be emotionally charged times for consumers. The emotional charge can be anywhere on a spectrum from positive to negative and varies with each individual consumer. For some individuals, change itself may be stressful, even if it means positive movement. For others, there is excitement at moving to a different level of care. Still for others, there is fear or anxiety about movement to a lower or higher level of care or discharging from the known element of current level of services. A written plan, or discharge summary, can be beneficial in helping with recall of discharge planning elements during this time.

Another strength of effective discharge planning and summarization is in the area of need identification. A discharge summary gives the next provider or caregiver to interact with a consumer a "blueprint" of the specific needs of the identified consumer in treatment. Discharge documentation can also provide for safe medication management. The discharge summary can identify the timing of the last dose of medication. The summary, or written discharge plan, can also specify any medication continuation needs and make precise arrangements or detail steps in continuing medication supply or securing prescriptions. Additionally, it can assist with reconciliation of medication to show pre-admission medications compared with post-discharge to ensure there are no harmful side effects, duplications or contraindications of medications, or omissions.

Every provider of services is driven by best practice standards, the standards of the profession, accreditation standards, and documentation requirements of the payer of services. Given this array of requirements and suggestions, it is often best to go with the highest standard that incorporates all driving forces for documentation for yourself as the provider. In this list to follow are examples of some the more standardized documentation requirements for a typical discharge summary/written plan or discharge information sheet:

- Consumer Specifics
  - o Name, date of birth, identifier number, address, phone number, applicable demographics
- Date of Discharge
- Discharging Provider Emergency Number
- Discharge Information
  - o Name of placement or return home, address, level of placement
  - o Discharge Diagnosis

- Medical Information
    - o Current medications—to include dosage, frequency, and discharge prescriptions
    - o Allergies
    - o Medical/dental conditions requiring follow-up
- History (Family, Psychiatric, and Treatment History as Applicable)
- Consumer SNAP (Strengths, Needs, Abilities, and Preferences)
- Consumer Treatment Preferences
- Safety and Crisis Precautions
    - o Include safety plans and/or crisis plans
    - o Include potential triggers and intervention strategies
- Treatment Goals and Progress/Lack of Progress toward Goals
- Summary of Services (and Frequency of Services) Provided at Current Treatment Provider
- Emergency Contact for Crisis
    - o Name, phone number, and standard contacts like 911 and local emergency room
    - o Include any emergency contact numbers for next provider, caregiver, or support in community
- Follow-up Appointments and Care
    - o Name, address, date and time of appointment and phone number of any psychiatric, therapeutic, or other appointments (these should be made prior to consumer's discharge and information coordinated between consumer and other caregiver)
    - o Include details of any after-care referrals and recommendations (including support groups, resource referrals, housing/occupational, parenting, education, medical/addiction, etc.)
- Special Instructions Given by Staff
- Signatures and Date (with area to document if given by phone or faxed and witness to this)
    - o Provider
    - o Consumer (document evidence of consumer participation)
    - o Parent or Guardian

Discharge summaries may also consider the consumer's current condition and any changes that have occurred as a result of intervention rendered. Anticipated symptoms, problems, or changes that may occur with discharge should be identified, as well as resources and planning to address these concerns. Another area that should be considered in the final discharge summary is the potential impact on the caregiver of caring for the consumer when the consumer returns home. Any caregiver needs, training, and resources should be identified on the summary with possible resolutions. Figure 7.1 provides a sample discharge summary.

Discharge Summary

IDENTIFYING INFORMATION

Consumer Name: _____ Case No.: _____

Date of Birth: / / Phone Number: _____

Address (number and street): _____

City: _____ State: _____ Zip Code: _____

Referral Date: Discharge Date:

Length of Services (first to last contact): Total Hours of Services:

Discharging Provider Contact Information:
Name:

Phone (include emergency contact):

Email/Address:

Reason for Referral to Services (Indicate referral method and treatment history):

Summary of Family History (Reference Initial Assessment and update as applicable):

Is the consumer/family currently at risk of out of home placement? No ☐ Yes ☐
If Yes, please explain:

Current/Ongoing Risk/Safety Issues (Attach safety plan):

Living Situation at Discharge: Private Residence ☐ Homeless Shelter ☐ Homeless ☐ Residential Care ☐ Jail/Correctional Facility ☐ Foster Care ☐ PRTF ☐ Institutional Setting/Nursing Home ☐ Other ☐

Figure 7.1 Sample Discharge Summary

Indicate address and name of placement/contact, if different from address listed on page 1:

Caregiver: Self ☐ Parents ☐ Foster Parents ☐ Spouse/Partner ☐ Grandparent ☐ Other Relative ☐ Friend ☐ Child Caring Institution ☐ Justice Department ☐ Other ☐

Indicate name/contact and relationship of caregiver:

<u>Strengths, Needs, Abilities, Preferences</u> (What changes have occurred in these areas as a result of program participation?)

Consumer Strengths	Family Resources	Formal/Informal Supports	Consumer Needs

Consumer Abilities:

Consumer Preference: What services has consumer identified as important (behavioral, community involvement, relapse prevention, social development)? Have other preferences been identified?

<u>Treatment Provision and Progress:</u>
What services, supports, care, and treatment were provided (narrative summary)?

Reason for Discharge or Transfer: Treatment Completed—no follow-up needed ☐ Treatment Completed—follow-up required ☐ Further Tx Needed—referred ☐ Further Tx Needed—no referral ☐ Admin Discharge ☐ Transferred or Referred Out of State ☐ Consumer Withdrew from Tx ☐ Incarcerated ☐ Other—discharge by consumer ☐ Death ☐ Consumer Moved ☐ Leave of Absence ☐ Other ☐

Figure 7.1 (Continued)

List initial and added goals/objective/interventions and summarize progress.
Additional goals can be added as needed.

Goal 1:
    Objective 1:
    Intervention 1:
    Intervention 2:

    Objective 2:
    Intervention 1:
    Intervention 2:

Summary Goal 1 (Status of Goal/Was it met?):

Goal 2:
    Objective 1:
    Intervention 1:
    Intervention 2:

    Objective 2:
    Intervention 1:
    Intervention 2:

Summary Goal 2 (Status of Goal/Was it met?):

Goal 3:
    Objective 1:
    Intervention 1:
    Intervention 2:

    Objective 2:
    Intervention 1:
    Intervention 2:

Summary Goal 3 (Status of Goal/Was it met?):

Progress Toward Recovery or Well-Being
Rate consumer outcome of recovery goals: None ☐ Minor ☐ Moderate ☐
Significant ☐ Accomplished ☐
Progress is evidenced by:

Gains Achieved During Program Participation (How did the consumer's life improve during program participation?):

Figure 7.1 (Continued)

Diagnosis (As indicated/applicable)

AXIS I:	AXIS IV:
AXIS II:	AXIS V:
AXIS III:	

Medical:
Current Medications (include dosage, frequency, and discharge prescriptions):

Allergies:

Medical/Dental Conditions Requiring Follow-up:

Follow-up Appointments:

After-care Recommendations/Plans for Referral:
Include the following needs or recommendation areas: community resource linkage; coordination with case manager; referrals made; behavioral health services needed; housing/occupational needs; parenting resources; educational needs; medical/addiction services; consumer specified goals, etc. Address long- and short-term goals and arrange for the initiation of these services where appropriate. Indicate detailed contact information to allow follow-up.

Recommendation	Contact Information (detail name of contact or organization, phone number, address, etc.)	Time Frame or Appointment Date
1. If emergency occurs, contact . . .	• If Medicaid: www.xxxxxx.com or call 1-800-555-0000 for behavioral health and support services • If life is in danger, contact 911 • For medical and behavioral health concerns, you may also contact your local health department at: • or the National Suicide Prevention Lifeline (24 hours/7days) 1-800-784-0000 or 1-800-000-TALK	As Indicated

Figure 7.1 (Continued)

2. Follow-up with any case plan recommendations made by Children/ Adult Services.	County Office: Case Worker: Contact Phone #:	Ongoing Until Completion
3. If you need local resources. . .	United Way 2-1-1 Resources Call 211 on telephone or www.211. org/[i]	As Indicated
4. *	*	*
5. *	*	*

Use additional rows to detail specific resources for consumers in relation to their specified goals, preferences, and needs. If a referral is indicated, the name, contact, and specific follow-up steps should be provided to ensure ease of follow-through. Additional rows can be added.

Discharged to: (a dictated or hand-written summary of the course of services, supports, treatment, or care incorporating the discharge summary information to be placed in the record within 30 days of discharge):

_____

Consumer Signature/Date
Print Name/Date:

_____

Parent/Guardian/Caregiver Signature/Credentials/Date
Print Name/Credentials/Date:

_____

Provider Signature/Credentials/Date
Print Name/Credentials/Date:

[i] The United Way/AIRS website and 2-1-1 information line provide referrals and free information for assistance with finding a counselor, housing assistance, food resources, healthcare referrals, and general resource coordination in your locale.

Figure 7.1 (Continued)

Areas of Support

SAMHSA (Substance Abuse Mental Health Services Administration) through the Recovery Support Strategic Initiative has delineated four major areas that support recovery from mental disorders and/or substance use disorders. These areas are Health, Home, Purpose, and Community. The health aspect includes managing one's symptoms or disease and making informed, healthy choices that support physical and emotional well-being. The home aspect is referring to a stable and safe place to live. Purpose refers to meaningful daily activities, such as a job, school, volunteerism, family caretaking, or creative pursuits; and the income, independence, and resources to allow the consumer to participate in society. Finally, community refers to the relationships and social networks that provide support, love, friendship, and hope (SAMHSA, 2012, p. 3).

When a provider is working with a consumer on discharge planning and summary, these four major areas that support recovery should be taken into account. One of the main goals of treatment should be to prepare the consumer to function as independently as possible and in the least restrictive environment possible. If all of these areas that serve to support recovery are taken into account, then the individual is given many of the tools to help prepare the consumer for the best possible outcomes.

Health

All people need to take care of both their physical health needs and behavioral health needs. These two types of needs are intricately linked, and are difficult to separate without ignoring an important piece of the puzzle of healthcare. Unmanaged high stress levels, lack of sleep each night, physical ailments, disease, and nutrition problems all can be linked to behavioral health issues. If a consumer has physical health issues that are impacting the person, it is important to identify needed steps to incorporate after-care in this area of recovery.

Home

Every person desires a stable and safe place to rest his or her head each night. The discharge process should take this basic human desire into consideration. When providing services in an office or clinic environment, it is critical to assess for living situation. If only a particular subset of the consumer's situation is addressed in treatment, and the consumer is returned to an environment that is not conducive to success or basic safety, the consumer is likely to fail and return back to the same treatment level, or higher level of care repeatedly. When providing services in the home or natural community, the provider is privy to the domicile of the consumer. There is no question as to the basic safety and stability of the home, as the provider is able to make firsthand observations in this area. When the consumer is in a transitional home, unsafe home, living on the streets, or environment with identified living concerns, this major life component should be figured into the process of transitioning to the next step in treatment. Whether that next step in treatment is discharge, movement to a lower level of care, or discharge from current services with a few supports in place, living situation and safety should be addressed.

Purpose

Purpose refers to those things that give a person a reason to live or to move toward something. Friedrich Nietzche spoke of purpose when he said, "He who has a why to live can bear almost any how." This German philosopher of the late 1900s illuminated the concept of purpose to surmise that if someone knows his or her purpose in life, then the person is self-encouraged to fight any obstacles in the path to achieve a goal. When a consumer is able to participate in society and has reason to make changes, the consumer has a motivation to reach a goal and is supported in recovery.

Community

Community refers to relationships. Relationships are those close associations or acquaintances between two or more people. Those relationships can be based on love, solidarity, family, neighborhoods, religious supports, business, or other social relationships. SAMHSA has identified community as one of the four supports for recovery from mental health and substance abuse disorders because the community surrounding the consumer has such a strong effect on the consumer. These communities can encourage and support or negatively trigger the consumer. Identifying healthy and supportive communities can be a fundamental part of the recovery process and discharge planning.

In this chapter, we have discussed the entire process of discharge and its commencement at the onset of treatment. Several concepts from earlier chapters have been elaborated upon as it bears reiterating the importance of each step of this process and how they are interlinked. Discharge planning should flow throughout every aspect of treatment and be reflected in documentation of planning, service provision, and finally in the discharge summary. After all, the goal of working with our consumers is to help them discharge and function in the natural community with the tools and supports they need to be successful!

Notes

1. Scope of practice is a term used to describe the procedures, actions, and treatment modalities that are permitted for a particular license or profession.
2. A step-down in services in the behavioral health arena refers to a decrease or reduction of services in terms of intensity and frequency. This is often accomplished in incremental steps to ease the transition to a lower intensity of service provision.

Reference

Substance Abuse and Mental Health Services Administration (SAMHSA). (2012). *SAMHSA's Working Definition of Recovery.* Retrieved October 30, 2013, from SAMHSA: http://store.samhsa.gov/shin/content/PEP12-RECDEF/PEP12-RECDEF.pdf

8

CHALLENGES AND HOW
TO OVERCOME THEM

Providing behavioral health services in home- and community-based settings has some inherent challenges. It is the opinion of this author that the
benefits of home- and community-based behavioral health service provision far outweigh the challenges; however, careful consideration must be
made of these potential impediments to service provision. In this chapter,
we will explore barriers to providing home- and community-based services and possible solutions to address these identified challenges.

Logistics

One of the first considerations of home- and natural community-based
service provision is how to coordinate actual logistics. When in a traditional office, agency, or hospital setting, the consumer travels to a specified location and receives treatment at a precise time. There is usually a
receptionist that welcomes the consumer, a waiting room to accommodate any delay in appointment fulfillment, and possibly additional "dou-
ble" bookings to minimize down time for the provider secondary to
cancellations/"no shows." In this model, the provider travels to one location at the start of the business day. This location is usually an office
within a hospital, clinic, or private practice. The provider typically has a
set schedule and is able to see consumers back-to-back throughout the
business day. This office-based model is a time saver for the provider and
has contingency planning built into the system to reduce down time. The
provider's time is protected. Consumers, however, may find themselves
spending time in an outer waiting room and potentially additional time
in inner office waiting rooms, if additional bookings or consumer allot-
ted times run over.

Let's consider home- and community-based service provision for a
moment. In this model, there is a reversal in the process in some
respects. The provider is the one traveling to the home-, school-, or
other community-based location and therefore has to make time to
accommodate logistics and travel time. As an in-home counselor for

many years, I would set my appointment times with my consumers based on consideration of convenience and available times based on both their schedule and my own. This meant, at times, making appointments after traditional hours so that families could be present in their entirety for a family therapy session. I would carry a notebook with me that had each of my consumer's face sheets[1] with the person's address and basic information. Behind each face sheet was a print out of a mapped location to the consumer's home (or other community-based location). That was part one and two of the planning. Who is to be seen at what time and where is the session to be held? Each day could be a new adventure, a new home, a new community, and new challenges. I savored the opportunity to have novel clinical scenarios and service locations, as compared to my more predictable experiences as an in-office therapist. For me, it reduced some of the monotony of often routine experiences and replaced them with a higher degree of change, challenge, and excitement. The reversal in the process is difficult for some providers, however. In this model, the provider is the one in traffic and trying to find the service location. This change offers an opportunity to obtain a whole new empathy for the consumer who is late to an appointment because he or she could not find a parking space or was late due to unanticipated traffic jams. The shoe is now on the other foot. The provider may now have some of those challenges the consumer previously experienced. The provider may also develop a deeper appreciation for the unique trials many of our consumers face in scheduling a myriad of appointments for themselves and their families.

Many consumers may have behavioral health, school, medical, Department of Family and Children Services, Department of Adult Protective Services, Juvenile Justice, probation, and court appointments that are all classified as "crucial and mandatory" components of their treatment. Their day is filled with logistics, scheduling, and trying to make it to appointments on time. All of this planning is a challenge to someone who is not experiencing behavioral health issues, or mental or substance use disorders. However, when you add one or more of these variables to the mix, the task of making, recalling, and keeping all of these appointments becomes a large barrier to procuring services for some consumers. When faced with a large number of mandatory appointments, many consumers choose to let the non-mandatory appointments slip, and this is often perceived by professionals as a lack of motivation for completing services. In the world of behavioral health, that overwhelmed consumer who inadvertently misses an appointment because he or she is overbooked may now be viewed as "noncompliant." It is true that some consumers may not have taken the steps necessary to prevent missed appointments or make contacts to cancel duplicated time slots. Others, though, are truly trying, to the best of their ability, to make all of their appointments. They are attempting this while trying to fulfill the requirements of those multiple agencies contacting them, go about their everyday life, deal with crisis, and manage all of these tasks with the added challenge of a behavioral health issue. When providers step back and experience the world of the consumer, their perspective and judgment around consumer behavior, or perceived motivations, may be challenged. Not all missed appointments are lack of motivation, lack of planning, or lack of desire to follow through. Some missed appointments are simply a consumer without a lot of confidence that was unable to say no to multiple calls from someone in authority to schedule appointments. Oftentimes, they are simply overwhelmed beyond their current coping abilities.

Having provided home- and community-based services and having supervised others who are providing these services, I have identified some methods to reduce the frustration and challenges with logistics. One of the more taxing, but crucial, pieces of this process is the pre-planning. The pre-planning is an essential part of providing services in the home and natural community. As an individual provider, or as a supervisor of a team, the first step is to map out the geographic areas where an individual staff member or provider is responsible for treatment. It is important to identify specific geographic areas of responsibility to prevent the very common mistake of working too far out of your geographic range. If you have multiple staff members, each can be assigned proximal areas of preference. If you are in private practice by yourself, you can base this decision on your own preferences for geographic travel parameters. Next, have pre-determined days the provider sets up appointments in specific communities. For example, while New York City, New York, may be one city, different providers may work in New York County (Manhattan), Richmond County (Staten Island), Bronx County (the Bronx), Kings County (Brooklyn), and Queens County (Queens). One county or geographic area may not be equal to another because of a number of variables. When setting up proximal geographic service provision areas, it is also important to consider traffic patterns and location. One city in a rural area may have the furthest points only one hour apart in rush hour traffic. Another, more urban, city may require a smaller coverage area to be able to cover travel during high traffic times. Other barriers, such as ferry travel or bridge travel, may also affect travel times. An additional consideration to assigning cases would be areas of provider clinical expertise. Alignment of expertise areas help ensure that the provider assigned to a particular consumer feels confident in working with the issues that have been pre-identified for the case. Consumer preference may also play into case assignment. Some consumers, for example, a female who has been the victim of domestic violence by a male, may feel most comfortable with a female provider. Each of these considerations should be considered early in the process to help this process move more smoothly. When working with the consumer to select the appointment times that are best for the consumer, the provider offers the set days for coordination in the geographic area. This allows the provider to serve a particular area with minimal travel time in between appointments, reducing both wasted time and travel costs.

Expense

Travel costs (i.e., gasoline consumption, personal automobile wear and tear, transit fares. etc.) brings us to one of the next challenges common in service provision in home- and community-based services. With this distributed locale for treatment, the provider faces the challenge of travel time and transit costs. Who pays for these necessary items? Sometimes they are not reimbursable items; however, there are some payers that do provide reimbursement to offset this cost. As a provider of services, it is essential to keep good records of your travel time, and travel costs to document these expenses. Some state payers, for example, will pay for travel time from specific locations. In other words, they may pay for travel time and mileage reimbursement from the agency's main office to the consumer's home or community setting. This is in contrast to reimbursing from the provider's home office to the consumer's home or community setting. Travel time, however, is traditionally reimbursed at a lower rate than clinical or service intervention time. Mileage reimbursement rates are variable by contract or payer, but are usually dependent on all or a percentage of state-published mileage reimbursement rates. There are other payers of service that do not reimburse for either travel time or mileage, but offer an increased reimbursement rate per unit or encounter for services provided in the community (versus those in the office or facility). This payment differential is intended to offset some mileage and travel expenses for home- and community-based service providers. Medicaid, for example, in many states offers a much higher reimbursement rate for home-, school-, and community-based interventions than clinic or facility-based. This increased rate is to offset the additional expenditures incurred by home and natural community providers. It is important to note that some larger agencies may have the resources to reimburse providers in the field for both travel time and mileage when it is not paid by a payer source. However, many smaller providers may not have this option. If providers are not reimbursed for mileage, or are paid less than the state mileage rate, they may be entitled to claim the difference in payment rates on their tax returns. Providers who use their car for business travel or utilize home offices should also consult a tax attorney for items that may be claimed on their tax return in their state.

We previously discussed cases where a payer reimburses for home-, school-, or community-based behavioral health services. There are some situations in which the payer does not reimburse, the consumer has a co-pay, or the consumer is self-paying for services. In these situations, there will be an exchange of payment. When this is the case, it is recommended that any monetary exchange take place at a main office or electronically to avoid completing these transactions in the home or natural community. There are several issues unique to home- and natural community-based service provision that should be considered when you deal with a monetary exchange. Primarily, these issues deal with safety in the field and clinical rapport. If the consumer is giving money directly to the provider in these community-based settings, it may confuse roles. In a traditional office, this exchange may take place with a representative from the financial department or a receptionist. The provider, in these situations, is usually somewhat removed from this role. In the home or natural community, it also makes sense to keep this role separate whenever possible. Additionally, if money is exchanged on site, there may be inherent safety issues with consumer family members or others in the community. It may bring awareness to others that a worker routinely carries cash and payment on his or her person. It is best to keep these roles separated to the best of your ability as a provider.

Documentation

Another issue that often appears on the forefront of challenges for providers, offering services in home- and community-based settings, deals with documenting their service provision. Many providers are concerned with reimbursement for documentation time for home- and natural community-based services. Very few payer sources reimburse for time spent on documentation. They do, however, often have very specific documentation requirements. Depending on the payer, there will be different requirements for progress note documentation. Some payers may be quite prescriptive in required components for both documenting clinical time/intervention and for the purposes of billing. Since this can be time-consuming, providers need to find the best way to document services in an environment where that time is rarely reimbursed by a payer source. How an agency or individual provider deals with this issue will depend on how records are kept and the size of the agency. Smaller agencies may keep paper records and may have more basic session notes. However, a smaller agency that has a myriad of payers may need an electronic record system to keep up with the demands of multiple payers' documentation requirements and accreditation or licensure standards. Many larger agencies have also had to adopt an electronic management information system to keep records accessible across geographic areas, multiple programs, multiple payers, and to meet audit demands.

If a provider utilizes paper records then the paper record format may be taken to the consumer's home or community setting and the basics can be filled in with the consumer during the last five to ten minutes of the session. If done correctly, this is a powerful tool to allow the consumer to be part of this process and to understand and recap the session direction. Providers that have electronic management systems can fill in main components of notes (primarily times, intervention, and response) on a portable digital device with the consumer. If a provider does not have remote access to Wi-Fi[2] (e.g., no Wi-Fi or is out of range of wireless coverage), it can be helpful to have a template of the progress note on the laptop and still be able to fill this out during the last few minutes of session. The note begun remotely can then later be uploaded or cut and pasted into an electronic management information system. This concurrent documentation approach allows the consumer to be a part of the process. It also allows note documentation in real-time versus trying to remember all components of the session later. Recalling the session at a later time can result in possibly losing detail or even merging two consumers' information. Concurrent documentation can also reduce frustration for the provider. It allows the provider to document the main components of the intervention during session time, thus reducing documentation time out of session. This system is also an effective way to utilize down time, such as missed appointments, to allow the provider to catch up on any additional documentation. With traditional clinic or facility settings, providers often use down time for documentation purposes. Home- and community-based providers can also make the best use of their down time with a concurrent documentation system. Ultimately, when providers are able to leave work and return to their own homes and spend time with their families, pets, or loved ones, they will be much better prepared to work with consumer issues. If providers leave a home or community setting and must continue documenting on their own time at night, they will inevitably feel their personal time is encroached upon. This encroachment of personal time can contribute to compassion fatigue[3] and/or provider burnout.[4]

HIPAA in the Field

We have talked about documentation, but another important consideration is keeping that consumer information protected while in the field. HIPAA (Health Insurance Portability and Accountability Act of 1996) has many purposes. The HIPAA Privacy Rule is intended to protect all individually identifiable information held or transmitted by a covered entity[5] or its business associate,[6] in any form or media, whether electronic, paper, or oral. The Privacy Rule calls this information Protected Health Information (PHI).[7] There are enforced civil monetary, as well as criminal, penalties for disclosing PHI outside of treatment, payment, and healthcare operations; where de-identified; using limited data sets; under authorization to release; to the individual; and under certain legal situations. The penalties, both monetary and criminal, increase as willful neglect increases and with the number of violations (U.S. Department of Health and Human Services, 2013).

In order to show that a provider is compliant with the intent of the HIPAA Privacy Rule, the covered entity must develop and implement written privacy policies and procedures that are consistent with the Privacy Rule. A covered entity must also designate a Privacy Officer that develops and implements privacy policies and procedures. There should also be a contact person who is responsible for the receipt of complaints and with providing information on privacy practices for the provider. There are many ways that providers can take strides to ensure, to the best of their ability, that consumers' protected health information (PHI) is only used for valid purposes. This requires, however, that all members of the behavioral health team know what PHI is and how to protect it. Workforce members (includes employees, volunteers, and trainees) should be trained on privacy policies and procedures and all necessary and appropriate steps for them to carry out their functions. A covered entity must apply appropriate sanctions against workforce members who violate the privacy policies and procedures or the Privacy Rule.

Let's look at a real example of how staff training might have prevented a breach of PHI for a consumer. In this scenario, a staff member requested a consumer medical record from a medical provider. The provider, in turn, mailed the information to the requesting provider. Sounds great so far, but something went wrong with this process. The individual who normally dealt with records requests was out sick and had someone else filling in for her position. The receptionist who normally sent out these records was very HIPAA savvy and knew exactly what steps were required in releasing patient's records. She had been properly trained. When she was out sick, however, someone else filled in who had not been trained on record release policy and procedure. The temporary employee sent the records in full, with release, to the requesting provider, but neglected to put the name of the company or the suite number on the package address area. Without a company name or suite number, the package was delivered to another suite and company. This other company's staff opened the package, in good faith, as they were unaware it was not for them. To find out what the record was, they would have to go through the paperwork to find out what it was, what it was about, and for whom it was truly intended. What just happened here was a breach in PHI for the consumer. All of his medical record could have been viewed by the recipient of the package, even though that receiver was not the intended recipient. In this example, the provider that breached PHI was contacted and the provider self-reported to HHS (U.S. Department of Health and Human Services) and contacted the consumer to notify him of the breach.

They had made good efforts to have systems in place to protect PHI and this was certainly a focus for them. The downfall was in the lack of training of all staff, including temporary staff.

As a home- and natural community-based provider, there are additional safeguards that must be put into place to protect consumers' PHI. When providers go into the community to see a consumer, they almost always have some sort of PHI with them. Often, they have a face sheet with the name and address of the consumer. This may have the phone number so providers can contact the consumer if they are running late or need to make a change in the schedule. Referral forms or face sheets may have dates of birth and insurance or medical record numbers. As a rule, it is best for community-based providers to travel with the least amount of PHI possible to conduct their job. If this information is in paper format all reasonable efforts must be taken to protect this information.

Another case scenario will help drive this point home. In this actual situation, a home- and natural community-based provider was traveling between appointments and was in an automobile accident. Through no fault of her own, her car was struck by that of another driver on her passenger side. The provider was not harmed in any way, but was really unsettled by the event. When roadside assistance and police arrived at the scene, she was removed from her car and sat in a shaded area on the side of the highway to allow her the opportunity to compose herself and shake off some of the shock of this unforeseen accident. As she got her license and driver's registration out of the car, a burst of wind sent most of the paperwork in her front seat flying onto the expressway. Some of the paperwork was retrieved; however, some was never recovered. We will look at how this may have been prevented momentarily.

Working in the home and natural community may mean that the provider has office space at a main office or it may mean there is a home office and the provider checks into a main office several times a week. If the provider has a home office, there may be some other points to consider. Telecommuting is a wonderful option for someone working non-traditional hours and can really be beneficial in retaining staff with non-traditional time commitments. Home offices, however, should have the same protections in place as the main office. Please consider one additional scenario to illustrate this point. An employee with a home office keeps most of his items on a computer with firewalls and password protection. He has been trained in Privacy Rule policy and procedure, and his company security officer has told him what computer protections need to be in place to protect any PHI he may have on his computer. This sounds like a solid plan, except, this provider has been taking home paperwork with PHI on it and putting it next to his computer until he has the opportunity to enter the information. In an actual scenario, this staff member was evicted from his apartment and all of his household possessions were placed by the curb. The terms *inopportune* and *life-altering* don't even begin to describe how this provider and his home agency felt on discovering his new circumstance. Unfortunately, to add insult to injury, PHI for consumers was included in the household items that were put on the curb and that were disbursed over the lawn.

Let's look at ways that protections could have been put in place to prevent both of these unfortunate circumstances. In both of the circumstances listed above, the car accident and the eviction, one or two safeguards may have protected PHI. First, all home- and community-based providers should minimize the amount of paper PHI taken into the field with them. Second, when necessary to take paper PHI into the field, the provider should make use of a locked file box for paperwork. This simple step may prevent paperwork from reaching the wrong hands. Providers can keep a locked file box in the trunk of their car and this will protect against many theft or accidental breaches. This same concept can be used in a home office. In a traditional office space that incorporates protection of PHI into the office culture, all PHI materials are picked up at the end of the day and put into a locked file cabinet or records room. This step helps prevent breaches that result from unauthorized staff having access to PHI. Similarly, with a home office, the provider can simply put paperwork with PHI on it in a locked file cabinet or lock box. These two steps will not protect against all possibilities of disclosure, but will seriously limit the possibilities of accidental PHI exposure. Every provider should make sure to maintain reasonable and appropriate safeguards to prevent intentional and unintentional use or disclosure of protected health information. This may include shredding documents before discarding them, securing medical records with lock and key or pass code, and limiting access to keys or pass codes.

We discussed paperwork, but also we must be aware of protecting electronic data. If providers utilize an electronic management system and/or mobile devices they should take the administrative safeguards such as protection from malicious software, password management procedures, log-in monitoring, firewall protection, and data backup plans. Additionally, providers should think about exposures on unsecure Internet Wi-Fi connections. Take the steps necessary to protect the consumers' information just like you would want your own data protected.

A final area to consider with PHI disclosures in the community is oral communication. Providers of home- and natural community-based behavioral health services may schedule to meet with a consumer in the home, at the school, at a government office, in court, or a community setting like McDonalds. When meeting in the home or natural community, the provider should be cognizant of two things. The first area providers should be aware of is their appearance, including accoutrement. If a provider has on a name badge that identifies the company the provider represents and his or her title, the provider is announcing to everyone nearby why he or she is there to see the consumer. While a badge and photo identification card are very important parts of being a home- and community-based provider, the provider should use discretion as to when it is necessary and unnecessary to make that connection apparent. A provider may take a young child or abused wife to a fast food establishment to talk because the consumer is fearful of speaking openly at home. When in this community setting, however, the consumer does not want to be identified as a consumer of behavioral health services. Likewise, a child in school will most likely not want his peers to know he is receiving services. Additionally, a provider should use discretion in conversational tone, volume, and content. A provider may use fake names of family members (agreed upon prior to discussion with consumer) or codes to discuss sensitive information in public areas. When possible, the provider should always choose locations where conversations cannot be overheard. Ensuring conversations can't be overheard, however, is not always possible. When it is not, all efforts should be made to be protective of PHI in conversation volume and content.

Job Stress

Providers who work in home- and natural community-based settings report some of the same job stressors as others in the behavioral health field. In addition, however, they may have additional job stressors that include the stress of working alone, potentially traveling through unsafe neighborhoods, heavy traffic, dangerous animals, and witnessing escalating arguments in a community environment. There are some things, however, that can be done to address and ameliorate some of these job stressors. Employers, in particular, can put certain support structures in place to retain employees who may be experiencing job stress. These structures include the following points (Department of Health and Human Services, 2010, p. 30).

- Provide frequent, quality supervision and agency support staff.
  o This point can't be overemphasized. Frequent, quality supervision helps to ensure that issues and concerns are addressed prior to escalation. A provider and supervisor will benefit from having an open relationship and discussion where the provider is able to be vulnerable and express real concerns and thoughts without fear of repercussion from the supervisor. Planning and preparation are important in the provision of any behavioral health services, but particularly in home- and natural community-based service provision. In these later environments, oftentimes, there is

a considerable amount of unpredictable circumstances. Planning and preparation can help the provider feel more prepared for these circumstances. Supervision time should be protected and offered at regular intervals. It may take on the form of face-to-face supervision as well as phone check-ins. A provider that works in a group or organizational practice may have this supervision as part of the company structure. If the provider is working in private practice, the provider can seek supervision outside of his or her own practice.

- Provide adequate job training and preparation, including continuing education opportunities.
    - o   It is difficult in this day and age for a provider to completely specialize in an area of behavioral health. While the provider may have clinical strength areas and be assigned cases based on those, working with consumers still has an element of unpredictability. A case that appears at the onset to be straightforward, such as clinical depression, may have many other issues that present once the provider begins to work with the consumer. After rapport building, the provider may learn, for example, that a mother with depression has domestic violence issues, drug use to self-medicate, educational issues for the children, and financial issues complicated by a recent job loss. Adequate job training and ongoing continuing education opportunities assist providers in identifying additional issues and stressors and addressing them when they are within their clinical scope of expertise. This training also helps providers to discern which areas may require additional specialty training and would best be referred out for specialty treatment. Larger organizations and provider groups may have their own training departments, while private practice or solo providers may wish to augment their training through CEUs (Continuing Education Units). CEU trainings can be face-to-face, via literature review, electronic, and through the use of electronic media (e.g., webinars).
- Hold regular staff meetings in which problems, frustrations, and solutions can be discussed.
    - o   Similar to individual or small group supervision, staff meetings can be quite an instrumental tool in identifying and preventing escalating issues. Having a time set aside for staff meetings, that is respected, allows providers the opportunity to anticipate scheduled opportunities to share any concerns or issues that they may have identified in their own cases. These group formats allow for exchange of ideas to address concerns and alternative solutions to identified problems. It is important to recognize

staffing and supervision as an opportunity to expand viewpoints and develop a sense of union. This is particularly applicable for providers that may be going to home or natural community environments on their own. In a traditional outpatient or facility setting, a provider may have the opportunity to walk down the hall and staff a case with a co-worker, seek immediate feedback during a particularly tough session, or have a water cooler discussion regarding a difficult case. When working in home- and natural community-based settings, the provider may not have these immediate support and feedback structures in place. For these community-based workers, it is important to set up needed clinical support structures through regular staffing, supervision (as detailed in the first point), and any other provider and advocacy groups that can provide support to the provider. Some states and countries have provider groups specific to home- and natural community-based provisioning of services that serve as advocates, connections for networking, and sounding boards for issues specific to the field. Where possible, it is advantageous for providers to join these groups and benefit from group advocacy and solutions.

- Include lunch breaks and sufficient travel time in worker's schedules and allow self-paced work.

  o This point may seem an unnecessary one to make in a traditional workplace, but is important to bring up in the world of home- and natural community-based behavioral health service provision. A provider who is self-paced and making his or her own schedule may think it is easier to see consumers back-to-back to make the day shorter. However, in all fields, there is a need for physical and mental rest after working for an extended period of time. Behavioral health service provision can be particularly taxing on the provider, as the provider is often working with consumer cases that are intense and emotionally charged. The provider needs a built-in time for lunch and small breaks to have an opportunity to recharge between sessions. They also need to allow for adequate travel time between appointments, so that they are not always rushed. Rushing from one location to another is a sure stress inducer. It only serves to make the provider stressed when the provider arrives at the session and the consumer is potentially irritated at the provider's late arrival. Pre-planning, to allow adequate travel time and breaks, helps keep the provider in a much better physical and emotional state to deal with the inherent stressors involved in provision of services to those with mental and substance use disorders.

- Most accreditation bodies require that companies that provide behavioral health services in the field have policies and procedures in place to ensure worker safety.
  - o Policy and procedure books are important to an organization to help set an expectation and clear direction base as to what the provider or organization does and expects in particular areas of functionality. Safety in the field is no different, by taking the time to detail what the organization's policy is and what steps (procedures) are to be taken in particular situations, there is no ambiguity as to expectations. A typical safety in the field policy and procedure may include points such as when safety training takes place, what to do in situations where there are identified potential safety concerns, contact expectations with supervisor, schedule submission requirements, and emergency response procedures. Policies and procedures should be individualized for the agency and for provision of home- and community-based services. All staff should receive detailed training on the company's policies and procedures and be aware of the specific steps to take during an emergency or dangerous situation. The policies and procedures should be so detailed in their written steps that any staff member can easily follow the procedures. In fact, staff should be polled during annual policy and procedure reviews to query what steps are taking place in the field during emergent or crisis situations. By comparing intended policies and procedures to those steps actually taken, the organization can capture opportunities for training or policy and procedure updates.
- Provide access to an Employee Assistance Program (EAP) or other means of counseling support.
  - o Provision of EAP (Employee Assistance Program)[8] or other counseling support for providers is not only relevant to home- and community-based providers, but rather to all providers of behavioral health services. In the field, providers often experience what is called "vicarious trauma." The concept refers to providers working with survivors who experience the emotional exposure of hearing the trauma stories of their consumers. As the providers witness the pain, fear, or endured trauma of their consumers, some of this exposure affects the providers in a way that may negatively alter their own behavior, interpersonal relations, belief systems, and job performance. Supervisors and colleagues should be aware of the signs and symptoms of vicarious trauma so they can identify the symptoms and assist the provider in seeking EAP or other forms of counseling support to address this vicarious trauma.
  - o EAP and counseling support is also important to address provider burnout. Burnout falls under the umbrella of compassion fatigue and is a state of emotional, mental, and physical exhaustion

caused by prolonged stress. It often occurs when a provider feels overwhelmed and is unable to handle the emotional burden of a position as a behavioral health professional. Supervisors and colleagues who are aware of the signs of burnout, and are in touch with the provider on a regular basis, can help identify the symptoms and assist the provider in getting EAP or support services to deal with the provider's feelings. This is an important area of recognition as there are often steps that may be taken to reduce provider burnout during early stages. When addressed early, the stressors are much less likely to become too overwhelming later. Providers experiencing burnout may have reduced energy levels, feel helpless, cynical, resentful, and this negative progression can often end in loss of motivation or interest in what caused the person to want to be a provider in the first place.

o   Lastly, EAP and other counseling support can help providers through situations where their own personal issues, triggers, or countertransference[9] occurs. Providers may have issues that they have dealt with in the past, but just like consumers, current cases may serve as triggers to their own issues. Additionally, a provider may be going through a difficult time personally that is affecting job performance. In these cases, the provider needs to seek counseling to address these concerns and secure self-care.

Safety in the Field

A final challenge to consider in providing behavioral health service in the home and natural community is safety in the field. Juxtaposed with the generally controlled environment of a hospital or private practice, working in a consumer's home and in the natural community can be relatively unpredictable. Some of the same reasons many providers love home- and natural community-based work become some of the same reasons there are additional risks associated with this type of service provision. Providers need to always be aware of their environment, as they never know what they will see or experience. We will look at some of the dangers inherent in going into consumers' homes and community-based settings and then address ways to set up best case scenarios for safety in the field in regard to each identified safety risk.

Physical Environmental Risks

One safety issue that presents itself more in home- and natural community-based work than elsewhere is the risk of fall. This is not a consideration you normally have to make in a standard work environment, but providers need to be observant and look for sidewalk and entryway defects when walking into a consumer's home or natural community-based setting. Cracks, holes in pavement or stairs, uneven surfaces, or other surprises, such as toys, may cause a trip. When a provider goes into a new community-based setting, the provider needs to watch for torn carpets or door mats that can cause a fall. Another non-standard consideration when transitioning from one work environment to another is the use of proper footwear appropriate to the weather. In snow, ice, or rain, the use of rubber-soled or traction shoes may prevent a fall.

Consumers may also have household items that are considered a safety risk. They may have firearms in the home or carry a gun. In this situation it is important for the provider to voice concerns and try to negotiate something that will make him or her feel safe in that environment. The provider can ask the consumer to put the gun away into a secure location during sessions.

Another safety issue that is not uncommon in home- and natural community-based behavioral health provision is safety with animals. Some of the risks of interacting with animals in consumers' homes can include allergic reaction, tripping over a pet, bites, or aggression. It is important for the provider to remember that even the friendliest pets can potentially become aggressive toward someone new to their environment or when they feel they are protecting their owner. Besides this potential physical threat, animals can distract a professional and interfere with clinical work and focus. A good rule is to avoid contact with pets unless the provider knows the animal well. Additionally, each provider should utilize steps to avoid a potentially dangerous animal safety situation; these include:

- A provider should never approach an unfamiliar pet and always stay still until it comes up to him or her.
- With a friendly animal, let the animal see and smell the provider's hand first and never disturb an animal that is sleeping, eating, or caring for young.
- If the provider has concerns about a consumer's pets, the provider should make sure to voice those concerns and make conditions around this type of contact.
- When the provider calls to confirm an appointment with a consumer, the provider can ask that animals be kept away during the visit.
- Every provider has the right to make restraint of animals a condition of service provision.

Hygiene Concerns

One concern that is often voiced by in-home providers of service is around the topic of hygiene and unsanitary living conditions. It is a realistic possibility that a home, where you are providing services, may be unsanitary and/or harbor some types of rodents or insects. Each provider or organization should train their employees on proper home hygiene and what they should do if they visit a home that is unsanitary.

Many consumers homes are clean and sanitary, but for the purposes of comprehensive readiness of the provider, it is important to address those homes that are either unhygienic or have lower-quality living conditions. Some homes, apartments, trailers, or living areas may have unregulated temperatures, poor indoor air quality, insects or rodents, or generally unsanitary conditions. The reasons are varied, but often are related to socioeconomic restrictions or unregulated behavioral health issues. Both a lack of resources and lack of ability to manage resources can result in some consumers living in conditions that many in our society would consider to be inferior or unacceptable. This topic is one that may hold an emotional charge for some providers of service. It is an area that, in fact, I consider a major determinant in deciding whether a provider is best fit to conduct sessions in a home and natural community environment. A provider should be able to maintain a professional composure in those homes that are unsanitary. If unable to do so, the provider's reaction of disdain toward the consumer's home can be detrimental to the consumer/provider relationship. As a budding in-home therapist, I experienced homes that challenged my ideas of cleanliness, of hygiene, and even of adequate basic living conditions. What I never forgot, though, was that this living structure I was visiting was a home to someone else. To many children, it may be the only way of living they know or with which they are familiar. Consumers experiencing significant behavioral health or substance abuse disorders may feel overwhelmed, despondent, and have simply lost the motivation to maintain the same sanitary conditions the majority of society views as standard. Job loss, mental illness, and relocation may have resulted in living in an apartment complex without heating, air-conditioning, and pest control. The consumers may find themselves in a losing battle of trying to fight roaches and mice, just to discover they find a way back in from a neighbor's apartment. Most families with unhygienic home conditions did not start out that way, they were embarrassed at first, and at some point just capitulated.

I have shared my personal opinion on this topic because I believe there comes a point in the careers of behavioral health professionals when they may cross this issue and how they deal with it speaks volumes to the consumer in front of them. When I went into a home that was unsanitary I would choose to sit in a wooden chair, at the kitchen table, or take a walk outside. At some point, we discussed the issues in the home, but never did I find it necessary to stand during a session or show disdain for the home of the consumer I was visiting. As a guest in the consumer's home, I always showed the person respect and respect was returned. I recall training a new therapist with whom I went to a consumer's home.

She was unable to conceal her repulsion to the roach crawling across the floor or the pile of dirty dishes in the consumer's kitchen. She visibly cringed, recoiled, and looked disgusted as she was introducing services to this family. My eyes glanced around the room and landed on the five-year-old peering around the corner. Earlier, he had announced he was going to leave the room and was bringing back a picture he had painted for his new therapist. His picture was on Manila paper and appeared to be finger painted with a yellow sun and flowers. When he peered around the corner and saw the disgusted look on his new therapist's face, he returned to his room and came back without the picture. At that moment he felt personally rejected. After all, this was his home, regardless of what it looked like to someone else. This home may have been all he ever knew, and it may have even been an upgrade to where he lived before and he was proud of it. If this new provider cringed at the very thought of being in his home, that single facial expression could convey to this child that what was important to him meant very little to her.

Once the provider has built rapport with the consumer, there are many methods available to deal with any hygiene or unsanitary situations that present themselves. The provider, however, that is unable to regulate responses to someone else in the person's home under these circumstances may not be the best fit to work with home- and natural community-based behavioral health service provision.

Transportation Risks

Another potential safety risk would be around transportation. When providers drive from one location to another location they can be at a higher risk for motor vehicle related injuries. There are multiple factors that play into this risk. Risk factors include lack of seatbelt use, driving while tired, poor weather conditions, poorly maintained automobiles, distracted driving, and rushing to an appointment. Each provider or agency should address these risks by having policy and procedure in place to reduce driving risks. Some considerations for policy and procedure may include proof of a valid driver's license, mandated use of seatbelts, and a five-year driving record for new employees with periodic rechecks after hiring. Training is also a critical piece of ensuring automobile safety. To reduce risk, training should be conducted on fatigue management and the dangers of distracted driving. This training would include avoiding distracting activities while driving (such as eating, adjusting radio, and texting). It should also address protocol on multitasking while driving. Sometimes just setting an expectation for staff around safety is a deterrent to risk-taking. Providers, for example, often correspond with consumers via text, email, or telephone. These contacts may be for the purposes of responding to a crisis, cancelling a session, or making a change to the start time of a session. All of these communications are significant and can change the course of the day's planning. Therefore, organizations need to set clear protocols on how providers respond to incoming calls, texts, and emails while driving. Simply by pulling over onto a side of the road to return the communication, the provider can reduce the risk of accidents that result from multitasking on the road. It is also a good idea to require that all staff have an emergency kit (flashlight, batteries, blanket, water, and flare) as well as a first aid kit in their car for use in unanticipated auto emergencies or road conditions. Additionally, providers should have maps or global positioning systems (GPS) in their cars to help avoid non-necessary time on the road (i.e., unable to find location) and provide alternative routes in case of an emergency.

Workplace Violence

A final area of safety risk consideration is workplace violence. Home- and natural community-based workers may be vulnerable as they face unprotected and unpredictable work environments each time they enter a consumer's home and community. The spectrum of violence can range from verbal abuse, to stalking, to threats of physical harm, to actual violent physical contact. Verbal abuse from the consumer, family members, or people in the community is a form of workplace violence. Verbal abuse may be subtle, such as asking for help beyond the scope of the job or it may be obvious, such as complaining about job performance or worker appearance or even threatening to cause harm.

In order to be safe in the community, providers should participate in violence prevention training and report incidents of violence, no matter how minor, to their employer. Those practicing independently should report violence to police. Employers can set their expectations by establishing a zero-tolerance policy for all incidents of violence. Additionally, they should train workers on recognizing and preventing workplace violence. Employers should make sure they investigate all reports of violence. Moreover, employers should work with police to identify dangerous neighborhoods where special precautions need to be taken and provide that information to providers in the field.

There are some practical steps providers can take to manage potentially violent situations. These include following basic personal safety protocols steps such as (Department of Health and Human Services, 2010):

- Provider should confirm with the consumer by phone before visit.
- Provider should be sure of the location of session.
- Provider should have detailed directions to a new consumer's home (as well as maps and GPS when possible).

146

- Providers should let their employer know their location and when to expect them to report back. This can be done electronically or through phone check-in system.
- Provider could consider working with a co-worker in high-crime areas, and if possible, schedule visits during daylight hours.
- Providers should keep their car in good working order and the gas tank full.
- When a provider is driving alone, they should have the windows rolled up and doors locked.
- Providers should park their vehicle in a well-lit area, away from large trees or shrubs where a person could hide.
- Providers should keep equipment, supplies, and personal belongings locked out of sight, in the trunk of the vehicle.
- Before getting out of the car, the provider should check the surrounding location and activity. If they feel uneasy, they should not get out of the car.
- The provider should have an extra set of keys in case keys are locked in the car.
- Providers of services should stay in their car, clear the immediate area, and contact their supervisor if they notice anything that might threaten their security, such as strong odors from a drug lab, gunshots, or shouting and sounds of fighting.
- Most importantly, a provider should make sure someone knows where they are at all times.

During the visit itself, providers should use basic safety precautions such as (Department of Health and Human Services, 2010, p. 36):

1. Provider should be alert.
2. The provider should evaluate each situation for possible violence.
3. The provider should watch for signals of escalation or possible violence, such as verbally expressed anger and frustration, threatening gestures, signs of drug or alcohol abuse, or the presence of weapons.
4. Providers should notify their employer if they observe an unsecured weapon in the consumer's home.

In a potentially violent situation, providers should maintain behavior that helps to diffuse anger such as (Department of Health and Human Services, 2010, p. 36):

1. Provider should present with a calm, caring attitude.
2. Providers should not match consumer threats.
3. A provider should avoid giving any orders.

4. The provider should acknowledge the consumer's feelings.
5. Providers should avoid behaviors that may be interpreted as aggressive (for example, moving rapidly or getting too close, touching unnecessarily, or speaking loudly).
6. A provider should keep an open pathway for exiting, when visiting a consumer's home.
7. Providers should always trust their judgment and avoid situations that don't feel right.
8. If a provider cannot gain control of an escalating situation, they should shorten the visit and remove themselves from the situation. If they feel threatened, they should leave immediately.
9. If the provider needs help, they should use their cell phone to call their employer or 911, depending on the severity of the situation.
10. If a crime is observed, the provider should contact the police.

Many of the tips and ideas presented previously are practical, hands-on precautions and protocols. These can be used in conjunction with internal supervision and worker safety policy and procedure. Suggestions for essential worker safety policies and procedures were discussed earlier in this chapter. In terms of internal supervision, however, individual providers and agencies often develop their own protocol around safety check systems and schedule submission to ensure that the provider's location is traceable and there are regular contacts with the provider's supervisor or designated contact. An example of such protocol may include submission of provider schedules in advance of sessions so that the provider's planned location is known and traceable. To account for changes in schedules or unanticipated circumstances, however, some organizations have regular contact points during the course of a provider's work day. The provider may, for example, be required to make contact with supervisor (by phone or electronic device) at designed points during the day.

There are, however, some Lone Worker Guidelines already in existence that are used in many countries as a standard for protocol. A lone worker is defined as someone who works by himself or herself without close or direct supervision. This definition is often used to describe anyone who works apart from colleagues. Some countries, such as the countries of the United Kingdom, Canada, and Australia, have specific legislation and standards regarding lone workers and those that employ them. The Management of Health and Safety at Work Regulations: Regulation 3 of the HSE (Health and Safety Executive of the United Kingdom) states that every employer must assess any work-related health and safety risks to employees. After identifying hazards and assessing the risk involved, the employer should put measures in place to avoid or control the risks (Health and Safety Executive, 2013).

The lone worker concept and regulations have translated into many training programs across the world that are used by multiple companies and varied training formats. Providers can purchase a pre-existing program or work internally to complete their own risk assessment and determine the steps necessary to provide protection to providers in the field. It is important to realize that safety solutions can be very simplistic for some providers. For some providers, the solution is to assess the risk and have contact systems in place, such as weekly schedules entered into a management information system, cell phone coverage with a supervisor 24 hours a day, and daily check-in calls. Within an organization, this can be done with the existing supervisory hierarchy. In private practice, however, an individual provider may wish to partner with another provider for safety check-ins. For some organizations, the solution may be much more detailed and include the use of notification and location tools. Solutions can be a discreet alarm button, which can be attached to clothing, or a simple phone application which can connect back to a main office or central help desk at a single touch. GPS (Global Positioning System) tools can also be utilized so that if the provider is not where he or she is scheduled to be, someone can check in to make sure everything is okay. Some providers may also wish to have a code word with their friends or colleagues for emergency purposes. That way, if they have a problem with someone they have met in a home- or community-based session, they can make the excuse to call a contact to covertly alert them they need help (with the obvious goal of not alerting the person they are with).

The purpose of this chapter has been to address concerns about home- and natural community-based service provision in an open and candid manner. Each identified challenge was also countered with several potential methods to address the concerns. It is important for each provider to personally, cost-wise, and clinically weigh the benefits that are covered elsewhere in this book against the challenges faced in providing behavioral health services in the home and natural community. Only then can providers make an informed choice around their preferred behavioral health service provision setting.

Notes

1. A face sheet, in behavioral health terminology, usually refers to a cover sheet to a multipage document (e.g., consumer record) that contains a brief summary of all the relevant points covered in the document itself.
2. Wi-Fi is short for wireless fidelity and refers to wireless networking technology that allows electronic devices (e.g., computer, phones, etc.) to communicate over a wireless signal.
3. Compassion fatigue occurs when providers experience a state of tension and preoccupation with consumer suffering. They become traumatized as a result of trying to empathize and help someone else.

4. Provider burnout usually includes the symptoms of emotional exhaustion, depersonalization, and reduced sense of accomplishment. Personal and work-related causes can contribute to burnout.
5. Covered entities, under HIPAA, include health plans, healthcare clearinghouses, and healthcare providers that transmit health information electronically.
6. A business associate, under HIPAA, is a person or organization, other than a member of a covered entity's workforce, that performs certain functions or activities on behalf of, or provides certain services to, a covered entity that involves the use of disclosure of individually identifiable health information.
7. PHI is protected health information (as defined by 45 CFR 160.103—Code of Federal Regulations in Section 13400 of Subtitle D Privacy of the HITECH Act). PHI is individually identifiable health information that is a subset of health information, including demographics of the individual that is created or received by a healthcare provider, health plan, employer, or healthcare clearinghouse and relates to a physical or mental health condition, provision, or payment of provision of healthcare to that individual. PHI can be used to identify the individual.
8. Employee Assistance Programs (EAPs) are employer-offered programs to help employees deal with personal issues that might be negatively effecting their work performance or well-being.
9. Countertransference is the redirection of the provider's own feelings (determined from the provider's own life, experiences, and unconscious) toward a consumer. It was first defined by Sigmund Freud in *The Future Prospects of Psych-Analytic Therapy,* as an address delivered before the second International Psycho-Analytical Congress in Nuremberg in 1910, first published in Zentralblatt, Volume Bd. 1.

References

Department of Health and Human Services. (2010, January). *NIOSH Hazard Review: Occupational Hazards in Home Healthcare.* Retrieved November 8, 2013, from DHHS (NIOSH) Publication No. 2010-125: www.cdc.gov/niosh/docs/2010-125/pdfs/2010-125.pdf

Health and Safety Executive. (2013). *Can a Person Be Left Alone at Their Place of Work?* (Contains public sector information published by the Health and Safety Executive and licensed under the Open Government Licence v1.0). Retrieved November 11, 2013, from HSE: www.hse.gov.uk/contact/faqs/workalone.htm

U.S. Department of Health and Human Services. (2013). *Health Information Privacy.* Retrieved November 6, 2013, from Health Information Privacy: www.hhs.gov/ocr/privacy/index.html

9

SUCCESS IN MY OWN
ENVIRONMENT

Home and Community Services Work

Each step outlined in the chapters in this book guides the consumer to success in his or her own living environment. The consumer is a key participant in the beginning assessment process and ongoing treatment planning. As a full contributor to planning, the consumer plays a key role in determining which areas of treatment he or she is ready to address and which areas to defer until he or she is better prepared to focus on them. Ideally, the consumer and provider work together and establish a frequency and type of treatment that best meets the individualized needs of the consumer. Most important, during this process, the consumer is taught skills and techniques the consumer is able to practice in his or her actual living environment and community. Additionally, when the behavioral health provider is knowledgeable, the provider works with the consumer to slowly reduce the intensity and frequency of services so that adequate time is given to each step in treatment. Ultimately, the consumer and provider work together toward discharge, or transition to a lower level of care, with all needed formal and informal support structures identified. The consumer is a full and contributing participant in the entire treatment process.

Consumers who are able to have in vivo[1] practice of coping skills and real life application of techniques are much more confident practicing those same skills later when they are without the provider and are in their home, school, or natural environment. When real life situations present themselves, the consumer who has received services in his or her own home and community, can refer back to practice experiences that occurred in those actual environments to bolster his or her responses to those situations. Modeling, in vivo practice, gradual step-down, and strong discharge planning (that includes formal and informal support structures), helps the consumer. Practice in real situations gives consumers more confidence in succeeding in the very environments in which they are schooled, going to work, walking to the corner store, and interacting with neighbors and friends, as well as adversarial contacts.

We can compare the experience of a consumer learning real life coping skills in an office to a student learning to drive on a computer. The individual who is taught how to drive on a computer is given the tools to know how to "academically" react in every potential scenario that may present itself in a virtual driving situation. Through simulations and testing, the student has validated his or her knowledge and built a strong skill base to utilize in a real life situation. Does this virtual training prepare the individual to drive? In many ways, it absolutely trains someone to drive, respond, and follow the rules of the road. However, when someone drives on an actual road he or she experiences situations in which there are time pressures and consequences much stronger than in the simulated situations. These pressures and real life scenarios may bring about a completely different reaction from the student driver. I can recall as a young driver taking all my required high school driving courses, learning to parallel park, and navigating traffic cones like a professional. It was not, however, until my brother taught me drive my father's 1963 Chevy II Super Sport around my grandfather's cow field (which, yes, was void of cows both just prior to and during the lesson) that I felt the off-road vibrations through the steering wheel and the gravity of being entirely responsible for the management of the power of a vehicle. In this real life scenario, I had authentic circumstances where my actions had the ability to help me succeed or to compound a difficult situation. The feeling between the simulation and the actual experience was vastly different. The feeling between virtual and real coping skill practice is also vastly different for our consumers. When a provider works with a consumer in the office and teaches the consumer coping skills to apply in the real world, the provider is giving the consumer a template of how to respond in a similar situation. There are many situations where recalling skills training works for consumers in real situations. Many providers, however, also work with their consumers on exercises where they are afforded the opportunity to practice these learned coping skills in a modeled scenario. This modeling technique, as opposed to learning skills via discussion and worksheets, can be quite effective. Modeling technique in an office setting can be used to reinforce healthy coping skills in a variety of situations. Most commonly, this technique is used to help children practice standing up to bullies, consumers practice confronting someone they have been unable to express their feeling to in the past, and teens and adults practice techniques for a job interview.

Let's look further, however, at how we can improve upon a system that is already quite effective. Suppose those skills that were practiced in the office environment were instead practiced in the community with the safety net of a behavioral health professional by the consumer's side. This real life practice experience allows the consumer to apply the new skills in novel situations and with different people. Practicing these skills in real life situations with unpredictable variables allows the consumer to truly strengthen the learning experiences. Each time the consumer is able to practice a learned skill, he or she is able to gain confidence in utilizing that skill. Additionally, each time the consumer is able to practice these skills in real life scenarios, the skill is reinforced and becomes part of more instant recall in stressful situations.

Disorders and Real Environment Practice Experiences

There are many situations in which service provision in the home, school, and natural community environment can assist a consumer in reaching goals. Earlier, we discussed a case study on John (Chapter 3), a consumer who was homeless and unable to keep standard office appointments. For John, providing services in his natural environment helped him get the assistance he so badly needed. The reasons why service location can make a big difference for consumers are diverse. Some of the consumers that can benefit most from home-, school-, and community-based services are those with challenges resulting from disorders that make it difficult to go to traditional service locations. For these consumers, challenges such obtaining transportation and getting time off of their jobs for appointments can be a significant barrier to obtaining services. Still other consumers can have behavioral health difficulties that only present in particular situations, in particular environments, and under stressors that are not easily duplicated in an office or hospital setting. In Chapter 3, a case study on Anna showed a consumer with identification difficulties that were more easily differentiated and addressed with home-based services.

Service Setting Case Study

Let's consider a case example where a consumer's disorder made it difficult for him to go to a traditional service location.

William

Behavioral Health History and Presentation

William is a 44-year-old married man with two sons. He has worked as an accountant, specializing in tax returns, for ten years. At this time, he has been on leave from his current job for five months. William is on leave due to symptoms associated with panic disorder and agoraphobia. When William describes one of his panic attacks it is usually characterized by a rapidly pounding heart, difficulty breathing, feelings of unreality, and tingling in his fingers. He has experienced panic attacks since 2005. He quite vividly remembers his first attack during which he had the fear he was dying of a heart attack or stroke and immediately presented to the emergency room at the local hospital. Since that time, he has experienced approximately one panic attack each week and often worries about the next attack.

William's panic symptoms have resulted in significant interference in his life. He has given up some of the activities he used to enjoy, unless he is accompanied by someone whom he considers safe, such as his oldest son or wife. Additionally, if he has experienced a panic attack in a public place, he avoids going back to that same place for fear he will experience another one.

During the last year, he began to experience heart palpitations and chest pain during his panic attacks. It was one of these intense panic attacks that led William to leave work one day, and he has since been unable to return to work due to fear of another severe panic attack. He is finding himself increasingly reliant upon doing things with his wife, due to fear he will be unable to get medical assistance during a panic attack. He feels very depressed about not being able to work. William's physician has prescribed him some anti-anxiety medication that he carries with him at all times. His primary care physician made a recommendation for cognitive behavioral therapy (CBT) in conjunction with medication management. William made an appointment to go to a traditional outpatient clinic for therapeutic intervention. However, he experienced a panic attack in the waiting room of the clinic during his initial appointment and has been unable to return to the clinic since that time.

Home-Based Treatment

William contacted a crisis line during one of his most recent attacks, and they made the referral for a provider who was able to offer services in the home environment. An intake coordinator contacted William for an initial assessment and was able to send someone to his home to meet with him and conduct an evaluation. After the initial assessment, it was determined that William would benefit from therapeutic intervention in the form of individual therapy. His therapist met with him to develop a treatment plan and prepared a format to address his clinical needs. The therapist utilized both CBT to challenge thoughts and exposure therapy to gradually expose William to some of the situations that triggered his fears. Through systematic desensitization, the therapist worked with William to teach him relaxation skills, create a step-by-step list of triggers, and create exposure scenarios through those identified steps. When William had first entered services and was involved in his own treatment planning, he had identified one overarching goal of returning to work. The therapist employed this goal and he and William worked together to identify 20 micro-steps that each progressed to the main goal of being able to return to the work environment where he had experienced a panic attack. First, William began working through the initial steps on the list. The primary step was simply going onto the company website. Even this step produced some anxiety for him. This was, however, part of a series of steps that William was able to progress through, one phase at a time. The goal of systematic desensitization is to stay in the fear-inducing situation until the fear subsides. That way, William could learn that the feelings themselves were not harmful and will go away. When the anxiety became too intense, the therapist would switch to relaxation techniques, then once relaxed, move back to progression in the identified steps.

Over the course of six months of therapy, William and his therapist worked on the progressive steps necessary to desensitize his anxiety and he was able to enter his work environment again. Each step of the way, the therapist was with William, as he progressively moved though each of the 20 steps. Not only did the therapist help William identify the progressive steps and instruct him on completion, he was actually there with him in the natural environment completing these steps. Once William mastered a step, the therapist would allow William to repeat the same steps, without a safe person (i.e., therapist). In doing so, William could experience completion of each step on his own and develop a sense of confidence and mastery of that situation.

Expanding Home-, School-, and Natural Community-Based Services

The President's New Freedom Commission on Mental Health stated in its report that: "Extending home- and community-based services (HCBS) as an alternative to residential treatment facilities could allow children to receive treatment in their own homes, surrounded by their families, at a cost per child that would cost less than the cost of institutional care" (New Freedom Commission on Mental Health, 2003, p. 40). Since the time of this report, many geographic regions have seen an expansion in home-, school-, and natural community-based service intervention and reimbursement for these services. The number of states, countries, and communities that have made a commitment to expand these services has also grown.

Demonstration Project

While many states, countries, and communities have found ways to expand these home and natural community services, there can be some challenges in setting these services up in areas that do not currently have them. In expanding these services into a geographic area, it makes sense to see what has worked in the past for others. One such effort began in 2005 when the U.S. Congress authorized a five-year demonstration project to see if children and adolescents served in a psychiatric residential treatment facility (PRFT) could successfully and cost-effectively be served in the community. The Centers for Medicare and Medicaid Services (CMS) selected ten states to compare effective ways of providing home- and community-based services (HCBS) as an alternative to PRTF placement. Using a "systems of care"[2] service delivery approach, the demonstration enabled consumers to either improve or maintain their functioning status, at less than a third of the cost of serving them in an institution. The functional status for the children and youth, served under the home- and community-based services demonstration, was measured in the domains of behavioral health, school functioning, juvenile justice, alcohol and other drug use, and social support. All participants in the demonstration project improved or maintained their functional status in these identified domains. Additionally, the children and youth with the highest levels of need, throughout periods measured during the project, consistently showed improved behavioral health status, less frequent interaction with law enforcement, better school performance, reductions in substance abuse, and better relationships with peers and family (Department of Health and Human Services: Office of the Secretary, 2013, p. 1).

The demonstration project targeted children and adolescents who might not have otherwise been eligible for Medicaid-funded, intensive community-based services, and supports available through existing waivers and funding. CMS awarded $217 million to ten states, with each state receiving between $15 million and $50 million each over the grant period (fiscal year 2007 through fiscal year 2011); and the remaining $1 million was awarded to fund an evaluation of the demonstration. "Each participating state was required to provide non-federal Medicaid matching funds. One of the ten states, Florida, did not continue in the demonstration after the first year due to difficulty securing the non-federal matching funds necessary to implement the program. The nine fully participating states were Alaska, Georgia, Indiana, Kansas, Maryland, Mississippi, Montana, South Carolina, and Virginia. The development of home- and community-based services in these states was built on historical funding to create systems of care from the Substance Abuse and Mental Health Services Administration (SAMHSA) Children's Mental Health Initiative (CMHI) grant program" (Department of Health and Human Services: Office of the Secretary, 2013, p. 2).

Box 9.1. Systems of Care Core Values

SAMHSA (2013) describes systems of care core values as:

1. Family-driven and consumer-guided, with the strengths and needs of the consumer and family determining the types and mix of services and supports provided.
2. Community-based, with the locus of services, as well as system management, resting within a supportive, adaptive infrastructure of structures, processes, and relationships at the community level.
3. Culturally and linguistically competent, with agencies, programs, and services that reflect the cultural, racial, ethnic, and linguistic differences of the populations they serve to facilitate access to and utilization of appropriate services and supports and to eliminate disparities in care.

Each state, country, and community has different funding available for the purposes of expanding home- and natural community-based services. In the United States, 90 percent of public behavioral health service funding comes from Medicaid and state general fund dollars. The other 10 percent is funded by Medicare, federal mental health service block grant funds, county funds, municipal funds, schools, and State Children's Health Insurance Program (S-CHIP) (NAMI, 2010). The list that follows is by no means inclusive of all available resources for funding home- and natural community-based services, but is intended to show some existing structures that are working. To follow are some examples of U.S. Medicaid plans that cover these services:

1905(a) Authority

Many of the services that were core to the success of the CMHI and PRTF Demonstration program can be covered through 1905(a) authority, generally through targeted case management or rehabilitative services. States that have used the 1905(a) authority as a foundation for their benefit design for children and youth with significant mental health conditions include: Massachusetts, Connecticut, New Mexico and Hawaii.

(SAMHSA and CMCS, 2013, p. 7)

1915(b) Authority

1915(b) Waivers are one of several options available to states that allow the use of managed care in the Medicaid Program. When using the 1915(b) authority, states have various options for implementing managed care including the authority to restrict the types of providers that people can use to access Medicaid benefits and the ability to use the savings to the state, from a managed care delivery system, to provide additional services or restrict the number or type of providers who can provide specific Medicaid services. Louisiana, Michigan, Iowa and California are examples of states that have used the 1915(b) authority (and sometimes a combination of 1915(b) and 1915(c) and other authorities) for their children's mental health delivery systems.

(SAMHSA and CMCS, 2013, p. 7)

1915(c) Authority

Some states have used the 1915(c) Home and Community-Based Services (HCBS) program to develop good benefit designs for children and youth with significant mental health conditions. The nine states that participated in the PRTF five-year demonstration grants utilized the 1915(c) waiver authority. These states included: Alaska, Georgia, Indiana, Kansas, Maryland, Mississippi, Montana, South Carolina and Virginia. Eight other states also use the 1915(c) authority for these children and youth. These states include: New York, Michigan, Wisconsin, Louisiana, Texas, Iowa, Kansas, and Wyoming. States have used these HCBS waivers to expand their array of home and community-based services and supports for this population with a view towards improving outcomes and reducing costs.

(SAMHSA and CMCS, 2013, p. 7)

1915(i) State Plan Amendment

Section 1915(i) state plan amendment (SPA) provides an opportunity for states to amend their state Medicaid plans to offer intensive home- and community-based behavioral health services that were previously provided primarily through 1915(c) HCBS waivers programs. Intensive care coordination, respite, parent and youth support partners, and other services can be offered under 1915(i) and serve children and youth with significant mental health conditions. Under 1915(i) states may not waive the requirement to provide services statewide, nor can they limit the number of participants in the state who may receive the services if they meet the population definition. Unlike the 1915(c) waiver program, the 1915(i) delinks the provision of services with participants meeting an institutional level of care. In order to target the initiative and limit costs, states may identify a specific population and establish additional needs-based criteria. For example, a state could develop needs-based criteria only for children and youth at risk of removal from their homes or in need of intensive community-based services and behavioral interventions in their homes, schools, or communities to control aggressive behavior towards self and others.

(SAMHSA and CMCS, 2013, p. 8)

1115 Authorities

Section 1115 of the Social Security Act gives the Secretary of HHS authority to approve experimental, pilot, or demonstration projects that further the objectives of the Medicaid and the Children's Health Insurance Program (CHIP). These demonstrations give states additional flexibility to design and improve their programs, to demonstrate and evaluate policy approaches, such as providing services not typically covered by Medicaid, and using innovative service delivery systems that improve care, increase efficiency, and reduce costs. Many section 1115 demonstrations include expansion of mental health services.

(SAMHSA and CMCS, 2013, p. 8)

Money Follows the Person (MFP)
Rebalancing Demonstration

MFP provides an opportunity for states to offer community-based services and supports to individuals transitioning from qualifying institutions to qualifying home- and community-based settings, including children and youth 21 years of age and under who have been in PRTFs or psychiatric hospitals for at least 90 consecutive days and are transitioning to community settings, including family homes, foster homes, alternative family-based homes, or other community-based settings. MFP allows an enhanced federal match equal to an additional 50 percent of the state share with an upper limit of 90 percent. The enhanced federal match on qualified Medicaid services is available for 365 days after each individual's discharge from the institution. The state may also provide additional supplemental transition services to support

159

the youth to successfully move into the community, including but not limited to household set-up, home modifications, or peer support. States are required to have the ability to meet the needs of the children and youth after the 365-day period.

(SAMHSA and CMCS, 2013, p. 9)

The MFP is a way for states to transition adolescent consumers from PRTFs back into the natural community. It has been successful in keeping the average service duration for adolescents needing intensive community-based services after discharge in the PRTF demonstration consistently close to 365 days—the allowable service duration of enhanced match under MFP. If the children and adolescents continue to need services and supports after 365 days in the community, services covered under other Medicaid authorities may be provided to address their needs (SAMHSA and CMCS, 2013, p. 9).

Balancing Incentive Program

The Balancing Incentive Program, created by the Affordable Care Act (Section 10202), authorizes grants to states to increase access to non-institutional, long-term services and supports (LTSS) and was effective as of October 1, 2011. The Balancing Incentive Program can help states transform their long-term care service systems by lowering costs through improved systems perfor-mance and efficiency, creating tools to help consumers with care planning and assessment and improving quality measurement and oversight. Enhanced federal match is available to states for four years. To participate in the Balancing Incentive Program, a state must have spent less than 50 percent of total Medicaid medi-cal assistance expenditures on non-institutionally based LTSS for fiscal year 2009. The Balancing Incentive Program also provides new ways to serve more people in home and community-based settings, helping states comply with their obligations under the integration mandate of the ADA. Most states that have approved applications under this program include mental health services in their rebalancing efforts.

(SAMHSA and CMCS, 2013, p. 10).

Community Mental Health Services Block Grant

Community Mental Health Services Block Grant is a federal program administered by the Center for Mental Health Services (CMHS). The grant is used to improve community-based services for consumers living with men-tal illness. Grants are awarded to states based on a funding formula (Sub-stance Abuse and Mental Health Services Administration, 2013, June 3).

State Mental Health Budget

State mental health budgets are separate from Medicaid budgets, and can be used to fund needed treatment and support not covered by Medicaid. These funds can be used for inpatient care, crisis services, and community-based behavioral health services for children and adults. In particular, this budget can be utilized to provide critical services for consumers who are uninsured, underinsured, or awaiting eligibility for Medicaid (NAMI, 2010).

Private Insurance

Private insurance often limits coverage to those behavioral health services provided in traditional clinic and medical settings. Advocacy is needed in this area to help ensure that more private insurance companies provide coverage for medically necessary home- and community-based services and supports. These services and supports can help keep consumers with serious behavioral health treatment needs, at home and in their natural communities. There are established advocacy groups in many communities that providers and consumers can join. Where these formalized groups do not currently exist, providers and consumers can advocate through their local behavioral health care payers for expansion of coverage. This advocacy is best accomplished by providing the payer evidence on the effectiveness of home- and community-based services as well as cost-saving analysis of these programs.

Creative Funding

It is important to recognize that in some states, countries, and communities, there is often very little funding for home- and natural community-based services. Therefore, in those geographic areas, they must redirect funds from high-cost services and away from those services that are not receiving positive outcomes. While financial drives are a consideration in service provision, consumer needs should ideally be what guides service delivery. Consumers needs dictate that they should be served in the least restrictive setting that meets their current level of clinical need. Therefore, some states, countries, and communities have come up with creative approaches to funding and expanding home- and natural community-based services. In these geographic areas, they may combine funds from projects, waivers, grants, and so on to merge together to cover costs of service. These funding sources can be from state mental health departments, Medicaid, federal grants, demonstration projects, child welfare departments, education departments, not-for-profit grants, private foundations, and justice systems. Additionally, some states, countries, and

161

communities have redirected funds from residential treatment to home- and natural community-based services whenever possible.

International Spotlight

We have discussed the possibilities of expansion of home- and community-based services in the United States, but there are many countries and communities around the world that can benefit from utilization of this model. The number of people worldwide with behavioral health and/or substance use issues continues to grow. In fact, the World Health Organization (WHO) reported that depression alone accounts for the largest percentage of global burden of disease and is the largest single cause of disability worldwide (WHO, 2013b, p. 8). There are many factors that contribute to the worldwide statistics on behavioral health, one of which is the significant numbers of emergency situations around the world. Many countries are affected by refugee crisis, heavy fighting, and natural disaster. Displacements, food shortages, and disease are all common during and after these emergencies. It is also not surprising that these emergencies impact behavioral health. This is because emergency situations can worsen existing mental health disorders at the same time that any existing local clinics or health infrastructures may be destroyed or weakened. Also, there are some new-onset mental disorders that can develop acutely during these times of psychological distress. The World Health Organization in its 2013 report on *Building Back Better Sustainable Mental Health Care after Emergencies* suggested that these emergency situations may actually provide an opportunity to improve local behavioral health services. The premise behind this growth is that after an emergency media focuses on the situation, senior government leaders acknowledge the gravity of the situation, and national and international agencies are usually willing to provide needed financial support. "The possibilities presented by emergency situations are significant because major gaps remain worldwide in the realization of comprehensive, community-based mental health care. This is especially true in low and middle-income countries, where resources are often scant. Countries faced with emergencies should not miss the chance to use available political will for change and to initiate mental health reform" (WHO, 2013a, p. 10). It is important to realize that global progress can be made in behavioral health reform during these times of crisis. Although it may seem strange to view crisis as an opportunity for growth, that is exactly what WHO found among ten diverse emergency-affected areas discussed in the report. The countries represented in the case examples included: Afghanistan—following the fall of the Taliban government in 2001; Burundi—in its development of modern behavioral health services; Indonesia (Aceh)—following the tsunami of 2004; Iraq—in behavioral health reform since 2004; Jordan—following a two-wave influx of war-displaced Iraqis into Jordan; Kosovo—after the inter-ethnic violence including the Kosovo war of 1999; Somalia—following multiple conflicts and emergencies; Sri Lanka—in the aftermath of the 2004 tsunami; Timor-Leste—building from a complete absence of behavioral health services in 1999; and the West Bank and Gaza Strip—making improvements in the last decade (WHO, 2013a). In each of the countries mentioned previously, behavioral health reform was a realistic part of crisis recovery. In these crises, humanitarian relief included a portion of available money allocated toward behavioral health reform. WHO asserts that global progress can occur with behavioral health reform more quickly if, in every crisis, efforts are made to build momentum for reform. WHO "has affirmed that mental health care in all countries—including those rebuilding from emergencies—should be centered on services that are accessible in the community" (WHO, 2004, p. 16). Some of the behavioral health growth has occurred in the form of community-based services. In other countries, these community-based behavioral health services may include traditional outpatient care; community centers; respite for families and caregivers; occupational, vocational, and rehabilitation support; home-based services; and peer support services.

It is estimated that between 76 percent and 85 percent of people with severe mental disorders receive no treatment in low-income and middle-income countries. The range for high-income countries, however, is also high; 35 percent to 50 percent receive no treatment for their behavioral health issues. Globally, annual spending on behavioral health is less than US$2.00 and less than US$0.25 per person in low-income countries. Then, of those allocated resources, 67 percent are used for mental hospitals with poor health outcomes and human rights violations (WHO, 2013b, p. 8). Redirecting this funding toward home- and natural community-based services can be a way to save on the costs of unnecessary hospital confinement and bring behavioral health services into the communities that have a shortage of available behavioral health providers and services. Globally, and particularly in low-income and middle-income countries, the number of specialized and general health workers dealing with behavioral health issues is extremely insufficient. Almost half the world's population lives in countries in which, on average, there is only one psychiatrist to serve 200,000 or more people (WHO, 2013b, p. 8). Currently WHO's Mental Health Gap Action Programme that began in 2008 is using evidence-based technical guides, tools, and training packages to expand behavioral health service provision in resource-poor countries. These services could be vastly expanded upon with home- and natural community-based supports. Where it is not possible to recruit or retain licensed or specialty staff, non-specialist providers can be utilized. Appendix B goes into more detail on this topic. Through training paraprofessionals and peers in recovery to work with others with behavioral health needs, two goals could be accomplished. The first goal of providing behavioral health services to more individuals would be addressed by bolstering the provider field with trained paraprofessional and peer staff. Additionally, by providing employment to these individuals, they have sustainable living sources and the money remains in the communities in need.

Consumers and Providers Working Together for Change

Consumers, families of consumers, and providers all want to see an expansion of effective services and supports for behavioral health consumers. The reality is that each of these groups can play a compelling role in the expansion of home- and community-based behavioral health services. To follow are some ideas for ways in which consumers, families, and providers may work to expand these services (adapted from NAMI, 2009).

1. Gather Data: Services are often provided in a wide array of settings, but data is not always collected to show how effective these services are to individual consumers in particular settings. It is important to collect outcome data on home- and natural community-based services to support the assertion for expanding these services.
2. Learn about Effective Home- and Natural Community-Based Services: There is a lot of data available to gain knowledge regarding which interventions have demonstrated evidence-based efficacy. One such source of information on these interventions is SAMHSA's (2013) National Registry of Evidence-based Programs and Practices (NREPP). This searchable online registry can be located at http:// nrepp.samhsa.gov/
3. Build a Community: Provider groups, consumer groups, state and community mental health authorities, welfare groups, justice system officials, educational leaders, judges, Medicaid officials, and law enforcement can all collaborate together. When key stakeholders work together, they can bring about change and reform. In working together each field can appreciate the benefits of home- and community-based service provision as they apply to its particular discipline, and any misconceptions, concerns, or questions can be addressed at the forefront of discussions.
4. Judicial Power: Many consumers with behavioral health issues have had involvement with the criminal justice system. Judges often have discretion to order behavioral health and/or substance use services and can influence the expansion of intensive home- and natural community-based services. Partnering with judges helps to expand provider and consumer collaboration efforts and also helps make

local judges aware of the home- and natural community-based services that are available.

5. Know your Medicaid and Financing Experts: Find out if Medicaid community-based financing experts are in your state. If not, you can advocate for state officials to bring in consultants who have worked in other communities with these same types of services. The experience of structuring funding for expanding home- and natural community-based services can provide needed direction in pursuing this locally.

6. Leadership: Find and support local leaders who are willing to put expansion of behavioral health services into the home and natural community on their agenda.

7. Success in Other Communities: Consumers, consumer families, and providers can communicate with key legislatures and officials on the rationale for expanding home- and natural community-based services. Personal stories about how services have benefited the consumer or the family can be a powerful tool to help bring about positive change. Providers can also tell their stories in order to show key officials how the services work and how location can make a difference.

8. Track Outcomes and Stories: Communities should track outcomes to ensure the investment being made into home- and natural community-based services shows improvement for consumers. Positive data and personal stories of success can help fortify a community's desire for continuation of funding of these services. Several studies have shown that the use of home- and natural community-based services results in monetary savings over out-of-home placement. This data should be documented and shared. Cost savings can be reinvested into the programs for training, supervision, and ongoing monitoring of effectiveness of interventions.

Putting It All Together

Those people who choose to go into the behavioral health field generally had a moment in their life or career development at which they decided they truly enjoyed helping other human beings. Perhaps they had experienced pain and struggles themselves and learned ways to cope that they could relay to others. Still others guided loved ones through difficult times and life decisions and felt this was a vocational calling. Some individuals decided in science class that they were fascinated with brain chemistry and how it affected mood and behavior. Additional others may have discovered they had a gift of relating to others and realized they needed to help those in vulnerable positions find their own voice and garner the strength to pursue their own goals. Regardless of the exact reason someone chooses to be a provider of behavioral health services, that connection with humanity and desire to help others is usually somewhere in the person's inspiration.

It follows that the provider who is motivated to help others and connect with them on a human level may be encouraged by serving the consumer in the least restrictive setting possible for the intensity of symptom presentation and severity of disorder. Service provision in the home and natural community is effective and is the best solution for many consumers. The provider can assess the consumer in the consumer's own surroundings and get a better idea of how the consumer functions in a familiar environment and what challenges are inherent in that setting. The provider can then begin to work more effectively with the consumer while retaining a rapport that is hard to emulate outside of the familiarity of the consumer's own living environment. The consumer recognizes that the provider is, at least for a short while, part of his or her surroundings and will be an integral part of his or her solution. When the provider is in the consumer's neighborhood and home the consumer can believe that the provider understands some of the consumer's unique challenges. Then, through person-centered planning, that consumer is given the opportunity to voice his or her own preferences for treatment and direction. The consumer and provider are in a partnership to help bring about positive change. This consumer-driven process continues as they approach discharge. The consumer has actively participated in identifying informal supports, formal supports for recovery, and the specific steps toward discharge. Ultimately, the consumer's living supports and structure have not been disrupted by an outside placement. Similarly, the consumer's and family's educational and vocational obligations are not interrupted by appointments during academic classes or employment times. Additionally, the consumer has learned to be successful in the very environment the consumer will experience daily by learning skills in vivo. Moreover, several research studies have shown that provision of intensive behavioral health services in the home and natural community are both effective and result in a cost-savings when compared to more restrictive settings. This book presented a detailed map as to how you can further your own efforts as a provider of home- and community-based services, begin serving consumers in their natural environments, address identified challenges to providing behavioral health services in the home and natural community, identify and bolster local funding sources, and use home- and community-based service models to bring services to underserved geographic areas. Now you can help change the tapestry of behavioral health provision *one home, one healing at a time.*

Notes

1. In vivo practice refers to practicing a behavior or skill in a real situation (in this case the consumer is able to practice learned coping skills in real situations in the home and natural community).
2. Systems of care is an organizational philosophy and framework that involves collaboration across agencies, the consumer, and families, for the purpose of improving access to community-based, competent services and supports.

References

Department of Health and Human Services: Office of the Secretary. (2013). *Report to the President and Congress Medicaid Home and Community-Based Alternatives to Psychiatric Residential Treatment Facilities Demonstration.* HHS. Retrieved November 20, 2013, from Department of Health and Human Services: www.medicaid.gov/Medicaid-CHIP-Program-Information/By-Topics/Delivery-Systems/Institutional-Care/Downloads/PRTF-Demo-Report-.pdf

National Alliance on Mental Health (NAMI). (2009). *Reinvesting in the Community: A Family Guide to Expanding Home and Community-Based Mental Health Services and Supports.* Retrieved November 1, 2013, from http://nami.org/Template.cfm?Section=Research_Services_and_Treatment&template=/ContentManagement/ContentDisplay.cfm&ContentID=76200

National Alliance on Mental Health (NAMI). (2010, January). *NAMI State Advocacy.* Retrieved November 28, 2013, from NAMI: www.nami.org/Content/NavigationMenu/State_Advocacy/About_the_Issue/Funding.pdf

New Freedom Commission on Mental Health. (2003, July 22). *The President's New Freedom Commission on Mental Health Report.* Retrieved November 15, 2013, from New Freedom Commission on Mental Health: http://govinfo.library.unt.edu/mentalhealthcommission/reports/FinalReport/downloads/FinalReport.pdf

Substance Abuse and Mental Health Services Administration (SAMHSA). (2013). *System of Care Core Values.* Retrieved December 10, 2013, from SAMHSA: www.samhsa.gov/children/core-values.asp

Substance Abuse and Mental Health Services Administration. (2013, June 3). *SAMHSA Block Grants.* Retrieved November 1, 2013, from SAMHSA: www.samhsa.gov/grants/blockgrant/

Substance Abuse and Mental Health Services Administration (SAMHSA). (2013, November 14). *NREPP.* Retrieved November 15, 2013, from NREPP: SAMHSA's National Registry of Evidence Based Programs and Practices: http://nrepp.samhsa.gov/Index.aspx

Substance Abuse and Mental Health Services Administration (SAMHSA) and CMCS. (2013). *Coverage of Behavioral Health Services for Children, Youth, and Young Adults with Significant Mental Health Conditions.* Retrieved November 15, 2013, from www.medicaid.gov/Federal-Policy-Guidance/Downloads/CIB-05-07-2013.pdf

World Health Organization (WHO). (2004). *Promoting Mental Health: Concepts, Emerging Evidence, Practice. Summary Report.* Geneva, Switzerland. Retrieved

November 20, 2013, from WHO: http://who.int/mental_health/evidence/en/promoting_mhh.pdf

World Health Organization (WHO). (2013a). *Building Back Better Sustainable Mental Health Care after Emergencies*. Geneva, Switzerland. Retrieved November 20, 2013, from WHO: http://apps.who.int/iris/bitstream/10665/85377/1/9789241564571_eng.pdf

World Health Organization (WHO). (2013b). *Mental Health Action Plan 2013–2020*. Geneva, Switzerland. Retrieved November 20, 2013, from WHO: http://apps.who.int/iris/bitstream/10665/89966/1/9789241506021_eng.pdf

APPENDIX A

Evidence-Based Practice Resources[1] That Are Accessible on the World Wide Web

Organization and Website	What It Does	What Is Listed
Child Trends www.childtrends.org	Child Trends provides data, analysis, and information to improve policies and programs serving children and youth.	• Description of interventions • Description of implementation • Databank with national trends and research on key well-being indictors for children and youth • Information on programs that work (and those that do not) • Evidence-based practice references
National Child Traumatic Stress Network (NCTSN) www.nctsnet.org	The NCTSN website has information on some clinical treatment and trauma-informed service approaches that are intended to reduce the impact of exposure to traumatic events on children and adolescents. NCTSN combines knowledge of child development and expertise in the full range of childhood traumatic experiences with evidence-based practice.	• Intended to be used for program planners working with children who have experienced trauma • Description of interventions and intervention implementation • Measures review database • Parent and caregiver resources • Guidance on staffing services

(*Continued*)

169

(Continued)

Organization and Website	What It Does	What Is Listed
National Guideline Clearinghouse (NGC), AHRQ www.guideline.gov/	NGC is a public resource for evidence-based clinical practice guidelines. NGC is an initiative of the Agency for Healthcare Research and Quality (AHRQ) of the U.S. Department of Health and Human Services.	• Intended to provide physicians, healthcare providers, health plans, purchasers, and integrated delivery systems with a mechanism to get detailed information on clinical practice guidelines • Descriptions of interventions • Description of evidentiary standards met • Description of intervention implementation
Office of Juvenile Justice and Delinquency Prevention: Model Programs Guide (MPG) www.ojjdp.gov/mpg/	The Office of Juvenile Justice and Delinquency Prevention developed the MPG to provide information on evidence-based juvenile justice and youth prevention, intervention, and re-entry programs.	• Resources include a literature review and program listing by topic area • A topic and sub-topic search (e.g., delinquency prevention/ community-based) results in program title, rating, and summary
Oregon Mental Health and Addiction Services www.oregon.gov/oha/ amh/pages/ebp/main.aspx	The office of Addictions and Mental Health Services (AMH) has created a listing of evidence-based treatment and prevention practices that have proven to be effective in behavioral health and addictions.	• Definition of evidence-based practice • Intended for consumers, policy makers, and providers of services • Provides descriptions of interventions • Tools for determining level of practice • Description of evidentiary standards met • Description of intervention implementation

Promising Practices Network www.promisingpractices.net/	Promising Practices Network (PPN) provides resources on research-based information that is proven to improve the lives of children and families.	• Summaries of effective programs in "Programs That Work" section • "Issue Briefs" to summarize research by topic area • "Expert Perspectives" section where child policy experts answer visitors' questions • Evidence-based information on service delivery provided
SAMHSA, National Registry of Evidence-based Programs and Practices (NREPP) www.nrepp.samhsa.gov	SAMHSA's National Registry of Evidence-based Programs and Practices (NREPP) was created to help the public learn more about evidence-based interventions. NREPP is a searchable database that includes voluntary rating and classification systems of interventions used in the field of behavioral health and substance abuse.	• Definition of evidence-based practice • Intended for promoting informed decision making and rating quality of research supporting intervention outcomes • Descriptions of interventions • Information on fidelity measurement • Searchable database
Social Care Institute for Excellence (SCIE) www.scie.org.uk/	SCIE works to identify information, research, and effective practice examples to assist providers, researchers, consumers, and policy makers. SCIE's focus includes social care for adults, children, and families. It also provides information related to human resource development, social work education, and e-learning.	• International site based out of London, England • Evidence-based practices are defined • Provides descriptions of interventions • Describes intervention implementation • Guidance on staff training • Evidence-based practice references

(*Continued*)

(Continued)

Organization and Website	What It Does	What Is Listed
Social Programs That Work, Coalition for Evidence-Based Policy, Council for Excellence in Government www.evidencebased programs.org/	The Coalition for Evidence-Based Policy seeks to identify social interventions that have undergone rigorous studies and have been shown to produce notable, long-term benefits to consumers and society. The purpose is to give policy officials the information they need to readily distinguish which few interventions are, in fact, backed by rigorous evidence.	• Definition of evidence-based practice • Intended for policy makers and providers • Interventions are organized by policy area • Descriptions of only those interventions shown in well-designed and independently randomized control trials • Describes intervention implementation • Provides guidance on staffing
Society of Clinical Child and Adolescent Psychology, American Psychological Association Division 53 www.effectivechild therapy.com/	The purpose of this site is to educate the general public and providers about the most current information on behavioral health treatment for children and adolescents. The site also provides valuable guidance to parents and caregivers about symptoms and specific treatment options.	• Definition of evidence-based practice • Intended for the general public, providers, parents, and caregivers • Descriptions of evidence-based practices listed by specific disorder • Information on online education as it pertains to children and adolescents
Suicide Prevention Resource Center (SPRC) www.sprc.org	The Best Practices Registry in Suicide Prevention Programs is a collaboration between SPRC and the American Foundation for Suicide Prevention (AFSP) to identify and classify effective suicide prevention programs using a multidisciplinary review process.	• Intended for providers, community leaders, survivors, advocates, researchers, and policy makers • Listing of evidence-based programs • Information on expert/consensus statements

	The Best Practices Registry on the site provides specific information on evidence-based programs.	• Description of evidentiary standards met • Description of intervention implementation • Marketing materials • Information on fidelity measurement
The California Evidence-Based Clearinghouse for Child Welfare www.cebc4cw.org/	The primary task of CEBC is to inform the public about research-based programs being marketed or used in California.	• Provides information about selected child welfare related programs • Screening and assessment tool overview • Implementation tools for evidence-based practices • Webinars and online training available
The Campbell Collaboration www.campbell collaboration.org	The Campbell Collaboration (C2) is an international network that produces systematic reviews in four major areas: social welfare, education, international development, and crime and justice. The Campbell Collaboration can help to support providers by summarizing individual studies and providing information on evidence-based interventions.	• Reviews (systemic) of the effects of interventions in social welfare, crime and justice, and education • International Site (based out of Oslo, Norway) • Approved reviews are freely accessible online • Library also gives approved protocols and user abstracts
The Cochrane Collaboration www.cochrane.org	The Cochrane Collaboration is an international network (in over 120 countries) that is dedicated to making updated information about the effects of healthcare available worldwide.	• Provides descriptions of interventions and reviews • International site with reviews available in multiple languages

(*Continued*)

(Continued)

Organization and Website	What It Does	What Is Listed
	It provides consumers, caregivers, advocates, providers of service, and policy makers updated information to assist them in making informed decisions regarding healthcare.	• Focus on helping providers, consumers, research funding agencies, health departments, international organizations, and universities make informed decisions on healthcare and problem behavior areas
The Guide to Community Prevention Services: The Community Guide www.thecommunityguide. org/index.html	The Community Guide is a resource to help stakeholders choose programs and policies to improve health and prevent disease in their community. Recommendations are provided by topic and include mental health, substance abuse (alcohol), social environment, and violence.	• The Community Preventive Services Task Force recommendations by topic • Presentation and promotion materials listed • Provides information on community preventive services that have been proven to be effective • Information provided on cost of interventions and likely return on investment
The National Implementation Research Network (NIRN) http://nirn.fpg.unc.edu/	NIRN's mission is to contribute best practices regarding the science of implementation across the human service domains of social services, health, and education. NIRN intends to help establish an evidence base for the implementation processes and practices of evidenced-based programs.	• Intended for researchers, program developers, consumers, and providers • Description of intervention implementation • Information on fidelity measurement • Guidance on staffing • Evidence-based practice references

Note

1. This list is representative of several such registries available via open access on the World Wide Web and is not intended to be exhaustive.

References

Department of Health and Human Services (HHS). (2013). *Prevention Evidence-Based Practice Registries*. Retrieved December 1, 2013, from HHS: Administration for Children and Families: www.childwelfare.gov/preventing/evidence/ebp_registries.cfm

Substance Abuse and Mental Health Services Administration (SAMHSA). (2012). *A Pocket Guide to Evidence-Based Practices (EBP) on the Web*. Retrieved November 10, 2013, from SAMHSA: www.samhsa.gov/ebpwebguide/index.asp

APPENDIX B

Evidence-Based Recommendations for Implementation of Behavioral Health and Substance Use Interventions by Non-Specialist Providers[1]

Area of Identified Challenge	Recommendations Based on Evidence-Based Guidelines
Depression: Adult with Depressive Episode/ Disorder	Brief, Structured Psychological Treatment • Depressive Episode/Disorder: Interpersonal therapy, cognitive behavioral therapy, and problem-solving treatment should be considered as treatment options. Therapy can be provided by specialists and interventions/training by non-specialist providers. • Moderate to Severe Depression: Problem-solving treatment should be considered in addition to use of antidepressants. Behavioral Activation[i] • Should be considered as treatment option with depressive episode/disorder. With moderate or severe depression, the intervention should be considered in addition to use of antidepressants. Relaxation Training • Should be considered as treatment option with depressive episode/disorder. With moderate or severe depression, the intervention should be considered in addition to use of antidepressants. Physical Activity • Physical activity should be encouraged as a part of treatment for depressed adults with inactive lifestyles. • With moderate or severe depression, the intervention should be used with antidepressants or brief, structured psychological treatments. Pharmaceutical Treatment • Should be considered on case-by-case basis under the direction of a specialist.

Child and Adolescent Behavioral Health Issues	Maternal Behavioral Health Interventions to Improve Child Development

Maternal Behavioral Health Interventions to Improve Child Development

- Parenting interventions that promote mother–infant interactions and include psychosocial stimulation can be used to improve child development outcomes. These interventions are particularly relevant in families where the child is poorly nourished, frequently ill, or at risk.
- To improve child development outcomes, mothers with depression or with any other behavioral health or substance use condition should be treated with appropriate interventions (see recommendations relevant to specific conditions).
- Additional psychosocial support such as home visits, psychoeducation, and knowledge expansion techniques (e.g., parenting education) should be offered to mothers with depression or with any other behavioral health or substance use condition.

Interventions for Preventing Child Abuse

- Home-based sessions can be offered to consumers for parent education purposes.
- Collaboration with school-based prevention programs (i.e., sexual abuse prevention and violence and injury prevention).

Interventions Intellectual Disabilities/Child and Adolescent

- Assessment of children suspected of intellectual and other developmental delays by brief, locally validated questionnaires.
- Clinical assessment to identify common causes of intellectual disabilities, under supervision of specialists where available. May offer referral as appropriate.
- Monitoring children's intellectual, social, and emotional development routinely as part of the mother and child health programs (using locally validated tools).

Community-Based Rehabilitation (CBR)

- Collaborating and facilitating referral to and from community-based rehabilitation (CBR) programs, if available, for care of persons with intellectual disabilities.

(Continued)

(Continued)

Area of Identified Challenge	Recommendations Based on Evidence-Based Guidelines
	Parent Skills Training for Emotional and Behavioral Issues in Children
	• Parenting training can be used to build skills in interacting with children with emotional and behavioral disorders. Such programs include positive parent–child interactions and emotional communication, the importance of time out and parenting consistency, the importance of using discipline that is not harsh, and requiring parents to practice new skills with their children during parent training sessions.
	Skills Training for Parents of Children with Intellectual Disabilities and Pervasive Developmental Disorders
	• Parenting training can be used to build skills in interacting with children with intellectual disabilities and PDD. Such training should use culturally appropriate training material relevant for these disorders to improve development, functioning, and participation of the children within the family and community.
	Interventions for Children with Attention Deficit Hyperactivity Disorder (ADHD)
	• Parent education/training should commence before starting medication for a child who has been diagnosed with attention deficit hyperactivity disorder (ADHD). Initial interventions may include cognitive behavioral therapy and social skills training.
	Somatoform Disorders
	• Brief psychological interventions, including cognitive behavioral therapy (CBT) should be considered to treat somatoform disorders in children (if specialists or adequate training and supervision by specialists can be made available).
	Behavior Change Techniques to Promote Behavioral Health
	• Non-specialized healthcare facilities should encourage and collaborate with school-based life skills education (e.g., peer pressure resistance, increasing self-esteem, reducing risk-behavior) to promote behavioral health in children and adolescents.

Pharmaceutical Treatment

- Should be considered on case-by-case basis under the direction of a specialist.

Psychosis and Bipolar Disorders

Psychoeducation, Family Interventions, and Cognitive Behavioral Therapy
Psychotic and Bipolar Disorders:

- Psychoeducation should be routinely offered to consumer and family members/caregivers.
- Cognitive behavioral therapy and family interventions can be considered if adequately trained professionals are available. These interventions should be continued as long as needed by the consumer and his or her family.

Psychosocial Strategies to Bolster Independent Living and Social Skills

- Psychosocial interventions can enhance skill building, coping skills development, and serve to support independent living goals. Consumers and their support systems should be involved in the design, implementation, and evaluation of these psychosocial interventions. Providers delivering psychosocial interventions should have an appropriate level of competence and, wherever possible, be regularly supervised by relevant specialists. Psychosocial interventions should be continued as long as needed by the consumer and his or her family.
- Having a home of their own can be an important goal for consumers. Providers can facilitate supported housing options for consumers. Careful consideration should be given to the consumer's functional capacity and the need for stability and support in advising and facilitating optimal housing arrangements.
- Social skills training can be an important psychosocial strategy and can be used along with other psychosocial interventions.

Vocational and Economic Inclusion

- Non-specialist healthcare providers can facilitate opportunities for consumers to be included in economic activities appropriate to their social and cultural environment.
- Facilitation of supported employment may be considered a critical service option for consumers with mental and substance use disorders if they have difficulty in obtaining or retaining standard employment.

(*Continued*)

(Continued)

Area of Identified Challenge	Recommendations Based on Evidence-Based Guidelines
	Strategies to Improve Community Attitude Toward Consumers • Anti-stigma campaigns can be planned and implemented with the involvement of consumers, their caregivers, and other supports. Through positive social contact with consumers who have behavioral health and substance use conditions, the wider community can be enhanced. Pharmaceutical Treatment • Should be considered on case-by-case basis under the direction of a specialist.
Self-Harm and Suicide	Triage • Non-specialist healthcare providers should ask consumers with behavioral health issues, substance abuse disorders, chronic pain or acute emotional distress associated with current interpersonal conflict, recent loss, or other severe life event, about thoughts or plans of self-harm. Planning for Safety (Providers can assist the consumer and family in some practical steps to address safety around self-harm issues): • Remove means for self-harm • Schedule regular contact • Reduce availability of drugs and alcohol • Assess for and utilize social supports • Utilize a structured problem-solving approach • In situations where the provider is concerned about imminent risk of self-harm, an urgent referral to mental health services should be made. If the service is not available, family, friends, and supports (formal and informal) should be gathered to ensure close monitoring of the consumer as long as the risk persists.
Trauma	Symptom Reduction in Consumers with PTSD • Provider can utilize graded self-exposure based on cognitive behavioral therapy principles. • Where specialists are available, individual or group cognitive behavioral therapy (CBT) with a trauma focus, eye movement desensitization and reprocessing (EMDR), or stress management should be considered for adults, children, and adolescents with PTSD. Non-specialists can conduct behavioral and skill-building techniques associated with these interventions.

Post-Trauma Exposure

- Psychological debriefing should be used for someone who recently was exposed to a traumatic event to reduce the risk of PTSD, anxiety, and depression.
- Provide access to support based on the principles of psychological first aid for those in acute distress that were recently exposed to a traumatic event.

Panic Attacks

- Treatment based upon cognitive behavioral therapy principles.
- Relaxation training should be considered a treatment for anxiety disorders (in absence of depressive episode/disorder)

Pharmaceutical Treatment

- Should be considered on case-by-case basis under the direction of a specialist.

---

i Behavioral activation is a behavioral treatment with a primary focus on changing behaviors to address problems individuals are experiencing.

Adapted from World Health Organization (WHO). (2012). *mhGAP Evidence Resource Centre*. Retrieved December 1, 2013, from WHO: www.who.int/mental_health/mhgap/evidence/en/

Note

1. Non-specialist refers to community-based health workers, trained paraprofessionals, and trained or certified peer specialists that can be used to provide needed intervention services in geographic areas where there is not a sufficient number of specialty staff. Specialists have a substantial role in training, supporting, and supervising non-specialist staff members.

APPENDIX C

Evidence-Based Programs and Practices Evaluated in Home-Based Settings for Children and Adolescents (Behavioral Health and Substance Use Issues)[1]

Name of Intervention	Description of Program or Practice
Active Parenting Now	Active Parenting Now is a video-based education program targeted to parents of 2- to 12-year-olds who want to improve their parenting skills. It is based on the application of Adlerian parenting theory, which is defined by mutual respect among family members within a democratically run family.
Active Parenting of Teens: Families in Action	Active Parenting of Teens: Families in Action is a school- and community-based intervention for middle school–aged youth designed to increase protective factors that prevent and reduce alcohol, tobacco, and other drug use; irresponsible sexual behavior; and violence.
Adolescent Community Reinforcement Approach (A-CRA)	The Adolescent Community Reinforcement Approach (A-CRA) to alcohol and substance use treatment is a behavioral intervention that seeks to replace environmental contingencies that have supported alcohol or drug use with prosocial activities and behaviors that support recovery.
AMIkids Personal Growth Model	The AMIkids Personal Growth Model (PGM) is a comprehensive approach to treatment for 10- to 17-year-old youth who have been adjudicated and, in lieu of incarceration, assigned to a day treatment program, residential treatment setting, or alternative school or who have been assigned to an alternative school after failing in a conventional school setting.
BrainTrain4Kids	BrainTrain4Kids is an interactive website (www.BrainTrain4Kids.com) that teaches children ages 7 to 9 years about the brain and the effects of drugs on the brain and body, building a foundation for later substance abuse prevention efforts.

Brief Strategic Family Therapy	Brief Strategic Family Therapy (BSFT) is designed to (1) prevent, reduce, and/or treat adolescent behavior problems such as drug use, conduct problems, delinquency, sexually risky behavior, aggressive/ violent behavior, and association with antisocial peers; (2) improve prosocial behaviors such as school attendance and performance; and (3) improve family functioning, including effective parental leadership and management, positive parenting, and parental involvement with the child and his or her peers and school.
Chestnut Health Systems–Bloomington Adolescent Outpatient (OP) and Intensive (IOP) Treatment Model	The Chestnut Health Systems–Bloomington Adolescent Outpatient (OP) and Intensive Outpatient (IOP) Treatment Model is designed for youth between the ages of 12 and 18 who meet the American Society of Addiction Medicine's criteria for Level I or Level II treatment placement.
Child–Parent Psychotherapy (CPP)	Child–Parent Psychotherapy (CPP) is an intervention for children from birth through age 5 who have experienced at least one traumatic event (e.g., maltreatment, the sudden or traumatic death of someone close, a serious accident, sexual abuse, exposure to domestic violence) and, as a result, are experiencing behavior, attachment, and/or mental health problems, including post-traumatic stress disorder (PTSD).
Children's Summer Treatment Program	The Children's Summer Treatment Program (STP) is a comprehensive intervention for children with attention deficit hyperactivity disorder (ADHD) and related disruptive behaviors. The program focuses on the child's peer relations, the child's academic/classroom functioning, and the parents' parenting skills—three domains that drive outcomes in children with these conditions.
Clinician-Based Cognitive Psychoeducational Intervention for Families	The Clinician-Based Cognitive Psychoeducational Intervention is intended for families with parents with significant mood disorder. Based on public health models, the intervention is designed to provide information about mood disorders to parents, equip parents with skills they need to communicate this information to their children, and open dialogue in families about the effects of parental depression.
Collaborative HIV Prevention and Adolescent Mental Health Project (CHAMP) Family Program	The Collaborative HIV Prevention and Adolescent Mental Health Project (CHAMP) Family Program is a 12-week, family-focused, developmentally timed intervention for fourth- and fifth-grade students in urban, low-income communities.

(Continued)

(Continued)

Name of Intervention	Description of Program or Practice
Early Risers "Skills for Success"	Early Risers "Skills for Success" is a multicomponent, developmentally focused, competency-enhancement program that targets 6- to 12-year-old elementary school students who are at high risk for early development of conduct problems, including substance use.
Familias Unidas Preventative Intervention	The Familias Unidas Preventive Intervention is a family-based program for Hispanic families with children ages 12 to 17. It is designed to prevent conduct disorders; use of illicit drugs, alcohol, and cigarettes; and risky sexual behaviors by improving family functioning.
Family Behavior Therapy	Family Behavior Therapy (FBT) is an outpatient behavioral treatment aimed at reducing drug and alcohol use in adults and youth along with common co-occurring problem behaviors such as depression, family discord, school and work attendance, and conduct problems in youth.
Family Matters	Family Matters is a family-directed program to prevent adolescents 12 to 14 years of age from using tobacco and alcohol. The intervention is designed to influence population-level prevalence and can be implemented with large numbers of geographically dispersed families.
Family Support Network (FSN)	Family Support Network (FSN) is an outpatient substance abuse treatment program targeting youth ages 10 to 18 years. FSN includes a family component along with a 12-session, adolescent-focused cognitive behavioral therapy—called Motivational Enhancement Therapy/Cognitive Behavioral Therapy (MET/CBT12)—and case management.
Footprints for Life	Footprints for Life is a universal intervention that is designed to help 2nd- and 3rd-grade students build a strong foundation of life skills rooted in key social competencies. The curriculum-based program focuses on planning and decision making, cultural competence, and interpersonal skills, such as handling peer pressure (e.g., refusal skills) and resolving conflicts peacefully.
Grief and Trauma Intervention (GTI) for Children	Grief and Trauma Intervention (GTI) for Children is designed for children ages 7 to 12 with post-traumatic stress due to witnessing or being a direct victim of one or more types of violence or a disaster, or due to experiencing or witnessing the death of a loved one, including death by homicide.

HOMEBUILDERS	HOMEBUILDERS is an intensive family preservation services program designed to improve family functioning and children's behavior and to prevent out-of-home placement of children into foster or group care, psychiatric hospitals, or correctional facilities.
Incredible Years	Incredible Years is a set of three interlocking, comprehensive, and developmentally based training programs for children and their parents and teachers. These programs are guided by developmental theory on the role of multiple interacting risk and protective factors in the development of conduct problems.
Keep a Clear Mind (KACM)	Keep a Clear Mind (KACM) is a take-home drug education program for elementary school students in grades four through six (ages 9 to 11) and their parents. KACM is designed to help children develop specific skills to refuse and avoid use of "gateway" drugs.
Michigan Model for Health	The Michigan Model for Health is a comprehensive and sequential health education curriculum that aims to give students ages 5 to 19 years (grades K through 12) the knowledge and skills needed to practice and maintain healthy behaviors and lifestyles.
Model Adolescent Suicide Prevention Program (MASPP)	The Model Adolescent Suicide Prevention Program (MASPP) is a public health–oriented suicidal-behavior prevention and intervention program originally developed for a small American Indian tribe in rural New Mexico to target high rates of suicide among its adolescents and young adults.
Multidimensional Family Therapy (MDFT)	Multidimensional Family Therapy (MDFT) is a comprehensive and multisystemic family-based outpatient or partial hospitalization (day treatment) program for substance-abusing adolescents, adolescents with co-occurring substance use and mental disorders, and those at high risk for continued substance abuse and other problem behaviors such as conduct disorder and delinquency.
Multidimensional Treatment Foster Care (MTFC)	Multidimensional Treatment Foster Care (MTFC) is a community-based intervention for adolescents (12 to 17 years of age) with severe and chronic delinquency and their families. It was developed as an alternative to group home treatment or state training facilities for youths who have been removed from their home due to conduct and delinquency problems, substance use, and/or involvement with the juvenile justice system.

(*Continued*)

(Continued)

Name of Intervention	Description of Program or Practice
Multisystemic Therapy (MST) for Juvenile Offenders	Multisystemic Therapy (MST) for Juvenile Offenders addresses the multidimensional nature of behavior problems in troubled youth. Treatment focuses on those factors in each youth's social network that are contributing to his or her antisocial behavior.
Multisystemic Therapy for Youth with Problem Sexual Behaviors (MST-PSB)	Multisystemic Therapy for Youth with Problem Sexual Behaviors (MST-PSB) is a clinical adaptation of Multisystemic Therapy (MST) that is specifically targeted to adolescents who have committed sexual offenses and demonstrated other problem behaviors.
Multisystemic Therapy with Psychiatric Supports (MST-Psychiatric)	Multisystemic Therapy with Psychiatric Supports (MST-Psychiatric) is designed to treat youth who are at risk for out-of-home placement (in some cases, psychiatric hospitalization) due to serious behavioral problems and co-occurring mental health symptoms such as thought disorder, bipolar affective disorder, depression, anxiety, and impulsivity.
Nurse–Family Partnership	Nurse–Family Partnership (NFP) is a prenatal and infancy nurse home visitation program that aims to improve the health, well-being, and self-sufficiency of low-income, first-time parents and their children.
Nurturing Parenting Program	The Nurturing Parenting Programs (NPP) are family-based programs for the prevention and treatment of child abuse and neglect. The programs were developed to help families who have been identified by child welfare agencies for past child abuse and neglect or who are at high risk for child abuse and neglect.
Parenting Fundamentals	Parenting Fundamentals (formerly called the Parenting Education Program) is a group-based parent education and skills training program for parents who speak English or Spanish and, often, have low incomes, are part of an immigrant family, and/or are involved with the court or social service system.
Parenting with Love and Limits (PLL)	Parenting with Love and Limits (PLL) combines group therapy and family therapy to treat children and adolescents ages 10 to 18 who have severe emotional and behavioral problems (e.g., conduct disorder, oppositional defiant disorder, attention deficit hyperactivity disorder) and frequently co-occurring problems such as depression, alcohol or drug use, chronic truancy, destruction of property, domestic violence, or suicidal ideation.
Parents as Teachers (PAT)	Parents as Teachers (PAT) is an early childhood family support and parent education home-visiting model. Families may enroll in Parents as Teachers beginning with pregnancy and may remain in the program until the child enters kindergarten.

Project ACHIEVE	Project ACHIEVE is a comprehensive school reform and improvement program for preschool through high school (students ages 3 to 18 years) that focuses on students' academic, social-emotional/behavioral, and social skills outcomes; school-wide positive behavioral support systems and school safety; positive classroom and school climates; and community and parent outreach and involvement.
Real Life Heroes	Real Life Heroes (RLH) is based on cognitive behavioral therapy models for treating post-traumatic stress disorder (PTSD) in school-aged youth. Designed for use in child and family agencies, RLH can be used to treat attachment, loss, and trauma issues resulting from family violence, disasters, severe and chronic neglect, physical and sexual abuse, repeated traumas, and post-traumatic developmental disorder.
Rock in Prevention, Rock PLUS	Rock in Prevention, Rock PLUS, is a 12-week classroom curriculum designed for grades 3 to 6 that uses music and the arts as interactive teaching tools to influence behaviors and attitudes related to the use of four targeted substances: alcohol, tobacco, marijuana, and inhalants.
SODAS City	SODAS City, a self-instructional software program for preadolescents and adolescents, is designed to help prevent participants' current and future use of alcohol and other substances, as well as the problems associated with this use.
SPORT	SPORT, a motivational intervention designed for use by all adolescents, integrates substance abuse prevention with health promotion to help adolescents minimize and avoid substance use while increasing physical activity and other health-enhancing habits, including eating well and getting adequate sleep.
Strengthening Families Program	The Strengthening Families Program (SFP) is a family skills training program designed to increase resilience and reduce risk factors for behavioral, emotional, academic, and social problems in children 3 to 16 years old.

Adapted from Substance Abuse and Mental Health Services Administration (SAMHSA). (2013). *NREPP: SAMHSA's National Registry of Evidence-Based Programs and Practices.* Retrieved December 1, 2013, from SAMHSA: http://nrepp.samhsa.gov/Search.aspx

Note

1. This listing is a representative sample of researched practices in behavioral health and addictions and is not inclusive of all EBPs.

APPENDIX D

Evidence-Based Programs and Practices Evaluated in Home-Based Settings for Adults (Behavioral Health and Substance Use Issues)[1]

Name of Intervention	Description of Program or Practice
Behavioral Day Treatment and Contingency Managed Housing and Work Therapy	Behavioral Day Treatment and Contingency Managed Housing and Work Therapy is a manualized program for adults who are homeless and have co-occurring substance use and non-psychotic mental disorders. The program, which is based on therapeutic goals management, helps participants to stop using substances and provides them with housing and work training.
Brief Self-Directed Gambling Treatment	Brief Self-Directed Gambling Treatment (BSGT) aims to help adults stop or cut back on problematic gambling, which is often chronic and long-term. It is designed for individuals who choose not to enter or are unable to access face-to-face treatment.
Choosing Life: Empowerment! Action! Results! (CLEAR) Program for Young People Living with HIV	The Choosing Life: Empowerment! Action! Results! (CLEAR) Program for Young People Living With HIV targets HIV-positive adolescents and young adults (ages 16 to 29 years) and is designed to prevent the transmission of HIV by reducing substance use and unprotected sex.
Community Advocacy Project (CAP)	The Community Advocacy Project (CAP) provides advocacy and individually tailored assistance to women who have been physically and/or emotionally abused by intimate partners as well as to their children, who may have been bystanders in abusive situations.
Compeer Model	The Compeer Model is designed for use with adults (including veterans and their families), youth (including children with an incarcerated parent), and older adults who have been referred by a mental health professional and diagnosed with a serious mental illness (e.g., bipolar disorder, delusional disorder, depressive disorder).

Depression Prevention (Managing Your Mood)	The Depression Prevention (Managing Your Mood) program is a computer-tailored intervention for adults who are experiencing at least mild symptoms of depression. The program is based on the Transtheoretical Model of Behavior Change (TTM), which conceptualizes change as a process that occurs over time and in five stages: precontemplation, contemplation, preparation, action, and maintenance.
Kognito At-Risk for College Students	Kognito At-Risk for College Students is a 30-minute, online, interactive training simulation that prepares college students and student leaders, including resident assistants, to provide support to peers who are exhibiting signs of psychological distress such as depression, anxiety, substance abuse, and suicidal ideation.
Kognito Family of Heroes	Kognito Family of Heroes is a 1-hour, online role-playing training simulation for military families of service members recently returned from deployment (within the past 4 years). The training is designed to: (1) increase awareness of signs of post-deployment stress, including post-traumatic stress disorder (PTSD), traumatic brain injury (TBI), depression, and suicidal ideation, and (2) motivate family members to access mental health services when they show signs of post-deployment stress.
ModerateDrinking.com and Moderation Management	ModerateDrinking.com and Moderation Management are complementary online interventions designed for non-dependent, heavy-drinking adults who want to reduce the number of days on which they drink, their peak alcohol use on days they drink, and their alcohol-related problems.
MoodGYM	MoodGYM is a free online program that aims to reduce mild to moderate symptoms of depression in adults by teaching them the principles of cognitive behavior therapy. The program is made up of five 20- to 40-minute modules, an interactive game, anxiety and depression assessments, a downloadable relaxation audio file, an online workbook for users to record their responses to quizzes and exercises and track their progress through the program, and a feedback assessment.
New York University Caregiver Intervention (NYUCI)	New York University Caregiver Intervention (NYUCI) is a counseling and support intervention for spouse caregivers that is intended to improve the well-being of caregivers and delay the nursing home placement of patients with Alzheimer's disease.
Oxford House Model	The Oxford House Model provides housing and rehabilitative support for adults who are recovering from alcohol and/or drug use and who want to remain abstinent from use. The model is a confederation of

(Continued)

189

(Continued)

Name of Intervention	Description of Program or Practice
	chartered community-based, self-supported rental homes that are operated under the umbrella of Oxford House World Services.
Pathways Housing First Model	Housing First, a program developed by Pathways to Housing, Inc., is designed to end homelessness and support recovery for individuals who are homeless and have severe psychiatric disabilities and co-occurring substance use disorders.
Program to Encourage Active, Rewarding Lives for Seniors (PEARLS)	The Program to Encourage Active, Rewarding Lives for Seniors (PEARLS) is an intervention for people 60 years and older who have minor depression or dysthymia and are receiving home-based social services from community services agencies.
Resources for Enhancing Alzheimer's Caregiver Health II (Reach II)	Resources for Enhancing Alzheimer's Caregiver Health II (REACH II) is a multicomponent psychosocial and behavioral training intervention for caregivers (21 years and older) of patients with Alzheimer's disease or dementia.
Transtheoretical Model (TTM)-Based Stress Management Program	The Transtheoretical Model (TTM)-Based Stress Management Program targets adults who have not been practicing effective stress management for 6 months or longer. TTM is a theory of behavior change that can be applied to single, multiple, and complex behavioral targets.

Adapted from Substance Abuse and Mental Health Services Administration (SAMHSA). (2013). *NREPP: SAMHSA's National Registry of Evidence-Based Programs and Practices.* Retrieved December 1, 2013, from SAMHSA: http://nrepp.samhsa.gov/Search.aspx

Programs from Appendix C that can also be used for Adult population (family interventions, parenting training, or young adult interventions):

Active Parenting Now, Active Parenting of Teens: Families in Action, Adolescent Community Reinforcement Approach (A-CRA), Chestnut Health Systems–Bloomington Adolescent Outpatient (OP) and Intensive (IOP) Treatment Model, Child–Parent Psychotherapy (CPP), Clinician-Based Cognitive Psychoeducational Intervention for Families, Early Risers "Skills for Success," Familias Unidas Preventative Intervention, Family Behavior Therapy, Incredible Years, Keep a Clear Mind (KACM), Model Adolescent Suicide Prevention Program (MASPP), Nurse–Family Partnership, Nurturing Parenting Program, Parenting Fundamentals, Project ACHIEVE, Strengthening Families Program

Note

1. This listing is a representative sample of researched practices in behavioral health and addictions and is not inclusive of all EBPs.

APPENDIX E

Evidence-Based Programs and Practices
Evaluated in Other Community-Based Settings
(e.g., natural community settings, schools, juvenile
justice, community meeting rooms, multimedia)
for Children and Adolescents (Behavioral
Health and Substance Use Issues)[1]

Name of Intervention	Description of Program or Practice
Across Ages	Across Ages is a school- and community-based substance abuse prevention program for youth ages 9 to 13. The unique feature of Across Ages is the pairing of older adult mentors (55 years and older) with young adolescents, specifically those making the transition to middle school.
Al's Pals: Kids Making Healthy Choices	Al's Pals: Kids Making Healthy Choices is a school-based prevention program that seeks to develop social-emotional skills such as self-control, problem solving, and healthy decision making in children ages 3 to 8 in preschool, kindergarten, and first grade.
Alcohol: True Stories Hosted by Matt Damon	Alcohol: True Stories Hosted by Matt Damon is a multimedia intervention designed to prevent or reduce alcohol use among young people in grades 5 through 12 by positively changing the attitudes of youth and their parents and other caregivers in regard to youth drinking.
American Indian Life Skills Development/ Zuni Life Skills Development	Suicide is the second leading cause of death among American Indians 15 to 24 years old, according to Centers for Disease Control and Prevention data. The estimated rate of completed suicides among American Indians in this age group is about three times higher than among comparably aged U.S. youth overall (37.4 vs. 11.4 per 100,000, respectively).
Big Brothers Big Sisters Mentoring Program	The Big Brothers Big Sisters Mentoring Program is designed to help participating youth ages 6 to 18 ("Littles") reach their potential through supported matches with adult volunteer mentors ages 18 and older ("Bigs").

(Continued)

Name of Intervention	Description of Program or Practice
Building Assets—Reducing Risks (BARR)	Building Assets—Reducing Risks (BARR) is a multifaceted school-based prevention program designed to decrease the incidence of substance abuse (tobacco, alcohol, and other drugs), academic failure, truancy, and disciplinary incidents among ninth-grade youth.
CAPSLE: Creating a Peaceful School Learning Environment	CAPSLE: Creating a Peaceful School Learning Environment, a school-wide climate change intervention for students in kindergarten through 12th grade, is designed to reduce student aggression, victimization, aggressive bystander behavior, and disruptive or off-task classroom behaviors.
Capturing Kids' Hearts Teen Leadership Program	The Capturing Kids' Hearts Teen Leadership Program, a curriculum-based intervention for middle and high school youth, is designed to improve students' emotional well-being and social functioning, including improving communication with parents, reducing feelings of loneliness and isolation, improving self-efficacy, and minimizing problem behaviors.
Celebrating Families!	Celebrating Families! (CF!) is a parenting skills training program designed for families in which one or both parents are in early stages of recovery from substance addiction and in which there is a high risk for domestic violence and/or child abuse.
Chicago Parenting Program	The Chicago Parent Program (CPP) is a parenting skills training program that aims to reduce behavior problems in children ages 2 to 5 by improving parenting self-efficacy and promoting positive parenting behavior and child discipline strategies.
Children in Between	Children in Between (CIB), formerly known as Children in the Middle, is an educational intervention for divorcing families that aims to reduce the parental conflict, loyalty pressures, and communication problems that can place significant stress on children.
Community Trials Intervention to Reduce High-Risk Driving	Community Trials Intervention to Reduce High-Risk Drinking is a multicomponent, community-based program developed to alter the alcohol use patterns and related problems of people of all ages. The program incorporates a set of environmental interventions that assist communities in (1) using zoning and municipal regulations to restrict alcohol access through alcohol outlet density control; (2) enhancing responsible beverage service by training, testing, and assisting beverage servers and retailers in the development of policies and procedures to reduce intoxication and driving after drinking; (3) increasing law enforcement and sobriety checkpoints to raise

actual and perceived risk of arrest for driving after drinking; (4) reducing youth access to alcohol by training alcohol retailers to avoid selling to minors and those who provide alcohol to minors; and (5) forming the coalitions needed to implement and support the interventions that address each of these prevention components.

Creating Lasting Family Connections (CLFC)/Creating Lasting Connections (CLC)	Creating Lasting Family Connections (CLFC), the currently available version of Creating Lasting Connections (CLC), is a family-focused program that aims to build the resiliency of youth ages 9 to 17 years and reduce the frequency of their alcohol and other drug (AOD) use.
Cultural Adaptation of Cognitive Behavioral Therapy (CBT) for Puerto Rican Youth	Cultural Adaptation of Cognitive Behavioral Therapy (CBT) for Puerto Rican Youth is a short-term intervention for Puerto Rican adolescents ages 13 to 17 years who are primarily Spanish speaking and have severe symptoms of depression.
Dare to Be You	DARE to Be You (DTBY) is a multilevel prevention program that serves high-risk families with children 2 to 5 years old. Program objectives focus on children's developmental attainments and aspects of parenting that contribute to youth resilience to later substance abuse, including parental self-efficacy, effective child rearing, social support, and problem-solving skills.
Emergency Room Intervention for Adolescent Females	Emergency Room Intervention for Adolescent Females is a program for teenage girls 12 to 18 years old who are admitted to the emergency room after attempting suicide. The intervention, which involves the girl and one or more family members who accompany her to the emergency room, aims to increase attendance in outpatient treatment following discharge from the emergency room and to reduce future suicide attempts.
Families and Schools Together (FAST)	Families and Schools Together (FAST) is a multifamily group intervention designed to build relationships between families, schools, and communities to increase well-being among elementary school children.
Family Foundations	Family Foundations, a program for adult couples expecting their first child, is designed to help them establish positive parenting skills and adjust to the physical, social, and emotional challenges of parenthood.
Healer Women Fighting Disease Integrated Substance Abuse and HIV Prevention Program for African American Women (HWFD)	Healer Women Fighting Disease Integrated Substance Abuse and HIV Prevention Program for African American Women (HWFD) targets African American women who are 13 to 55 years old and at risk of contracting HIV/AIDS and transmitting HIV through unsafe sexual activity and substance abuse.

(*Continued*)

(Continued)

Name of Intervention	Description of Program or Practice
Healthy Alternatives for Little Ones (HALO)	Healthy Alternatives for Little Ones (HALO) is a 12-unit holistic health and substance abuse prevention curriculum for children ages 3 to 6 in child care settings. HALO is designed to address risk and protective factors for substance abuse and other health behaviors by providing children with information on healthy choices.
Hip-Hop 2 Prevent Substance Abuse and HIV (H2P)	Hip-Hop 2 Prevent Substance Abuse and HIV (H2P) is designed to improve knowledge and skills related to drugs and HIV/AIDS among youth ages 12 to 16 with the aim of preventing or reducing their substance use and risky sexual activity.
I'm Special	I'm Special is a substance abuse prevention program for third and fourth graders. The primary goal of the program is to develop and nurture each child's sense of uniqueness and self-worth. It further enhances the protective and resiliency factors of children by teaching them appropriate ways for dealing with feelings; steps for making decisions; and skills for healthy living, effective group interactions, and resisting drugs, as provided through the program's "no use" message.
Joven Noble	Joven Noble is a youth development, support, and leadership enhancement curriculum designed to strengthen protective factors among male Latino youth ages 10 to 24. The curriculum aims to promote the character development of young men and facilitate continued "rites of passage" development with the goals of reducing and preventing unwanted or unplanned pregnancies, substance abuse, community violence, and relationship violence.
Lead & Seed	Lead & Seed is an intervention for middle and high school youth designed to increase their knowledge and problem-solving skills for preventing and reducing alcohol, tobacco, and other drug (ATOD) use; guide them in developing strategic prevention plans for use in their schools and communities; and help them implement these plans.
Parent Corps	Parent Corps is a culturally informed, family-centered preventive intervention designed to foster healthy development and school success among young children (ages 3 to 6) in families living in low-income communities.
Parenting through Change	Parenting through Change (PTC) is a theory-based intervention to prevent internalizing and externalizing conduct behaviors and associated problems and promote healthy child adjustment. Based on the Parent Management Training—Oregon Model (PMTO), PTC provides recently separated single mothers with

	14 weekly group sessions to learn effective parenting practices including skill encouragement, limit-setting, problem solving, monitoring, and positive involvement.
Parenting Wisely	Parenting Wisely is a set of interactive, computer-based training programs for parents of children ages 3 to 18 years. Based on social learning, cognitive behavioral, and family systems theories, the programs aim to increase parental communication and disciplinary skills.
Point Break	Point Break is a 1-day workshop for middle and high school students that aims to promote resiliency, break down educational and social barriers between youth, and ultimately, reduce campus violence by teaching the value of conflict resolution and respect for others.
Project MAGIC (Making a Group and Individual Commitment)	Project MAGIC (Making a Group and Individual Commitment) is an alternative to juvenile detention for first-time offenders between the ages of 12 and 18. The program's goals include helping youths achieve academic success; modifying attitudes about alcohol, tobacco, and other drugs; and enhancing life skills development and internal locus of control.
Project SUCCESS	Project SUCCESS (Schools Using Coordinated Community Efforts to Strengthen Students) is designed to prevent and reduce substance use among students 12 to 18 years of age. The program was originally developed for students attending alternative high schools who are at high risk for substance use and abuse due to poor academic performance, truancy, discipline problems, negative attitudes toward school, and parental substance abuse.
Reality Tour	Reality Tour is a volunteer-driven substance abuse prevention program that is presented to parents and their children (ages 10 to 17) in a community setting over the course of one approximately 3-hour session.
Red Cliff Wellness School Curriculum	The Red Cliff Wellness School Curriculum is a substance abuse prevention intervention based in Native American tradition and culture. Designed for grades K through 12, the curriculum aims to reduce risk factors and enhance protective factors related to substance use, including school bonding, success in school, increased perception of risk from substances, and identification and internalization of culturally based values and norms.
Residential Student Assistance Program (RSAP)	The Residential Student Assistance Program (RSAP) is designed to prevent and reduce alcohol and other drug (AOD) use among high-risk multiproblem youth ages 12 to 18 years who have been placed voluntarily or involuntarily in a residential child care facility (e.g., foster care facility, treatment center for adolescents with mental health problems, juvenile correctional facility).

(Continued)

(Continued)

Name of Intervention	Description of Program or Practice
Reward and Reminder	Reward and Reminder, a population-level intervention targeting whole communities, counties, or states, is designed to promote the community norm of not selling tobacco to minors. By using rapid and public rewards and recognition for clerks and retailers/ outlets that do not sell tobacco to minors, Reward and Reminder aims to reduce illegal sales of tobacco, perceived access to tobacco, and tobacco use prevalence rates.
SAFEChildren	Schools and Families Educating Children (SAFEChildren) is a family-focused preventive intervention designed to increase academic achievement and decrease risk for later drug abuse and associated problems such as aggression, school failure, and low social competence.
SANKOFA Youth Violence Prevention Program	The SANKOFA Youth Violence Prevention Program is a strengths-based, culturally tailored preventive intervention for African American adolescents ages 13 to 19. The goal of the school-based intervention is to equip youth with the knowledge, attitudes, skills, confidence, and motivation to minimize their risk for involvement in violence, victimization owing to violence, and other negative behaviors, such as alcohol and other drug use.
Say It Straight (SIS)	Say It Straight (SIS) is a communication training program designed to help students and adults develop empowering communication skills and behaviors and increase self-awareness, self-efficacy, and personal and social responsibility.
Strong African American Families (SAAF)	Strong African American Families (SAAF) is a culturally tailored, family-centered intervention for 10- to 14-year-old African American youths and their primary caregivers. The goal of SAAF is to prevent substance use and behavior problems among youth by strengthening positive family interactions, preparing youths for their teen years, and enhancing primary caregivers' efforts to help youths reach positive goals.
Systematic Training For Effective Parenting (STEP)	Systematic Training for Effective Parenting (STEP) provides skills training for parents dealing with frequently encountered challenges with their children that often result from autocratic parenting styles.
TeenScreen	The Columbia University TeenScreen Program identifies middle school– and high school–aged youth in need of mental health services due to risk for suicide and undetected mental illness. The program's main objective is to assist in the early identification of

	problems that might not otherwise come to the attention of professionals.
Too Good for Violence	Too Good for Violence (TGFV) is a school-based violence prevention and character education program for students in kindergarten through 12th grade. It is designed to enhance prosocial behaviors and skills and improve protective factors related to conflict and violence.
Trauma Affect Regulation: A Guide for Education and Therapy (TARGET)	Trauma Affect Regulation: Guide for Education and Therapy (TARGET) is a strengths-based approach to education and therapy for survivors of physical, sexual, psychological, and emotional trauma. TARGET teaches a set of seven skills (summarized by the acronym FREEDOM—Focus, Recognize triggers, Emotion self-check, Evaluate thoughts, Define goals, Options, and Make a contribution) that can be used by trauma survivors to regulate extreme emotion states, manage intrusive trauma memories, promote self-efficacy, and achieve lasting recovery from trauma.
Triple P—Positive Parenting Program	The Triple P—Positive Parenting Program is a multilevel system or suite of parenting and family support strategies for families with children from birth to age 12, with extensions to families with teenagers ages 13 to 16.
Wyman's Teen Outreach Program	Wyman's Teen Outreach Program (TOP) aims to reduce teens' rates of pregnancy, course failure, and academic suspension by enhancing protective factors. TOP is delivered over 9 months (a full school year) to middle and high school students who voluntarily enroll in the program in school or in an after-school or community-based setting.
Youth Partners In Care—Depression Treatment Quality Improvement (TPIC/ DTQI)	Youth Partners in Care—Depression Treatment Quality Improvement (YPIC/DTQI) is a 6-month quality improvement intervention to improve depression outcomes among adolescents by increasing access to depression treatments, primarily cognitive behavioral therapy (CBT) and antidepressants, in primary care settings.

Adapted from Substance Abuse and Mental Health Services Administration (SAMHSA). (2013). *NREPP: SAMHSA's National Registry of Evidence-Based Programs and Practices.* Retrieved December 1, 2013, from SAMHSA: http://nrepp.samhsa.gov/Search.aspx

Programs from Appendix C that can also be used for community-based interventions:

Active Parenting Now, Active Parenting of Teens: Families in Action, Adolescent Community Reinforcement Approach (A-CRA), Chestnut Health Systems–Bloomington Adolescent Outpatient (OP) and Intensive

(IOP) Treatment Model, Child–Parent Psychotherapy (CPP), Clinician-Based Cognitive Psychoeducational Intervention for Families, Early Risers "Skills for Success," Incredible Years, Model Adolescent Suicide Prevention Program (MASPP), Nurturing Parenting Program, Parenting Fundamentals

Note

1. This listing is a representative sample of researched practices in behavioral health and addictions and is not inclusive of all EBPs.

APPENDIX F

Evidence-Based Programs and Practices Evaluated in Other Community-Based Settings (e.g., natural community settings, jail or detention settings, community meeting rooms, multimedia) for Adults (Behavioral Health and Substance Use Issues)[1]

Name of Intervention	Description of Program or Practice
Behavioral Day Treatment and Contingency Managed Housing and Work Therapy	Behavioral Day Treatment and Contingency Managed Housing and Work Therapy is a manualized program for adults who are homeless and have co-occurring substance use and non-psychotic mental disorders. The program, which is based on therapeutic goals management, helps participants to stop using substances and provides them with housing and work training.
Border Binge Drinking Reduction Program	The Border Binge Drinking Reduction Program provides a process for changing the social and community norms associated with underage and binge drinking that has proven effective at reducing alcohol-related trauma caused by young Americans binge drinking across the U.S.–Mexican border.
Brief Self-Directed Gambling Treatment	Brief Self-Directed Gambling Treatment (BSGT) aims to help adults stop or cut back on problematic gambling, which is often chronic and long-term. It is designed for individuals who choose not to enter or are unable to access face-to-face treatment.
Brief Strengths-Based Case Management for Substance Abuse	Brief Strengths-Based Case Management (SBCM) for Substance Abuse is a one-on-one social service intervention for adults with substance use disorders that is designed to reduce the barriers and time to treatment entry and improve overall client functioning.
Celebrating Families!	Celebrating Families! (CF!) is a parenting skills training program designed for families in which one or both parents are in early stages of recovery from substance addiction and in which there is a high risk for domestic violence and/or child abuse.

(Continued)

199

(Continued)

Name of Intervention	Description of Program or Practice
Challenging College Alcohol Abuse	Challenging College Alcohol Abuse (CCAA) is a social norms and environmental management program aimed at reducing high-risk drinking and related negative consequences among college students (18 to 24 years old).
Chicago Parent Program	The Chicago Parent Program (CPP) is a parenting skills training program that aims to reduce behavior problems in children ages 2 to 5 by improving parenting self-efficacy and promoting positive parenting behavior and child discipline strategies.
Children in Between	Children in Between (CIB), formerly known as Children in the Middle, is an educational intervention for divorcing families that aims to reduce the parental conflict, loyalty pressures, and communication problems that can place significant stress on children.
Choosing Life: Empowerment! Action! Results! (CLEAR) Program for Young People Living with HIV	The Choosing Life: Empowerment! Action! Results! (CLEAR) Program for Young People Living With HIV targets HIV-positive adolescents and young adults (ages 16 to 29 years) and is designed to prevent the transmission of HIV by reducing substance use and unprotected sex.
Communities Mobilizing for Change on Alcohol (CMCA)	Communities Mobilizing for Change on Alcohol (CMCA) is a community-organizing program designed to reduce teens' (13 to 20 years of age) access to alcohol by changing community policies and practices. CMCA seeks both to limit youths' access to alcohol and to communicate a clear message to the community that underage drinking is inappropriate and unacceptable.
Community Advocacy Project (CAP)	The Community Advocacy Project (CAP) provides advocacy and individually tailored assistance to women who have been physically and/or emotionally abused by intimate partners as well as to their children, who may have been bystanders in abusive situations.
Community Trials Intervention to Reduce High-Risk Drinking	Community Trials Intervention to Reduce High-Risk Drinking is a multicomponent, community-based program developed to alter the alcohol use patterns and related problems of people of all ages. The program incorporates a set of environmental interventions that assist communities in (1) using zoning and municipal regulations to restrict alcohol access through alcohol outlet density control; (2) enhancing responsible beverage service by training,

testing, and assisting beverage servers and retailers in the development of policies and procedures to reduce intoxication and driving after drinking; (3) increasing law enforcement and sobriety checkpoints to raise actual and perceived risk of arrest for driving after drinking; (4) reducing youth access to alcohol by training alcohol retailers to avoid selling to minors and those who provide alcohol to minors; and (5) forming the coalitions needed to implement and support the interventions that address each of these prevention components.

Compeer Model

The Compeer Model is designed for use with adults (including veterans and their families), youth (including children with an incarcerated parent), and older adults who have been referred by a mental health professional and diagnosed with a serious mental illness (e.g., bipolar disorder, delusional disorder, depressive disorder).

Computer Assisted System for Patient Assessment and Referral (CASPAR)

The Computer Assisted System for Patient Assessment and Referral (CASPAR) is a comprehensive assessment and services planning process used by substance abuse clinicians to conduct an initial assessment, generate a treatment plan, and link clients admitted to a substance abuse treatment program to appropriate health and social services available either on site within the program or off site in the community.

Contracts, Prompts, and Reinforcement of Substance Use Disorder Continuing Care (CPR)

Contracts, Prompts, and Reinforcement of Substance Use Disorder Continuing Care (CPR) is an after-care intervention for adults that begins in the final week of residential substance abuse treatment.

Creating Lasting Family Connections CLFC/Creating Lasting Connections (CLC)

Creating Lasting Family Connections (CLFC), the currently available version of Creating Lasting Connections (CLC), is a family-focused program that aims to build the resiliency of youth ages 9 to 17 years and reduce the frequency of their alcohol and other drug (AOD) use.

Creating Lasting Family Connections Fatherhood Program: Family Reintegration (CLFCFP)

The Creating Lasting Family Connections Fatherhood Program: Family Reintegration (CLFCFP) is designed for fathers, men in father-like roles (e.g., mentors), and men who are planning to be fathers. The program was developed to help individuals who are experiencing or are at risk for family dissonance resulting from the individual's physical and/or emotional separation (e.g., incarceration, substance abuse, military service).

(Continued)

201

(Continued)

Name of Intervention	Description of Program or Practice
Creating Lasting Family Connections Marriage Enhancement Program (CLFCMEP)	The Creating Lasting Family Connections Marriage Enhancement Program (CLFCMEP) is a community-based effort designed for couples in which one or both partners have been physically and/or emotionally distanced because of separation due to incarceration, military service, substance abuse, or other circumstances.
Critical Time Intervention	Critical Time Intervention (CTI) is designed to prevent recurrent homelessness and other adverse outcomes among persons with severe mental illness. It aims to enhance continuity of care during the transition from institutional to community living.
Customized Employment Supports	Customized Employment Supports (CES, formerly known as Comprehensive Employment Supports) was developed to help methadone treatment patients, who are likely to have irregular work histories, attain rapid placement in paid jobs and increase their legitimate earnings.
DARE to Be You	DARE to Be You (DTBY) is a multilevel prevention program that serves high-risk families with children 2 to 5 years old. Program objectives focus on children's developmental attainments and aspects of parenting that contribute to youth resilience to later substance abuse, including parental self-efficacy, effective child rearing, social support, and problem-solving skills.
DARE to Be You (DTBY) Bridges Program	The DARE to Be You (DTBY) Bridges Program brings together families of children in kindergarten through second grade (ages 5 to 7) and their teachers to support the transition to formal schooling. The goals of the program are to (1) build strong relationships between parents and teachers, and (2) enhance the skills of parents, teachers, and children to improve children's success in school and prevent later problems such as aggression and substance abuse.
Dialectical Behavior Therapy	Dialectical Behavior Therapy (DBT) is a cognitive behavioral treatment approach with two key characteristics: a behavioral, problem-solving focus blended with acceptance-based strategies, and an emphasis on dialectical processes.
Double Trouble in Recovery	Double Trouble in Recovery (DTR) is a mutual aid, self-help program for adults ages 18 to 55 who have been dually diagnosed with mental illness and a substance use disorder. In a mutual aid program, people help each other address a common problem, usually in a group led by consumer facilitators rather than by professional treatment or service providers.

Enhance Wellness	Enhance Wellness is an outpatient intervention for older adults with chronic health conditions such as heart disease, high blood pressure, arthritis, and rheumatism. The program's goal is to help men and women better manage their illnesses and minimize related problems such as unnecessary use of prescription psychoactive medications, physical inactivity, depression, and social isolation.
Family Foundations	Family Foundations, a program for adult couples expecting their first child, is designed to help them establish positive parenting skills and adjust to the physical, social, and emotional challenges of parenthood.
Family Wellness: Survival Skills for Healthy Families	Family Wellness: Survival Skills for Healthy Families is a psychoeducational program designed to help families (including children ages 8 and up) strengthen their connection with each other and reinforce healthy ways of interacting.
Friends Care	Friends Care is a stand-alone after-care program for probationers and parolees exiting mandated outpatient substance abuse treatment. The after-care program is designed to maintain and extend the gains of court-ordered outpatient treatment by helping clients develop and strengthen supports for drug-free living in the community.
Healer Women Fighting Disease Integrated Substance Abuse and HIV Prevention Program for African American Women (HWFD)	Healer Women Fighting Disease Integrated Substance Abuse and HIV Prevention Program for African American Women (HWFD) targets African American women who are 13 to 55 years old and at risk of contracting HIV/AIDS and transmitting HIV through unsafe sexual activity and substance abuse.
Healthy Living Project for People Living with HIV	The Healthy Living Project for People Living With HIV promotes protective health decision making among individuals with HIV—heterosexual women, heterosexual men, gay men, and injection drug users—to reduce substance use and the risk of transmitting HIV.
ICCD Clubhouse	The ICCD (International Center for Clubhouse Development) Clubhouse Model is a day treatment program for rehabilitating adults diagnosed with a mental health problem. The goal of the program is to contribute to the recovery of individuals through use of a therapeutic environment that includes responsibilities within the Clubhouse (e.g., clerical duties, reception, food service, transportation, financial services), as well as through outside employment, education, meaningful relationships, housing, and an overall improved quality of life.

(Continued)

(Continued)

Name of Intervention	Description of Program or Practice
IMPACT (Improving Mood—Promoting Access to Collaborative Treatment	IMPACT (Improving Mood—Promoting Access to Collaborative Treatment) is an intervention for adult patients who have a diagnosis of major depression or dysthymia, often in conjunction with another major health problem.
Interactive Journaling	Interactive Journaling is a goal-directed, client-centered model that aims to reduce substance abuse and substance-related behaviors, such as recidivism, by guiding adults and youth with substance use disorders through a process of written self-reflection.
JOBS Program	The JOBS Program is intended to prevent and reduce negative effects on mental health associated with unemployment and job-seeking stress, while promoting high-quality re-employment. Structured as a job search seminar, the program teaches participants effective strategies for finding and obtaining suitable employment as well as for anticipating and dealing with the inevitable setbacks they will encounter.
Mental Health First Aid	Mental Health First Aid is an adult public education program designed to improve participants' knowledge and modify their attitudes and perceptions about mental health and related issues, including how to respond to individuals who are experiencing one or more acute mental health crises (i.e., suicidal thoughts and/or behavior, acute stress reaction, panic attacks, and/or acute psychotic behavior) or are in the early stages of one or more chronic mental health problems (i.e., depressive, anxiety, and/or psychotic disorders, which may occur with substance abuse).
Motivational Interviewing	Motivational Interviewing (MI) is a goal-directed, client-centered counseling style for eliciting behavioral change by helping clients to explore and resolve ambivalence. The operational assumption in MI is that ambivalent attitudes or lack of resolve is the primary obstacle to behavioral change, so that the examination and resolution of ambivalence becomes its key goal.
National Alliance on Mental Illness (NAMI) Family-to-Family Education Program	The National Alliance on Mental Illness (NAMI) Family-to-Family Education Program is a 12-session course for family caregivers of individuals living with serious mental illness. The curriculum-based course covers a range of topics, including

participants' emotional responses to the impact of mental illness on their lives, current information about many of the major mental illnesses, current research related to the biology of brain disorders, and information on the evidence-based treatments that are most effective in promoting recovery.

Network Therapy	Network Therapy is a substance-abuse treatment approach that engages members of the patient's social support network to support abstinence. Key elements of the approach are: (1) a cognitive behavioral approach to relapse prevention in which patients learn about cues that can trigger relapse and behavioral strategies for avoiding relapse; (2) support from the patient's natural social network; and (3) community reinforcement techniques engaging resources in the social environment to support abstinence.
New York University Caregiver Intervention (NYUCI)	New York University Caregiver Intervention (NYUCI) is a counseling and support intervention for spouse caregivers that is intended to improve the well-being of caregivers and delay the nursing home placement of patients with Alzheimer's disease.
Oxford House Model	The Oxford House Model provides housing and rehabilitative support for adults who are recovering from alcohol and/or drug use and who want to remain abstinent from use. The model is a confederation of chartered community-based, self-supported rental homes that are operated under the umbrella of Oxford House World Services.
Parent Corps	Parent Corps is a culturally informed, family-centered preventive intervention designed to foster healthy development and school success among young children (ages 3 to 6) in families living in low-income communities.
Parenting Through Change	Parenting Through Change (PTC) is a theory-based intervention to prevent internalizing and externalizing conduct behaviors and associated problems and promote healthy child adjustment. Based on the Parent Management Training—Oregon Model (PMTO), PTC provides recently separated single mothers with 14 weekly group sessions to learn effective parenting practices including skill encouragement, limit-setting, problem solving, monitoring, and positive involvement.
Pathways Housing First	Housing First, a program developed by Pathways to Housing, Inc., is designed to end homelessness and support recovery for individuals who are homeless and have severe psychiatric disabilities and co-occurring substance use disorders.

(Continued)

(Continued)

Name of Intervention	Description of Program or Practice
Prevention and Relationship Enhancement Program (PREP)	The goal of the Prevention and Relationship Enhancement Program (PREP) is to modify or enhance those dimensions of couples' relationships that research and theory have linked to effective marital functioning, such as communication, problem-solving skills, and protecting positive connections and expectations.
PRIME for Life	PRIME for Life (PFL) is a motivational intervention used in group settings to prevent alcohol and drug problems or provide early intervention. PFL has been used primarily among court-referred impaired driving offenders, as in the two studies reviewed for this summary.
Prize Incentives Contingency Management for Substance Abuse	Prize Incentives Contingency Management for Substance Abuse is a variation of contingency management, or reinforcement that awards prizes for abstinence and treatment compliance. It is based on a construct central to behavioral psychology known as operant conditioning, or the use of consequences to modify the occurrence and form of behavior.
Program of All-Inclusive Care for the Elderly (PACE)	The Program of All-Inclusive Care for the Elderly (PACE) features a comprehensive and seamless service delivery system and integrated Medicare and Medicaid financing. Eligible individuals are age 55 years or older and meet the clinical criteria to be admitted to a nursing home but choose to remain in the community.
Project MAGIC (Making a Group and Individual Commitment)	Project MAGIC (Making a Group and Individual Commitment) is an alternative to juvenile detention for first-time offenders between the ages of 12 and 18. The program's goals include helping youths achieve academic success; modifying attitudes about alcohol, tobacco, and other drugs; and enhancing life skills development and internal locus of control.
Prolonged Exposure Therapy for Post-traumatic Stress Disorder	Prolonged Exposure (PE) Therapy for Post-traumatic Stress Disorder is a cognitive behavioral treatment program for adult men and women (ages 18 to 65+) who have experienced single or multiple/continuous traumas and have post-traumatic stress disorder (PTSD).
Psychiatric Rehabilitation Process Model	The Psychiatric Rehabilitation Process Model is a process guiding the interaction between a practitioner and an individual with severe mental illness. Manual driven, the model is a client-centered, strengths-based intervention designed to build clients' positive social relationships, encourage self-determination of goals, connect clients to

needed human service supports, and provide direct skills training to maximize independence.

Psychoeducational Multifamily Group	Psychoeducational Multifamily Groups (PMFG) is a treatment modality designed to help individuals with mental illness attain as rich and full participation in the usual life of the community as possible.
Residential Student Assistance Program (RSAP)	The Residential Student Assistance Program (RSAP) is designed to prevent and reduce alcohol and other drug (AOD) use among high-risk multi-problem youth ages 12 to 18 years who have been placed voluntarily or involuntarily in a residential child care facility (e.g., foster care facility, treatment center for adolescents with mental health problems, juvenile correctional facility).
Reward and Reminder	Reward and Reminder, a population-level intervention targeting whole communities, counties, or states, is designed to promote the community norm of not selling tobacco to minors. By using rapid and public rewards and recognition for clerks and retailers/outlets that do not sell tobacco to minors, Reward and Reminder aims to reduce illegal sales of tobacco, perceived access to tobacco, and tobacco use prevalence rates.
SAFEChildren	Schools and Families Educating Children (SAFEChildren) is a family-focused preventive intervention designed to increase academic achievement and decrease risk for later drug abuse and associated problems such as aggression, school failure, and low social competence.
Say It Straight (SIS)	Say It Straight (SIS) is a communication training program designed to help students and adults develop empowering communication skills and behaviors and increase self-awareness, self-efficacy, and personal and social responsibility.
Self-Help in Eliminating Life-Threatening Diseases (SHIELD)	Self-Help in Eliminating Life-Threatening Diseases (SHIELD) is a training program for adult men and women who are current or former drug users with or without HIV. SHIELD trainees become peer educators on risky behaviors for HIV infection, serving as indigenous outreach workers for others in their immediate social network (i.e., sex and drug partners, family members, friends) and/or community network.
Service Outreach and Recovery (SOAR)	Service Outreach and Recovery (SOAR), a multicomponent program for indigent and residentially unstable clients, aims to reduce drug and alcohol use and increase participation in formal substance abuse treatment programs and 12-step self-help groups such as Alcoholics Anonymous and Narcotics Anonymous.

(Continued)

(Continued)

Name of Intervention	Description of Program or Practice
Systematic Training for Effective Parenting (STEP)	Systematic Training for Effective Parenting (STEP) provides skills training for parents dealing with frequently encountered challenges with their children that often result from autocratic parenting styles.
Team Solutions (TS) and Solutions for Wellness (SFW)	Team Solutions (TS) and Solutions for Wellness (SFW) are complementary psychoeducational interventions for adults with a serious mental illness. TS teaches life and illness management skills, while SFW focuses on physical health and wellness.
Telephone Monitoring and Adaptive Counseling (TMAC)	Telephone Monitoring and Adaptive Counseling (TMAC) is a telephone-based continuing care intervention for alcohol and cocaine dependence that is designed to follow a client's initial stabilization in a 3- to 4-week intensive outpatient treatment program.
Trauma Affect Regulation: A Guide for Education and Therapy (TARGET)	Trauma Affect Regulation: Guide for Education and Therapy (TARGET) is a strengths-based approach to education and therapy for survivors of physical, sexual, psychological, and emotional trauma. TARGET teaches a set of seven skills (summarized by the acronym FREEDOM—Focus, Recognize triggers, Emotion self-check, Evaluate thoughts, Define goals, Options, and Make a contribution) that can be used by trauma survivors to regulate extreme emotion states, manage intrusive trauma memories, promote self-efficacy, and achieve lasting recovery from trauma.
Triple P—Positive Parenting Program	The Triple P—Positive Parenting Program is a multilevel system or suite of parenting and family support strategies for families with children from birth to age 12, with extensions to families with teenagers ages 13 to 16.
Wellness Initiative for Senior Education (WISE)	The Wellness Initiative for Senior Education (WISE) is a curriculum-based health promotion program that aims to help older adults increase their knowledge and awareness of issues related to health and the aging process.
Wellness Recovery Action Plan (WRAP)	Wellness Recovery Action Plan (WRAP) is a manualized group intervention for adults with mental illness. WRAP guides participants through the process of identifying and understanding their personal wellness resources ("wellness tools") and then helps them develop an individualized plan to use these resources on a daily basis to manage their mental illness.

Youth Partners in Care—Depression Treatment Quality Improvement (TPIC/DTQI)	Youth Partners in Care—Depression Treatment Quality Improvement (YPIC/DTQI) is a 6-month quality improvement intervention to improve depression outcomes among adolescents by increasing access to depression treatments, primarily cognitive behavioral therapy (CBT) and antidepressants, in primary care settings.

Adapted from Substance Abuse and Mental Health Services Administration (SAMHSA). (2013). *NREPP: SAMHSA's National Registry of Evidence-Based Programs and Practices.* Retrieved December 1, 2013, from SAMHSA: http://nrepp.samhsa.gov/Search.aspx

Programs from Appendix C that can also be used for Adult population (for parenting) in natural community settings:

Active Parenting Now, Active Parenting of Teens: Families in Action, Adolescent Community Reinforcement Approach (A-CRA), Chestnut Health Systems–Bloomington Adolescent Outpatient (OP) and Intensive (IOP) Treatment Model, Child–Parent Psychotherapy (CPP), Clinician-Based Cognitive Psychoeducational Intervention for Families, Early Risers "Skills for Success," Incredible Years, Model Adolescent Suicide Prevention Program (MASPP), Nurturing Parenting Program, Parenting Fundamentals

Note

1. This listing is a representative sample of researched practices in behavioral health and addictions and is not inclusive of all EBPs.

INDEX

Bold indicates a table; italics indicates a figure.

Adult Needs and Strength Assessment (ANSA) 86
Affordable Care Act 160
Alexander, J. 62
American Foundation for Suicide Prevention (AFSP) **172**
American Psychiatric Association (APA) 3
American Society of Addiction Medicine (ASAM) 10
Americans with Disabilities Act of 1990 (ADA) 3, 160
anxiety 59, 118–19, **181**, **186**, **189**, **204**; disorder 57, 100n4, **181**; Generalized Anxiety Disorder (GAD) 59
Assertive Community Treatment (ACT) 37–8, 45, 48, 64–5, 71–2
assessment 12, 15–16, 35, 41, 70, 81, 88, 99, 113; comprehensive 5, 39–40; home-based 40–1; strengths-based 17, 84–7, 89, **90–1**, 114
Attention Deficit Hyperactivity Disorder (ADHD) 36, 59, **178**, **183**
Ayurvedic **30**, **32niii**

Balancing Incentive Program 160
Baum, F. 80
Bavolek, S. 62
Beck, A. 57
Behavioral Activation **176**, **181ni**
BERS (Behavior and Emotional Rating Scale) 86
Borderline Personality Disorder (BPD) 58

California Evidence-Based Clearinghouse for Child Welfare (CEBC) 53, **173**
Campbell Collaboration (C2) **173**
Care Management Organization (CMO) 23
case management 17, 41, 157, **184**; Brief Strengths-Based (SBCM) **199**; Intensive (ICM) 38, 41, 69, 70
Center for Medicaid and CHIP Services (CMCS) 7, 19–20, 23, 43, 157–60
Center for Medicare and Medicaid Services (CMS) 19, 23,156
Center for Mental Health Services (CMHS) 19, 160
Child and Adolescent Needs and Strengths- Mental Health (CANS-MH) 86
Children's Health Act 4
Children's Health Insurance Program (CHIP) 7, 157, 159
Children's Mental Health Initiative (CMHI) 156–7
Child Trends **169**
child welfare 49n1, 53, 73, 161, **173**, **186**
Chinese 56; medicine **32**
Chinese Classification of Mental Disorders (CCMD) 3, 8n8
civil commitment 4, 20n1
clubhouses 42, **203**
cognitive behavioral therapy (CBT) 57, 58, **178**, **180**, **193**
Community Based Rehabilitation (CBR) **177**

Community Mental Health Act (1963) 2
community mental health centers 2, 7n4, 14
Community Mental Health Services Block Grant 160
Community Preventive Services Task Force **174**
compassion fatigue 134, 141, 149n3
Comprehensive Community Mental Health Services for Children and Their Families Program 19
continuing education units (CEUs) 139
co-occurring disorders 5, 69, 71, **184–6, 188, 190, 199, 205**
covered entity 134–5, 150n6
crisis residence 16
crisis stabilization 14, 18, 44
Critical Time Intervention (CTI) 35, **202**
culture 3, 27–8, **31**, 75
Curanderismo **31**

Day Treatment *11*, 14–15, 72, **188, 199, 203**
Department of Adult Protective Services 130
Department of Child Services, Division of Family and Children, or Division of Child Welfare *see* Department of Family and Children Services
Department of Family and Children Services 35, 49n1, 130
depression 5, 58–60, 74, 162, **176, 189, 197, 204, 209**; bipolar 100n6; post-partum 59
detention centers 6, *11*, 17
diagnosis 2–3; dual 5; Integrated Dual Diagnosis Treatment (IDDT) 69
Diagnostic and Statistical Manual (DSM) 3, 8n7
Dialectical Behavior Therapy (DBT) 58, **202**
Dickens, C. 79
discharge: planning 98–9, 112, 115–18; process 18, 112–14; summary 118–20
documentation 118–19, 133–4
domicile 22, 80, 127

ecomap 111
emergency treatment 14
Empirically Supported Treatments (ESTs) *see* Evidence-Based Practice (EBP)

Employee Assistance Program (EAP) 141–2, 150n8
Evidence-Based Practice (EBP) 51–61, 65–6, 70–5; resources **169–74**
Evidence-Based Treatments (EBTs) *see* Evidence-Based Practice (EBP)
Exposure and Response Prevention (ERP) 59
exposure therapy 58–9, **206**
Eyberg, S. 63

Farm Crisis Response Council 27
family support services 19, 46
family 12, 44; Brief Strategic Family Therapy (BSFT) 61–2, **183**; education and support services 56, 61; Family to Family (NAMI) 56, **204**; Functional Family Therapy (FFT) 62; psychoeducation (FPE) 55
folk healers 28, **29–32**
foster care *11*, 15, 159; Multidimensional Therapeutic Foster Care (MTFC) 73, **185**; therapeutic 15, 43, 72–3, 83

goal 85, 87–9, 91, 93–4, 97–100, 116, 127

Health and Safety Executive of the United Kingdom (HSE) 148
health professional shortage areas (HPSA) 27
HIPAA (Health Insurance Portability and Accountability Act) 25, 114, 134–5, 150n5–6
Home and Community Based Services (HCBS) 155–6, 158
HOMEBUILDERS 66, **185**
hospitalization: inpatient 11–14, 25, 34; partial 14, 18

Intensive Family Intervention (IFI) 45–6
international 33, 162; Center for Clubhouse Development (ICCD) 42, **203**
International Classification of Diseases (ICD) 3, 8n6
Interpersonal Therapy (IPT) 59–60

justice: juvenile 62, 73, 130, 156. 164; Office of Juvenile Justice and Delinquency Prevention **170**

Kallawaya **31, 32niv**
Kazdin, A. 63
Kennedy, J. F. 2
Kiwanis 109

Latin American Guide for Psychiatric
  Diagnosis (GLADP) 3, 8n9
Lions Club 109
Linehan, M. 58
logistics 65, 129–31
Long-Acting Injectable (LAI) 74
Lone Worker Protocol 148–9

Marx, A. 45, 64
Medicaid 39, 67, 110, 132, 156–61
medical services 48, 70, 109
medication management 12, 14,
  16–18, 48, 54, 65, 119
Mendota Mental Health Institute 45
mental health courts 4
Mental Health Parity Act of 1996
  (MHPA) 4
Mental Health Parity and Addiction
  Equity Act of 2008 (MHPAEA) 4
mentoring: Big Brother Big Sisters of
  America 66, **191**
Miller, W. 60
mobile crisis teams 14–15, 44
Money Follows the Person (MFP)
  159–60
Morita Therapy 30, **32ni**
Motivational Enhancement Therapy
  (MET) 60, **184**
Motivational Interviewing (MI) 60, **204**
Multi-Systemic Therapy (MST) 66–7,
  186

Naikan 30, **32nii**
National Alliance on Mental Illness
  (NAMI) 56, 110, **204**
National Child Traumatic Stress
  Network (NCTSN) **169**
National Guideline Clearinghouse
  (NGC) **170**
National Implementation Research
  Network (NIRN) **174**
National Institute of Mental Health
  (NIMH) 74
National Prevention Council 40
National Survey on Drug Use and
  Health 5, 22–3, 26
New Freedom Commission on Mental
  Health 27, 84, 91

Nietzche, F. 127
non-specialist 33, 163, **176–81**
Nurturing Parenting Program (NPP)
  62–3, **186**

objective 94–6, 100
Obsessive Compulsive Disorder
  (OCD) 58–9, 117
outpatient treatment 6, 140; intensive
  (IOP) 17–18, **183**; traditional *11*,
  16–7, 163

paraprofessional 24, 28, 43–4, 48,
  163–4
Parent Child Interaction Therapy
  (PCIT) 63
Parent Management Training (PMT)
  63–4, **194, 205**
Patterson, G. 64
peer: specialists 17, 54, 65; supports
  12, 28, 45, 47, 67, 160, 163
pharmacological treatment *see*
  medication management
Praed Foundation 86
President's New Freedom Commission
  91, 155
Profiles of Student Life: Attitudes and
  Behaviors (PSL-AB) 86
Providence Service Corporation 41
provider burnout 134, 141–2, 150n4
Psychiatric Residential Treatment
  Facility (PRTF) 18, 20n3, 38,
  159–60; demonstration project 19,
  23, 156–8
psychoeducation 40, 42, 55, 65, 70,
  177–8, 183, 203, 207–8
psychosocial 44, 54–5, **177–8**;
  rehabilitation 13, 71
psychotropic medication 73–4

rapport 16, 35, 78–9, 85, 113, 166
Recovery Support Strategic Initiative
  126
residential: treatment *11*,13, 18;
  Virtual Residential Program (VRP)
  41, 68
Resource Support Meeting 102–8
respite 15–6, 44

safety 118, 141–50
Santeria **29**
Scales for Predicting Successful
  Inclusion (SPSI) 86

INDEX

school based: services *11*, 47, **178**, **196–7**; prevention 40, **177**, **192**
shaman **29**, **31**
short break 16
Social Care Institute for Excellence (SCIE) **171**
SMART (Specific, Measurable, Attainable, Realistic, Time-Specific) 95, 100
SNAPS (Strengths, Needs, Abilities, and Preferences) 86, *88*, 100, 113–15
Stein, L. 45, 64
Strengths and Difficulties Questionnaire (SDQ) 86
strengths-based 85, 89, **90–1**, **199**
step-down 117–18, 128n2
Substance Abuse and Mental Health Services Administration (SAMHSA) 4–5, 7, 19–20, 22–3, 26, 56, 126–7, 156; NREEP 42, 53–4, 164, **171**
Suicide Prevention Resource Center (SPRC) **172**
supported: employment (SE) 38, 46, 71, **177**, **202**; housing 38, 70–1, **177**; living 46
support group 12, 47, 75, 110, 117–18
supports 126–7; formal 13, 25, 42–3, 97, 105–6, 109–10, **180**; informal 13, 25, 28, **29–31**, 42–3, 55, 97–8, 100, 105–6, 111, **180**; natural 41, 68, 91, 97, 100
systematic desensitization 154–5
systems of care 20, 156–7, 167n2

telemedicine 48, 49n5
Test, M. 45, 64
The Cochrane Collaboration **173**
therapeutic day care 16
therapeutic group home 15

trauma 2, 27–8, 59, **180**, **197**, **208**; informed **169**; post-traumatic stress disorder (PTSD) 2, 57–59,100n4, **180**, **183–4**, **187**, **189**, **206**; psychological 57; vicarious 141
tribes 28, **31**; Alaskan Native **29**; American Indian **29**, **185**
treatment planning 16–17, **29**, **30–32**, 42, *57*, 66, **90–1**; person-centered **88–9**, 92, 102

U.S. Department of Education 6
U.S. Department of Health and Human Services (HHS) 2, 7, 135, **170**
U.S. Health Resources and Services Administration 27
U.S. House of Representatives 6
U.S. Department of Housing and Urban Development 6, 110
U.S. Department of Justice 3, **170**
U.S. Surgeon General 1, 43

Vietnam 2, 32, 56
Vodou **33**
Voodoo, Voudou, or Vodon *see* Vodou
vocational 42–3, 46, 65, 72, **177**; rehabilitation 55, 110; support 38, 54–5, *88*, 163; training 54, 110

Wellness Management and Recovery (WMRP) 69
Wellness Recovery Action Plan (WRAP) 208
Wolfgang von Goethe, J. 93
World Health Organization (WHO) 33, 162–63; Mental Health Gap Action Programme (mhGAP) 33
wraparound services 42, 68–9